THE EMERGENCE
OF MODERN
SOUTH AFRICA

THE EMERGENCE OF MODERN SOUTH AFRICA

State, Capital, and the Incorporation of Organized Labor on the South African Gold Fields, 1902–1939

DAVID YUDELMAN

CONTRIBUTIONS IN COMPARATIVE COLONIAL STUDIES, NUMBER 13

Greenwood Press
WESTPORT, CONNECTICUT • LONDON, ENGLAND

Library of Congress Cataloging in Publication Data

Yudelman, David.
  The emergence of modern South Africa.

  (Contributions in comparative colonial studies,
ISSN 0163-3813 ; no. 13)
  Bibliography: p.
  Includes index.
  1. Industrial relations—South Africa—History.
2. Gold miners—South Africa—History. 3. Industry
and state—South Africa—History. 4. South Africa—
History—1909–1961. I. Title. II. Series.
HD6976.M732S628 1983   331'.0968   82-9375
ISBN 0-313-23170-2 (lib. bdg.)   AACR2

Library of Congress Catalog Card Number: 82-9375
ISBN: 0-313-23170-2
ISSN: 0163-3813

First published in 1983

Greenwood Press
A division of Congressional Information Service, Inc.
88 Post Road West
Westport, Connecticut 06881

Printed in the United States of America

10 9 8 7 6 5 4 3 2 1

To my late Mother

He in a few minutes ravished this
fair creature, or at least would have
ravished her, if she had not, by a timely
compliance, prevented him.

—Henry Fielding, *Jonathan Wild*

Contents

Figures

Tables

Series Foreword

An integrated empire requires predictive capacity over the supply of labor. So, too, does the modern concept of the state, whether capitalist or socialist. Organized labor immediately becomes an issue where the state (or empire) and capital have divergent goals: who organizes the labor, and to what ends? The modern state is often far more interventionist than the traditional empire was, and in both capitalist and communist societies, the state and capital often work through a symbiotic relationship. Ideological Marxism to the contrary, there are genuine choices involved here and all is not inevitable. The choices in a nation that has once been a colony may well differ from the choices made in an integrated nationalist state. Further, where deep-rooted elements of racism also intervene to help define conventional wisdom about both labor and the steps necessary to attain predictive capacity over it, issues often labeled "neocolonial" quickly arise. No situation is better suited to pose the types of questions that have led to both pro- and anti-Marxist conclusions and, more recently and increasingly, to conclusions simply best referred to as non-Marxist.

David Yudelman, of the Department of Political Studies at the University of Witwatersrand, has explored both the facts and the theory of this dilemma, with specific reference to gold production in South Africa. He has sought to place the issue of race in South Africa into a larger framework, as George Fredrickson, John Cell, and other historians have done recently, so that one does not impose an intellectual apartheid upon the economic and social facts. By a careful examination of the conflict between capital and labor in the first four (and more) decades of this century, Dr. Yudelman has reinterpreted a central debate in southern African history. He has placed more emphasis on the continuity of development and less on alleged "turning points" and "watersheds" in the conflict between capital and labor, and he has woven a terse, tight, and intriguing analysis of value to all scholars of nationalism, of imperialism, or of the role of extractive economies in colonialism. The controversial conclusions presented here should add richly to the growing debate over the fundamental patterns of South African (and colonial African) history.

Robin W. Winks

Preface

This study is a history concerned with the nature of the relationship between a modern state and big business, and with the dynamics of the process through which decisions were made and power exerted. But, besides being a very specific study drawn largely from basic primary sources, it attempts to throw some light on several very broad theoretical and contemporary world issues. Though it is not primarily concerned with the nature of the South African state today and its problematic place in the modern world, it suggests that a careful reexamination of the state's past can give us new insights about its far from deviant present. And though the study is not primarily concerned with "macrotheoretical issues" such as the elusive distinction between "early" and "late capitalist societies," or between "legitimation" and "ideology" (if that debased term retains any meaning at all), it is hoped that case studies from the colonies can refine and broaden these essentially Eurocentric conceptualizations.

South Africa, it is argued, should not be seen as deviant, the "polecat of the world," as it suits some to portray it. In many ways, it is the precursor and model of developments in the "advanced industrial societies" rather than their flotsam. The early growth of a symbiotic (some might, inaccurately, refer to it as "corporatist") relationship between the state and capital in South Africa leads one to question whether the general distinction between "early" and "late capitalism" is anything more than a descriptive label of limited relevance. Earlier than most, for specific historical reasons, the South African state was exposed to the overriding problem of resolving the tension between legitimation and accumulation. It needed to legitimate itself vis à vis the white population, in Habermas's sense of mobilizing constituencies of political acquiescence not only by words—"ideology"—but also by actions, such as the broadening of representative institutions, trade unions, and franchises. (The exclusion of the black population from this legitimation process has been largely instrumental in creating the myth that South Africa is an anachronism in the modern world, a deviant state.) And at the same time, the South African state needed, both for itself and for others, to protect the accumulation process, to ensure continued industrial growth.

This tension between legitimation and accumulation, which is such an old problem in South Africa, is in many ways the central problem of the industrial world today—on both sides of the Berlin Wall. It is not an entirely new problem in Europe, of course, as the corporatist literature on fascism and the welfare state testifies; but the "corporatist" South African state—complete with parastatals and institutionalized symbiotic relationship with private capital—developed earlier. Even more interesting, it developed to a great extent in response to the same conflicting imperatives of political mobilization and economic growth.

This study does not pretend to have conceptualized acceptable alternatives to such models as "early" and "late capitalism." It is, in fact, indebted to that literature even while it bites the hand that feeds it. But it does suggest that in some ways, Europeans and North Americans seeking to understand themselves might profit by reversing the normal procedure. As de Tocqueville demonstrated, the colonies can illuminate the metropoles. Those wishing to understand the modern state cannot afford to ignore either the Latin American or the South African experience.

Notwithstanding the above, I should like to acknowledge my personal debt to the metropole in the persons of Michael Oakeshott and Hannah Arendt, both of whom have greatly influenced my thinking, though not always in ways they might have wished. George Palmer taught me a great deal about the relationship of business and government, about critical analysis, and even attempted to teach me to write reasonable prose. Emelia da Costa gave me a perspective on Latin American problems and fruitful insights on their relevance to my concerns. Helen Lunn and Maryna Fraser read and commented on the manuscript. And Robin Winks was both an acerbic critic and a supportive editor.

Abbreviations

ARGME	—	Annual Report of the Government Mining Engineer
ARTCM	—	Annual Report of the Transvaal Chamber of Mines
BRA	—	Barlow Rand Archives
GME	—	Government Mining Engineer
LGM	—	Low-grade mines
MM	—	Secretary for Mines Archives (in South African State Archives)
PM	—	Secretary to Prime Minister Archives (in South African State Archives)
SAIF	—	South African Industrial Federation
SAMWU	—	South African Mine Workers' Union
TCM	—	Transvaal Chamber of Mines
TMA	—	Transvaal Miners' Association

THE EMERGENCE
OF MODERN
SOUTH AFRICA

Introduction: Historical and Comparative Perspectives

We don't want to . . . end up with a situation which gets out
of control. . . . Whilst management and labour are trying to
come to terms with one another [I see] a series of, let's call
them disputes, and some disruption. . . . I think that at this
point in time, managements in this country have got to get it
right, because if they get it wrong the first time up then they
really will have a problem which is going to be extremely difficult to resolve.

—Dick Goss, Managing Director,
South African Breweries, Ltd., 1981[1]

PAST AND PRESENT

The most crucial problems shared by the South African state and
large-scale business in the 1980s are how to defuse the revolutionary potential of the work force and how to create jobs on an
unprecedented scale. This is strikingly similar to the problems faced
in the early part of this century, when the critical political tasks
were to incorporate organized labor into the state structure without
wrecking the capitalist economy and to create jobs for a dangerously large number of unemployed and radical workers.

Then, as now, the state was confronted with a militant, increasingly organized labor force and widespread unrest, which seemed
to pose a threat to its very existence. Both government and big
business knew that change was urgently required and unavoidable,
but they also knew that it posed a mortal threat if they did not "get
it right" the first time.

There are, of course, important differences. The labor force that
posed a threat then was white; now it is black. The South African
state then was, at best, a fledgling industrial state; today it is one of

the more powerful and sophisticated in the world community. The South African economy then was almost totally dependent on the mining industry; now, though still highly dependent on mining, it is infinitely more flexible and diversified. Finally, South Africa was then a respected member of the "world community"; today it is a political outcast.

The differences should not be allowed to obscure the connection between the problems of the past and the present, nor the fact that the events of the first few decades of this century will shape the events of the next two decades and are already doing so. Though history rarely, if ever, repeats itself, men tend to be enslaved by it all the same. Thus, there is little doubt that many of the patterns, alliances, tactics, strategies, and outcomes of the power struggles of 1902–1939 are of direct relevance in analyzing and even anticipating events in South Africa in the 1980s. But one needs to take the point further: men are frequently bound in the present, not merely by the past, but also by their inaccurate perceptions of the past. This study attempts to identify broadly held fallacies about twentieth-century South Africa. It argues that, contrary to the widely accepted view of South Africa's past, organized (white) labor was decisively subjugated and co-opted by an alliance of state and capital in the early part of the twentieth century; and that, partly as a result, a symbiotic relationship of state and capital was cemented, which has endured to the present. It tries to show how this new relationship was reinforced by the development of an increasingly subtle, stable decision-making process.

The historic patterns established in the shaping of the South African state will be crucial in the immediate future, though one cannot predict precisely how. A *modus vivendi* was worked out in the early years, not only for the relationship of the state to organized labor, but also for the relationship of the state to capital. Though the destiny of organized (black) labor in the next two decades will probably be very different from that of organized (white) labor before World War II, it will be determined largely within the same parameters that were established sixty years ago.

NATIONAL AND INTERNATIONAL

A reevaluation of South Africa's past is vital, then, for an intelligent appraisal of its present and its future. But the need for revision goes further than that. Contemporary South Africa is almost inevitably seen as a deviant, even bizarre, case among modern industrial states. The heavy overemphasis on the unique aspects of South African society, such as its highly institutionalized and rigid system of race discrimination, has tended to blind observers to the way South Africa fits into an international comparative perspective. Historians of South Africa have compounded the problem. They have perceived modern South Africa as a uniquely racial situation, and they have consequently (and mistakenly) proceeded to ransack the past seeking racial origins of the ostensibly unique present. It is necessary to correct the misconceptions of the past, not only for the sake of the past itself, nor merely in the hope of achieving a better understanding of the present, but also to restore South Africa to a position where its experience is relevant to the rest of the world and vice versa.

One cannot, of course, deny the importance of race both to South Africa's past and present; the study has a good deal to say about how and why race was important. But it tries to do that by placing South Africa in a broad analytic framework rather than by seeing it as a colorful but aberrant piece of exotica growing wild in the otherwise rationally cultivated garden of industrial civilization. It focuses on issues of importance to various societies, such as the way the state increasingly intervenes to dampen the conflict between capital and labor in large-scale industrial enterprise. The growth of the South African state, then, is not merely of interest to those attempting to understand South Africa's past and present; it also provides a comparative perspective that illuminates the development of other states.[2]

This does not mean that South Africa can be reduced to one more "case study" to be filed away with all the others in the tidy social scientist's taxonomy. The fact that it is not deviant does not mean that it is therefore typical. Its importance from a comparative perspective lies more in the additional dimensions it can give the so-called typical state than in the degree to which it conforms to the typical. The pervasive convergence of interest between and within the state and capital in modern South Africa is almost without equal in the modern industrialized world. Even the United States, usually cited as the archetypal example of state-capital collaboration, displays far more divergence.

The rhetoric, of course, has been all in the other direction. The state and capital in South Africa are traditionally seen to be at war, as are politics and economics, and Afrikaner nationalists and Anglophone capitalists. Academics, ranging ideologically from far left to far right, have reinforced the image by overwhelmingly plumping for one or another version of the war. They vehemently dispute where the cleavage is situated: some would even see it as a war within capital over who should control the state. But they agree on the central thesis: they focus on conflict rather than on convergence of interest. For this reason, the open alliance of the state and capital—as symbolized by the summit meetings of senior political and business leaders at the Carlton Hotel in Johannesburg in November 1979 and in Cape Town in November 1981—has appeared to observers of all political shades to herald either a new era of collaboration or an unprecedented breakthrough.

But in fact, the major thing that is new about the relationship is the openness of the liaison and the cessation of the traditional adversary rhetoric. Unlike the marriage of individuals, state-capital relationships everywhere tend to be characterized by public antipathy and private passion.[3] In the United States, when General Motors was seeking a closer relationship with the state, it was eminently sensible to argue in public that, as Charles Erwin Wilson told the Senate Armed Forces Committee in 1952, "What is good for the country is good for General Motors, and what's good for General Motors is good for the country." But in South Africa, where the major mining houses have been locked into an inextricable embrace with the state since the first decade of the twentieth century, there is no need for such public exhortations. They could even be positively damaging. More than forty years before Wilson's celebrated statement, the head of South Africa's largest mining house group, Julius Wernher, was using much the same terminology: "We are so big in South Africa that anything that is good for the country is good for us."[4] Wernher was expressing a literal truth in a sense that could never have applied to General Motors and the economically diversified, established federal state. What General Motors was canvassing for—a greater identity of interest between the state and big business—Wernher already possessed. And precisely for that reason, he confined his observation to a private letter to one of his partners and almost invariably kept a low profile in his relations with the state.

THEORETICAL AND CONCEPTUAL

South Africa exhibited the symbiosis of the state and big business earlier and more decisively than did most other industrial states. This was so in spite of the relative backwardness of both its state and its industry in relation to those of the advanced industrial countries. The reasons are complex and will be elaborated below, but three central characteristics of the South African situation can be briefly isolated. Seen in combination, they explain a good deal about the early maturation of the state-capital relationship:

1. The unusual concentration and homogeneity of capital resulting largely from the peculiar nature of the mining industry, and of the gold mining industry in particular;
2. the unusual concentration of political power in the hands of a minority group—the Afrikaners—which was relatively impermeable to direct infiltration by capital; and
3. the extremely divided nature of the working class, which was split, not only on race, urban-rural, and skill criteria, but was also composed largely of (black and white) migrants.

This combination meant that, unlike the early situations of the advanced industrial states, neither the state nor capital could effectively dominate the other in South Africa. It also meant that neither peasants nor proletarians presented a serious threat to the state and capital, provided that the latter two elements collaborated. The state-capital relationship in South Africa, then, was not characterized by the dominance of Afrikaner nationalism, as the liberal, nationalist, and pluralist schools of thought have all argued. Nor was it characterized by the dominance of capital, as the Marxists and neo-Marxists suggest. Rather, it was (and is) characterized by symbiosis. Individually, neither the state nor big business could attain hegemony in South Africa; combined, they very early established an effective dominance. The dominance has endured until the present, surviving important changes in the composition of both the state and capital.

This study focuses on what has been conventionally seen as the greatest issue of *conflict* between the state and capital: the subjugation and co-optation of organized white labor. Never before or since has organized labor in South Africa been so ostensibly politically powerful, and the state so desperately in need of its support. Never before or since has big business acted so uncompromisingly to alienate organized labor. On this issue, above all others, one would expect conflict between the state and capital. But, it will be argued, a symbiotic relationship can be demonstrated even at the exact point where the tension between legitimation (the state's need to mobilize political support) and accumulation (capital's need to maintain growth, profitability, or even solvency) was at its height. If the symbiotic nature of the state and capital can be demonstrated where conflict is at its greatest (precisely where one would expect cooperation to be nonexistent or negligible), then one has gone a long way to establishing symbiosis as the most significant characteristic of the state-capital relationship generally. And this applies further afield than in South Africa.[5]

What is being examined here, then, is symbiosis at its weakest link. The challenge to the symbiotic relationship of the state and capital in South Africa since 1970 comes from a similar quarter to that of the period 1907–1924. Today, of course, a far more advanced state and more diversified, flexible capital face a challenge from black labor which, though voteless and not yet fully organized, dwarfs the threat of organized white labor sixty years ago. The differences in the protagonists and in their world situation are vast, but there can be little doubt that the attempt is being made in South Africa today to depoliticize organized labor and to reproduce the outcomes to the events of 1902–1939. Even some of the basic techniques—for example, the subtle blending of subjugation and cooptation—are similar. New techniques, such as the partial withdrawal of the state from the economy—à la Reaganism—and from sections of the polity—through decentralization and a more federalized constitution—are also being mooted. But both new and old techniques are employed to resolve the same tension between legitimation and accumulation that has always plagued modern South Africa.

It should be emphasized that the South African case, now as well as then, is exceptional only in degree, not in kind. Elsewhere, state and capital are also probing the limits of symbiosis and toying with ideas of partial, voluntary state emasculation. Thatcherism and Reaganism are merely the tentative dawn of this new trend.[6] South Africa, like other nations, will think long and hard before making any drastic changes in the state-capital relationship. Nevertheless, for reasons of its own, which are bound up with the history of the state-capital relationship elaborated in this study, it is likely to move further and faster than the United States, the United Kingdom, or other advanced industrial states on which it is ostensibly modeled. South Africa should be closely observed, not only because its fate *per se* is of general interest, but also because it is, in some way, anticipating trends developing more slowly elsewhere.

The major influence behind the telescoped development of modern South Africa, the leap from a fledgling quasi-state to a surprisingly advanced industrial state within the space of eighty years— a process that took centuries in Europe—was the South African gold mining industry. This study focuses on the developing relationship of capital and organized (white) labor in a crucial period on the mines and shows how the industry both shaped and was shaped by the rapidly maturing state. It rejects the theory that the protracted capital-labor conflict between 1907 and 1924 was essentially a racial issue caused by the substitution of poorly paid black labor for exceptionally well-paid white labor. Rather, the overriding issues were the struggle for industrial dominance between capital and labor and the state's growing intervention in the conflict.

The equally widely held "turning-point" theory, which argues that international mining capital won the "battle" of 1922 (by crushing the Rand Revolt) only to lose the "war" of 1924 (when a new government ostensibly representing Afrikaner nationalists and white labor was elected), is also rejected. The events of 1922–1924 marked a decisive defeat for organized labor, a definite victory for the expanding interventionist state, and a qualified but important victory for mining capital. They did not constitute a turning point, the study demonstrates, because they merely continued and extended the long-standing state-capital alliance and the process by which the state was subjugating and co-opting organized labor. Neither did the increasing state support for import-substitute industrialization after 1924 mark a turning point: it was a wholly logical development of previous governments' preoccupations with stabilizing revenue and capital accumulation and expanding employment opportunities for the white electorate, thus legitimizing the state.

The turning-point theorists—and it is difficult to find anyone analyzing twentieth-century South Africa, from Fichtean national-

ist to Althusserian Marxist, who is *not* a turning-point theorist—
almost universally base their argument on the concept of zero-sum.
They correctly observe conflict, but they incorrectly assume that
conflict to be fundamental. They look only for winners and losers,
dominators and dominated, and fail to grasp the mutual dependence of the state and capital. In fact, neither the state nor capital
(nor any fraction thereof) could individually dominate economy or
society; but by each contributing something distinctively different,
they were able to exercise a joint domination that was otherwise
not feasible.[7]

This study also analyzes in detail the virgin territory of South
Africa's decision-making process and the far-from-virgin territory
of the relationship of "economic power" (that of mining capital) to
"political power" (the state). It is argued that the developing South
African state—in common with other industrial states elsewhere—
was faced with two major imperatives, which were, to some extent,
mutually contradictory. In the first place, because it was account-
able to the electorate, the state tended to expand its role to all sectors of the economy, and in particular, to politically sensitive areas
such as the creation of jobs and the control of conflict between capital and labor. Some social scientists refer to this expansion as being
part of the state's growing "legitimation imperative." In the second
place, because its growth required financing, the state had to protect its sources of revenue. The South African economy was overwhelmingly dependent on a single product (gold), so the state was
even more than usually impelled to intervene in crisis situations to
guarantee the gold mines' viability. This second need can be
(loosely) referred to as the state's "accumulation imperative." It
was pointed out earlier that the state's need to mobilize popular
support can, and does, bring it into conflict with capital's drive to
make profits. But the state also has a vital interest in the profitability of capital, in its ability to be taxed and provide revenue. In
other words, there is also an *internal* conflict within states between
their legitimation and accumulation imperatives.

A state may, for example, have the theoretical choice between
compelling the employment of expensive local labor in an industry
or allowing the industry to use poorly paid migrant labor. The first
option would make the state popular with the electorate; the second would ensure its sources of revenue through taxation and other

forms of appropriation from the industry. The degree of conflict between the state's legitimation and accumulation imperatives will vary, but the sharper the conflict, the more is revealed about the inner nature of the modern industrial state and where power actually lies. This is one reason for the importance of the early decades of this century for those seeking to understand modern South Africa. The period lays bare the depth and strength of the mutual dependence of the state and capital (their symbiosis), even during a time of ostensibly intense conflict; it also shows in stark relief the inner legitimation and accumulation tensions of the South African state and its limited options in resolving them. The options are at least as limited now as they were then, and for many of the same reasons.

NOTES

1. David Keefe, (ed.), *Insight into 1981: Transcription of the Simpson-Frankel Investment Conference*, Carlton Hotel, Johannesburg, 28 January 1981, Johannesburg, 1981, pp. 37–38. S. A. Breweries is one of the largest employers of labor in South Africa.

2. Predictably, treatments of South Africa in comparative perspective tend to focus on race relations. See George H. Fredrickson, *White Supremacy: A Comparative Study of American and South African History*, New York, 1981, for an historical treatment. For a sociological treatment, see Pierre L. van den Berghe, *Race and Racism*, New York, 1967. Stanley Greenberg, *Race and State in Capitalist Development: Comparative Perspectives*, New Haven, 1980, is an example of a useful attempt to take the comparative perspective one step further. Though it suffers somewhat from theoretical incoherence, it is a formidable and valuable compilation of diverse and important data.

3. Today's public honeymoon of the state and big business may well turn out to be brief, as there are good political reasons not to publicize it. On the other hand, the long-standing private affair of seventy-five years is almost certain to endure for years to come.

4. A. P. Cartwright, *Golden Age: The Story of the Industrialization of South Africa and the Part Played in It by the Corner House Group of Companies, 1910–1967*, Cape Town, 1968, p. 16.

5. The aim here, of course, is not to "prove" a law that will apply inexorably to all state-capitalist relationships, as Michels's Iron Law aspires to apply to all parties. Rather, it is hoped that symbiosis could prove useful heuristically, drawing attention to possible alternative methods of concep-

tualization of state-capital relationships in a wide variety of geographical and historic contexts.

6. For a recent treatment of the need to reassess the relationship of the state to capital, which compares the situation in several different states, see Richard Rose and Guy Peters, *Can Government Go Bankrupt?* London, 1979.

7. For an outline of the differences between the zero-sum and symbiotic approaches, see David Yudelman, "Capital, Capitalists and Power in South Africa: Some Zero-Sum Fallacies," *Social Dynamics*, Vol. 6, No. 2, December 1980, pp. 59–67.

A Critique of the Historiography of Modern South Africa

Thus when we fondly flatter our desires
Our best conceits do prove the greatest liars
       —Michael Drayton, *The Barrons' Wars*

Contemporary South Africa is widely seen as a bizarre exception to general trends of development in both the industrialized and the third worlds. It is portrayed internationally as a combination of seventeenth-century fanaticism (Calvin's variety) and twentieth-century technology (Dr. Strangelove's variety). The image is, of course, convenient for those anxious to distance themselves from, and to avoid obvious comparisons with, the dark sides of their own societies, past or present. For South Africa exhibits in almost caricatured form the ugly face of most developing industrial states: the concentration of a disproportionate amount of growing wealth in the hands of a minority, the decline in civil and human rights, the centralization of power, and the systematic exploitation of the powerless. It is far more comfortable to relegate such a creature to a lunatic asylum than to conceive of living with it as a blood relative.

Both academics and popularizers concentrate on South Africa's highly developed system of legalized race discrimination. In itself, this emphasis can be easily justified: after all, the phenomenon of a modern industrial state that has built institutionalized race discrimination into its very foundations is problematic for anyone in the modern world attempting a comprehensive explanation of the relationship between class and color, economic and political power, or ideology and action.

The problem arises in the tendency to believe that what is unique is necessarily salient. Because the contemporary South African situation is ostensibly deviant, the argument goes, we must search out its origins in deviant features of South Africa's past. Quests such as these result, for example, in the attempt to explain modern apartheid by blaming it all on a mythical white Afrikaner tribe still metaphorically carrying its Bible in one hand and rifle in the other as it marches unwillingly into the twentieth century.

The Afrikaner, in general, has thus been credited with a far larger role in the evolution of contemporary South Africa than he deserves. This is partly the fault of Afrikaner nationalist mythology, which has portrayed him as the divinely ordained protector of the values of Western Christian civilization and, like the American frontiersman, the hero of an epic story of pioneering survival.[1] But it is equally the fault of Anglophones, who have portrayed the Afrikaner as the villain, the fanatic who created or at least perfected institutionalized race discrimination in the shape of apartheid.[2]

Of course, Anglophone academics sometimes reject this crude caricature, are sympathetic to the Afrikaner, and are critical of fellow Anglophones; but even these still tend to argue that the whites of British extraction have passively accepted race discrimination rather than being partly responsible for creating it. In fact, Anglophones, including British Imperialists, played a crucial role in laying down both the administrative and the ideological foundations for modern institutionalized race discrimination.[3]

South African Anglophones are not significantly more liberal than are Afrikaners on race questions. They are quite prepared, however, to use apartheid[4] as a pretext for indirectly expressing their culturally chauvinistic distaste for the Afrikaner while continuing to enjoy the benefits of white supremacy. The institutional basis of race discrimination predates the official apartheid policy by decades, but the two are eagerly conflated by the opponents of Afrikaner nationalism.

Even those liberal Anglophone academics who genuinely abhor race discrimination share the responsibility for unconsciously obfuscating its origins, development, and contemporary function.[5] Politically isolated and with very little chance of widespread support from any significant number of the white electorate, the liberals have attempted to avoid ivory tower isolation by passing lightly over the role of their fellow Anglophones. The great majority of these, particularly those who have been large-scale employers of Africans, supported and still support race discrimination.[6]

The conscious or unconscious tendency to overemphasize the deviant nature of past events in the hope of explaining or shifting responsibility for the present is not, of course, unique to South Africa. Historians in the United States, for example, have put far too much emphasis on plantation slavery in attempting to explain their contemporary race relations problems.

Nor are all historians of South Africa equally guilty of the tendency to brand South Africa as bizarre and deviant. Some, in fact, have done exactly the opposite by showing precisely how South Africa is best understood in a comparative context. Significantly, these studies tend to pre-date the high noon of the apartheid era.[7]

This group, however, is small. In general, there has been an insufficient awareness of the connections between the processes taking place in South Africa and those taking place elsewhere. There has been a pervasive tendency to look inward and indulge in ultimately sterile debates about which groups or special interests should be assigned the credit or blame for the unique features of the present. Even the debate on the relationship between industrialization and race relations, which showed great potential for providing a comparative perspective on South Africa's problems by looking at change as *process*, has degenerated into an ideological and academic wrangle.[8]

All this is not to dispute that valuable work has been done on South Africa or to deny that it is the task of historians and social scientists to be alive to differences as well as similarities, to change as well as continuity. It merely suggests that most of the work suffers from a tendency to be isolationist. Even when that work deals with such "universal" problems as race relations, it seeks origins or causes in situations unique to South Africa. Processes common to South Africa and other countries (such as expansion of the role of the state, industrialization, and dependence) go largely ignored or are dealt with as though they were unique.

SCOPE OF THIS STUDY

There are, of course, any number of comparative perspectives that would exhibit the manifest "normality" of contemporary South Africa. Some have already been tried. South Africa, for example, has been seen as a modernizing oligarchy.[9] This study attempts to understand modern South Africa by examining the tran-

sition from a fledgling state to a fully interventionist state.[10] As
such it may be regarded as a small contribution to a large general
literature,[11] which will attempt to keep in mind comparative perspectives on developments elsewhere. It will also attempt to show
how the pattern of subjugation and co-optation of organized (that
is, white) labor followed in South Africa is connected to patterns
that were evolving throughout the industrial capitalist world at the
time.

The formation of the International Labor Organization (ILO) in
the early 1920s, for example, was only the most visible sign of
widespread international cooperation between capitalist states and
organized employers. This cooperation began before World War I
and really accelerated after 1917, when the Bolshevik revolution
shocked employers and brought on waves of militancy among the
working class everywhere. The subjugation and co-optation of
organized labor in South Africa and elsewhere is intimately related
to the development of interventionist states throughout the industrial world.

A related but distinct issue is the transformation of the South
African state from fledgling status (with its legitimacy questioned
and its sovereignty seriously threatened) to a state commanding
relatively unquestioned sovereignty (recognized by most of the
electorate, at least, as legitimate, and consequently achieving relative stability for as long as the mass of voteless blacks remained
politically inactive).

South Africa, of course, exhibits peculiarities as well as regular-
ities. Two of the most obvious—the extremely divided and hetero-
geneous nature of the working class and of society in general, and
the unique character and importance to the state of the gold mining
industry—will be dealt with at some length.

A detailed study will also be made of the decision-making process. In South Africa, to date, nearly all such studies have been
confined to the *public* part of the process—to examining legislative
decisions.[12] With few exceptions, this criticism applies to the literature of decision making elsewhere as well. The most important
part of the decision-making process in the modern capitalist state
occurs at the executive and administrative levels,[13] but these are
precisely the levels most neglected because of their relative inacces-
sibility. The existence of unusually rich primary source materials

has made it possible to examine in depth these levels of decision making in South Africa.

Finally, the role of the state and the political parties in labor disputes will be examined in detail. This is an area that has been largely neglected, not only by political scientists dealing with South Africa, but also by those dealing with other countries,[14] though it is absolutely vital for understanding the modern industrial state and society.

The major organizing concept employed here is the notoriously treacherous "state." The "state" is here defined to encompass the executive, legislative (Parliament), the civil service, judiciary, police, army: the institutions that make and enforce public policy, symbolically and actually. It is "the continuous administrative, legal, bureaucratic, and coercive systems" that seek to structure relations between government and society, as well as relations within a society.[15] The latter definition would include relations such as those between capital and labor. The state is a complex of mechanisms of domination and control, with the exclusive legal monopoly on the use of force and a territorial basis. This is a "minimum description" of the state for working purposes, and one of the themes of this study will be to trace the expansion of the South African state's activities, both within the above categories and into entirely new areas. By early 1924, for example, the Secretary for Mines and Industries, H. Warington Smyth, was referring publicly to the state's new role "as wealth producer" and as creator of employment.[16] An attempt will be made to go beyond a description of the component parts of the state to a broader conceptualization that draws on and possibly even adds something to the contemporary literature on the capitalist state in advanced industrial countries.

The term "state," as used here, should be distinguished as sharply as possible from the "government," which is generally used merely to signify the executive branch of the state. The "government" is deliberately defined narrowly to mean the executive heads of the ruling party in Parliament. This is, moreover, general usage: for example, the "government" is commonly said to introduce legislation in Parliament.

Finally, there is "society," which refers to all collective human activity and its artifacts within a given geographic area. No analysis of society as a whole will be attempted, and the focus will be on those aspects of society that fit into the ambit of state and government. The analytic use of "society" is largely implicit, though it should be recognized at the outset that the structure of society places broad but powerful limits on the options open to any state.

Three structural levels can therefore be distinguished: (1) the government, or executive, which ostensibly initiates and shapes state policy but which does not necessarily finally control it; (2) the state, a complex of systems structuring relations between government and society as well as within society; and (3) society, which would take in all groups, those represented in varying degrees in the state (such as capital and organized white labor) and those unrepresented (such as migrant black labor).

The focus here is on the state's relationship to gold mining capital, their dealings on the issue of organized white labor, and how labor-capital relations came to be structured by the state. Extensive primary research has been done on other aspects of the state-mining capital relationship, such as black migrant labor, taxation, mineral law, revenue, and the structure of the state and industry. The results of this additional research confirm the findings published here, but they are not elaborated in detail. However, there are occasions when, for example, the rights of black labor are bartered for the rights of white labor or the capital-labor conflict spills over into other areas such as the protective policy advocating import-substitute industrialization. Thus, it has been necessary, on occasion, to deal with topics outside the relationship of the state, capital, and organized labor.

The position of blacks in the mining industry has not been the focus here, except when the black mine labor issue impinged directly on the white mine labor issue (as in the case of the "white labor policy" or the 1920 black miners' strike). This is not, of course, to suggest that black labor is less important than is white labor to the industry; but black labor was not a "political" issue in the sense that white labor was, and the fundamental question of equal political and economic rights for blacks was never seriously considered or debated among the white government or white electorate.[17] Blacks were treated as objects of policy, not subjects, and were often used as an issue to mobilize support from diverse groups in the electorate. The black "issue" was the one on which most whites could agree. For this reason, the point is repeatedly made that color discrimination was more a tactical than a strategic issue for the state. Naturally, for blacks, color discrimination was by far the most important issue, and it is a significant commentary on the economic and political structure that the fundamental long-term questions posed by the presence of this group in society were ignored by the state.

The perpetuation, institutionalization, and even expansion of the unsettled and migrant nature of the black labor force prevented urban blacks from developing any viable political base. This meant that they could be and were dealt with by the white state largely in terms of its own priorities. The position of large numbers of black laborers in South African society and their elimination as political actors or even as a contested political issue among whites is absolutely vital.[18] The entire relationship of the state, capital, and organized white labor was wholly based on the premise that blacks were not a politically contested issue. If they had been, this study would have been entirely different. When black miners, on occasion, acted politically in spite of the constraints on them, the whole state-industry relationship immediately developed a fluidity and a potential for radical change that was previously unthinkable (see Chapter 4).

HISTORICAL BACKGROUND: THE STATE AND THE GOLD MINES

The transformation of South Africa from a largely rural, subsistence economy in the nineteenth century to a twentieth-century industrial state is intimately bound up with the development of mining, particularly gold mining. In 1867, large deposits of diamonds were discovered, which began the process of railway building and the creation of the infrastructure on which a modern state is built. In 1886, large-scale deposits of gold-bearing ore were discovered on the Witwatersrand and, as one historian puts it with some justification: "From 1886 the story of South Africa is the story of gold."[19]

The state was involved in the development of the industry almost from the beginning, particularly in providing the conditions for the organization and recruitment of the black labor supply, the vast bulk of which was brought to the Rand from hundreds of miles away.[20] The discovery of gold greatly hastened the development of the transport infrastructure: three railway lines connecting the Rand to commercial ports on the coast—in Mozambique, Natal, and the Cape—were completed in the early 1890s. These lines were initially built solely because of the mines, though their use quickly became more general, and branch lines expanded. The railways became a major force uniting the South African economy and, after unification of the four provinces in 1910, its political structure.

The state here, as in other industrializing countries, played a major role in building the railways, which were largely publicly financed.[21] The gold mines, then, became the major force shaping the economic and political development of the Transvaal (then called the South African Republic) in the late nineteenth century. The Transvaal state, too, began a rapid transformation from a marginal and weak position to one of relative centrality in Transvaal society.[22]

At the turn of the century, war broke out between the South African Republic and Britain, partly because of the new situation resulting from the discovery of gold. The war ended in 1902, with the nominally unconditional surrender of the republic. The British Government hoped to shape the reconstruction of the Transvaal by using the gold mines to (1) generate employment and encourage British immigration, thereby ensuring white Anglophone domination of the new electorate when the Transvaal attained self-governing status; and (2) generate revenue to finance the reconstruction of the Transvaal, which the British had systematically devastated during the war in their efforts to subdue the Afrikaner (Dutch-speaking) local population.[23]

The development of the gold mining industry did not, however, live up to British expectations. One of the main reasons was an initially acute postwar shortage of unskilled migrant black labor on which the low-grade, labor-intensive industry depended. Attempts then being made to mine lower-grade ore at deeper levels created even worse labor shortages. The British response to that problem was to allow the importation of indentured Chinese labor, which had some limited success in reviving the industry but which contributed to the fall of the Conservative government in Britain and to the early granting to the Transvaal of responsible government in 1907. An Afrikaner coalition, dominated by landowners and tenant farmers, then took political power in the Transvaal, aided by a suffrage restricted to white males.

The new government repatriated the Chinese but also helped to recruit sufficient black labor to expand operations. Mining costs were crucial, and attention shifted to white labor, which was very highly paid relative to black labor. Mining capitalists attempted, from about 1906, to cut white wages and increase white productivity. The white miners responded by organizing into mass unions, by going into politics, and by increasing the use of strikes.

In 1910, the Union of South Africa was formed, with the Transvaal as the motor force in the formally unified economy. A loosely organized, coalition-type party, the South African party (henceforth S.A. party) formed the first government and remained in power until 1924. It advocated conciliation between Anglophones and Afrikaner whites, loyalty to the Imperial connection, and accelerated economic development, including the encouragement of gold mining.

In the opposition were (1) the Unionist party, almost exclusively Anglophone, suspicious of Afrikaner political motives, business-oriented but basically in agreement with the S.A. party's policies; (2) the Labour party, a fairly militant enemy of big business drawing its support from urban white workers and the lower middle class. It was formed largely by trade unionists but led by a former mine manager, Colonel Frederic Hugh Page Creswell; and (3) the National party, an early offshoot of the S.A. party. It represented diverse Afrikaner interest groups under the integrating banner of Afrikaner nationalism and drew its strength mainly from the rural electorate.

The gold mines became almost as vital to South Africa after Union as they had been to the Transvaal alone, and the pattern of conflict between capital and organized (white) labor continued until 1922, with World War I merely muting the struggle. There were major strikes in 1913 and 1914 of such magnitude that they seemed to threaten the very existence of the fledgling South African state.

Finally, in 1922, a renewed cost crisis precipitated the boiling over of almost two decades of bitter conflict between capital and organized labor. A widespread strike of gold miners and coal miners (and other scattered groups) rapidly broke into violence and developed into the full-scale civil insurrection known as the Rand Revolt. White miners formed armed "commandos" (military groups), sabotaged railway installations with dynamite stolen from the mines, and fought pitched battles with the police, the army, and mine officials.[24] The revolt was forcibly put down, and the strikers returned to work on their employers' terms. Probably more than 200 persons—strikers, government forces, and bystanders—were killed, and nearly 600 were wounded.[25]

The following year, 1923, an electoral pact was entered into by the two opposition parties, the Labour and the National parties. The Labour party sought mainly to protect unionized white workers' jobs from the attacks of capitalists and from competition by blacks, while the National party sought, *inter alia*, to expand drastically employment of unskilled Afrikaner "poor whites" who were flocking to the cities. These respective goals were not always compatible (see Chapter 7).

In 1924, after some by-election setbacks, General Jan Smuts, the leader of the S.A. party, which had absorbed the Unionist party in 1921, called a general election. The S.A. party polled the most votes (47 percent against the National party's 36 percent), but the larger electoral weight given to the rural constituencies—increasingly the National party's stronghold—more than counteracted this difference. The S.A. party lost 19 seats and the National party emerged with 63 seats compared to the S.A. party's 53. The Labour party, with 18 seats, was very much the junior partner in the new Pact government.

THE PERIODIZATION OF THE MODERN
SOUTH AFRICAN STATE

The change of government in 1924 has been almost universally interpreted as one of the two major "turning points" in modern South African history (the other is the election of the National party government in 1948). It has been seen, often implicitly, as changing not merely the government, but also the form of the state and the groups it represented. This study rejects the turning-point theory and attempts to place the Pact's election in an entirely different perspective. This perspective is a radical departure from the literature, and the reader should perhaps be warned that it implies (and even necessitates) a broad revision of twentieth-century South African history as a whole.

This is because the 1924 turning point is at the heart of virtually all attempts to periodize the modern South African state. Afrikaner nationalists have seen it as the culmination of the march of Afrikaner consciousness from the country into the towns, which was made irreversible by the Afrikaner takeover of the state in 1948. Liberals have seen 1924 as a decisive victory for racist white workers that entrenched the legislative color bar and elevated race discrimination to the prime motivation of the South African state. Marxists have seen the 1924 turning point as a victory for capital's policy of dividing the working class on racial lines, the triumph of the propagators of false (racial) consciousness, and the death of class-based politics. More specifically, neo-Marxists have argued that 1924 marks a vital victory in the struggle for control of the state by local businessmen ("national capital") over foreign mining capital ("metropolitan bourgeoisie"). Rather heretically, then, they have tended to focus on divisions *within* capital rather than between capital and labor.

Thus, to reject 1924 as a turning point, as this study does, is necessarily to suggest that the modern South African state has to be periodized in an entirely different way from that suggested by the existing literature. This, in turn, means that modern South Africa as a whole has to be conceptualized differently. It is necessary, therefore, to examine in detail how the 1924 turning-point theory gained almost universal currency and has continued implicitly or explicitly to dominate in schools of thought that cover the entire ideological spectrum.

An important part of the Pact's election manifesto were the promises to protect the interests of those white workers who had jobs and to create jobs for those who did not. The jobless comprised mainly the hundreds of thousands of unskilled "poor whites" who had, within the last generation, migrated to the urban areas from the country and who constituted over 25 percent of the white population. The Pact's courtship of the employed and unemployed whites has led to the unsubstantiated assumption that its election in 1924 was largely due to the electorate's hostility to the S.A. party's handling of the 1922 strike and revolt. This, in turn, assumes that the overall electorate was primarily motivated by sympathy for the aspirations of the white working class. The relationship between the 1922 revolt and the 1924 election result was, however, complex, and it is probable that the connection between the two was not crucial (see Chapter 6).

Within two years of its election, and with much fanfare, the Pact government passed various new labor laws. It brought labor in unorganized, small industries under state control. It reestablished the state's power to reserve certain mining jobs for whites. It also introduced administrative measures aimed at creating more jobs for unskilled whites at the expense of blacks, and at higher wages than those paid to blacks.

Largely for these reasons, the Pact's election has been seen as a turning point in South African history in which the white miners, who had lost the "battle" of 1922, finally won the "war" of 1924. The Rand Revolt is seen as the major cause of the Pact government's accession to power, and the new government is seen as genuinely, though not exclusively, representative of white workers. Even more important, the Pact's election is seen as imposing similar priorities on the state as a whole.

The literature is suprisingly unanimous on this, both in content and in the imagery with which it is expressed. The cliché of "the battle won but the war lost" is trotted out by the most varied of commentators with a regularity that conjures up ringing bells and Pavlov's salivating dogs. Examples from the two most influential treatments of South African mine labor to date, the first liberal and the second Marxist, could be interchanged without any sacrifice of meaning. Francis Wilson argues that "although the miners lost the battle, as the Chamber of Mines did in fact lay off a number of white workers, they won the war." Frederick Johnstone puts it this way: "The white workers had lost a battle in 1922, but they had not lost the war," and "the pendulum had thus come full circle. The state, which in 1922 had served as the instrument for the repression of the white workers, was now in the hands of their representatives. . . ."[26] The same point is made by numerous others, using the same metaphor.[27] Superficially, of course, there are some grounds for this view. Organized labor *was* represented in the Pact government, and the Pact did pass important legislation, which purported to strengthen the position of white miners and white workers in general.

If the actual impact of the Pact government is examined, however, as opposed to its rhetoric, one sees nakedly confirmed the adage that "politics is the means by which the will of the few becomes the will of the many." For the truth of the matter is that the smashing of the 1922 strike and revolt dealt white miners a blow from which they had not yet recovered by the beginning of World War II.

White employment did not return to 1921 levels until 1928; the proportion of blacks to whites in the industry—which is alleged by nearly all historians to be the cause of the 1922 strike—increased sharply and did not return to 1921 levels until 1937. White cash earnings per capita did not return to former levels until after World War II, nor did the proportion of total mine revenue spent on white wages. Significant strikes became almost unheard of: in the four years from 1919–1922, a total of 2.8 million man-days were lost to industries through strikes, most of them in the mining industry; in the next eighteen years, fewer than 250,000 man-days were lost.[28]

The only qualification necessary is that 1920–1921 was a period of high inflation: the drop in *monetary* wages is therefore exaggerated to the degree to which deflation occurred after 1921. Even taking this into account, the white worker took ten years to regain his 1921 per capita wage in real terms (that is, adjusted for price inflation). More important, however, is the fact that he lost ground to the black miner; proportionately more blacks were employed and the white/black earnings-gap ratio dropped. (More will be said about this later.)

Lest it be argued that labor figures cannot be abstracted from the overall fortunes of the industry, it should be pointed out that tons of ore treated and revenue show a steady growth from 1923 on, as do dividends. And the major reason for this was the simultaneous increase in white labor's productivity and the decrease in white labor's wages. In short, the mining capitalists benefited considerably from the aftermath of the 1922 revolt at the expense of white miners and have continued to do so ever since. (See Table 1.)

Most indicators, then, show that the white miners lost both the battle and the war in 1922.[29] The Pact's election did not mark any victory for them, though it has been argued that they might well have suffered more if the Pact had not been elected.[30] The wages of white workers outside the gold mines were also cut. Though gov-

Table 1 Organized White Labor, Before and During the Pact, 1921–1929

	1921	1922	1923	1924	1925	1926	1927	1928	1929
Number of whites employed on the gold mines ('000)	20.9	13.9	17.7	18.5	19.3	19.7	20.6	21.3	21.6
Black/white ratio on gold mines (:1)	8.2	11.4	10.1	9.7	9.1	9.2	9.0	9.1	8.8
Index of real wages: white miners (1910=1,000)	965	794	825	853	833	866	876	884	893
Union membership, all white workers ('000)	108.2	81.9	86.9	87.1	93.6	67.2	58.4	64.8	69.9

Sources: Annual Reports of the Government Mining Engineer and of the Transvaal Chamber of Mines 1939; Official Yearbooks of the Union of South Africa; *Union Statistics for Fifty Years, 1910–1960*, Pretoria, 1970. There have been changes in Chamber of Mines statistical series over the years, which accounts for some minor discrepancies between, for example, this table and table 5 below.

ernment policies did increase white employment outside the mines, the new jobs were mainly for unskilled, nonunionized workers (see Chapter 7). The election of the Pact, therefore, represented a "seizure" of the South African state neither by white miners nor by white workers in general.

The converse of the above theory—that the mining capitalists won the battle of 1922 but lost the war of 1924—is, if anything, even more widely argued.[31] That argument sees 1922 as the desperate last attempt of big business (otherwise known as "Imperial," "metropolitan," or mining capital—the mines at the time were largely owned by European stockholders) to dominate the state directly for its own purposes.

Mining capitalists lost, it is argued, because a coalition of organized white labor and other interests (variously specified as Afrikaner nationalists, poor farmers, indigenous bourgeoisie, urban and/or rural landholders) wrested power from its grasp and favored the economic and class interests they represented above those of the mining industry.[32]

That argument is as incorrect as its converse. The most important reason has already been discussed: the crushing of white labor, which brought working costs on the gold mines tumbling 23.9 percent from 25 shillings and 10 pence a ton milled in 1921 to 19 shillings and 8 pence in 1924. Costs did not climb above 20 shillings again before World War II. Even in real terms, costs stayed below 1921 levels for the entire 1920s. In terms of its overall fortunes, the gold mining industry recovered well after the strike and continued its recovery throughout the Pact government's first five years, with tons of ore treated, revenue, profits, and dividends all showing steady growth.

The upturn in the fortunes of mining capital was eventually halted by the Depression rather than by the actions of the Pact government in siphoning off profits (or surplus) for other sectors of the economy. To repeat, the mining capitalists benefited considerably from the 1922 revolt and continued to do so until at least World War II, through a significant and lasting cut in working costs relative to revenue.

A slightly more sophisticated version of the argument that the mining capitalists lost the war in 1924 suggests that, although white miners may not have benefited, the Pact appropriated part of the surplus or profits from the gold mines to subsidize the development of "national capital"—that is, for locally owned agricultural and/or manufacturing industries. The Pact victory, the argument goes, meant that "national capital" became the dominant capitalist group (or "hegemonic fraction of capital") by seizure of control of the state.[33]

To prove this dubious proposition, a significantly higher rate of appropriation, or taxation, from the gold mining industry to other sectors of the economy after 1924 would need to be demonstrated. The gold mining industry, after all, had "subsidized" other sectors of the economy since Union in 1910 and even before.[34]

To demonstrate a higher rate of appropriation, moreover, is exceedingly difficult: indirect subsidization (such as differential railway rates, differential state infrastructural spending) would have to be taken into account, as would the effects on different sectors of the economy of state "nondecisions" as well as state decisions. Areas apparently unrelated to revenue (such as gold law or mineral rights) would need to be researched to assess fully the level of appropriation of profits and surplus by the state in the context of vital concessions made to the mining industry in other areas.

A superficial attempt has been made to prove that the pact appropriated significantly more from the mining capitalists than did the S.A. party and that it therefore represented a coalition of new "national capitalist" interests that were using the newly captured state for gain. This attempt is of little value because of its highly procrustean treatment of the statistics and the uncritical way it accepts mining industry propaganda.[35] Moreover, it can be shown that the direct opposite was true, as state revenue from gold mining as a percentage of total revenue actually *declined* quite steeply under the Pact: from 8.4 percent in 1923 and 7.2 percent in 1924, it stayed under 6 percent for the remainder of the 1920s.[36] (See Table 11.)

It is not proposed to argue, however, that state appropriation from the gold mines and transfers to other sectors did not increase at all under the Pact government—this was, after all, a long-established trend under previous governments, reversed only by the cost crisis of 1919–1921. But it is clear that even if the appropriation did increase, it did not do so radically, especially taking into account the much-publicized Pact program of protection and secondary industrialization (that one would normally expect to be paid for by large increases in taxation of the gold mines).

The mining capitalists, it is true, complained as always about being used as a milch cow for other sectors, but they did not allege a substantial increase in discrimination under the Pact. Such moderate increases in appropriation are quite compatible with a fundamentally unaltered state policy, as mining capital would have accepted, even welcomed, a higher level of taxation or appropriation if, by so doing, it protected its vital interests. Nevertheless, the neo-Marxists, in common with other schools of thought, argue the turning-point theory: they say that the election of the Pact marks a new state as well as a new government, a state in which "national capital" takes over from "metropolitan" (mining) capital as the dominant group ("hegemonic fraction").[37]

THE NEED FOR AN ALTERNATIVE APPROACH

The turning-point and battle-war theories have been dealt with at some length for two main reasons. First, they serve as an analytic introduction to the literature on the South African state and the gold mining industry, as virtually everyone who has dealt with these subjects has to some extent espoused these theories. Second, they reveal a fundamental misconception of the nature and role of the state that goes far beyond the interpretation of an individual event.

Various empirical arguments have been advanced for the rejection or radical alteration of the turning-point and battle-war theories. These will be amplified in the body of this study and documented in detail. The question remains why the turning-point theory is nearly universally held, in spite of readily available evidence to the contrary. Some have even argued the theory while supplying, in appendices, statistics that clearly controvert their thesis.[38] This suggests that the root of the problem may be more conceptual and analytic than empirical. In that case, the misinterpretation of the significance of the Rand Revolt can be seen as merely a stark and dramatic example of a more pervasive, less obvious tendency in the entire historiography.

Three possible sources of conceptual and analytic confusion will now be outlined. This is not done with the intention of denigrating work on which this study is building; rather, it is with the hope of suggesting added dimensions or possibly even alternative approaches to a whole range of ostensibly unrelated historical and contemporary issues. Two of the most hotly debated of these issues today are the general issue of industrialization and race relations (or social change) referred to above, and the perennial historic issue of the degree to which either Afrikaner nationalism or monopoly capitalism is to be credited (or debited) with the emergence of institutionalized race discrimination after World War II.

SOURCES OF CONCEPTUAL CONFUSION 1: INADEQUATE THEORIES OF THE STATE

The first possible underlying source of confusion is the way the state has been conceptualized. It has already been suggested that the state should be sharply differentiated from the government. Thus, a change of government, such as the Pact takeover, does not necessarily imply a change in the form of the state. As Trotsky once said, "Every policeman knows that though governments may change, the police remain."

In the case of parliamentary systems of government organized around political parties (especially where these parties represent only a small minority of society), this is particularly true. Viable parliamentary systems in which opposing parties have genuinely radical differences are rare. Nevertheless, liberals, nationalists, and Marxists alike have assumed that the change of government in 1924 expressed a significant change in the balances of power between capital and labor and within capital.

The striking similarities between the liberal and neo-Marxist views of contemporary South Africa have been commented on in another context.[39] It should also be pointed out that their conceptions of the state have significant similarities. Granted, the classic Marxist view of the state is instrumentalist (it sees the state as the tool of an economic class or "fraction" thereof), whereas the liberal view corresponds more to the idea of the state as a neutral arbiter of social conflict. What they share, however, is the idea that the state merely *represents* some other entity, whether it be a class or the public good or society as a whole. They refuse to accept, or fail to see, that in addition, the state can become at least partially autonomous, with distinct interests of its own. Both liberal and Marxist theories, in short, see the state as a "dependent variable" shaped by the near autonomy of society.[40]

This view leaves little room for analysis of the dynamic nature of the state in advanced capitalist states. The "representational" theorists would argue that there may be changes in the composition of groups that seize control of the state, but there is little room in their theory for changes in the nature and role of the state itself. It is seen as an unchanging, passive instrument that varies only with changes in the hands that wield it or changes of contestants between whom it arbitrates.

The liberal school of thought in South Africa has done little theoretical analysis of the state that goes much beyond Adam Smith and John Maynard Keynes.[41] Afrikaner nationalists have considered the subject at somewhat greater length, experimenting in the 1930s, in particular, with "organic" theories of the state that emerged from national socialist sources in Europe.[42] These are Fichtean theories of the mystical expression of the *volkswil* through the state, however, rather than serious analyses of the modern state. More recently, an attempt has been made to fuse Afrikaner nationalist views with conservative libertarian views of the state.[43]

The Marxists, or more accurately, the neo-Marxists, have made the most comprehensive effort to deal with the South African state. The bulk of this group is heavily influenced by the work of Nicos Poulantzas, a European Marxist who has attained some degree of influence in the Anglophone world, partly through a protracted debate with other Marxists in the columns of the *New Left Review*.[44] Part of the dispute concerns his uncompromising insistence that the state has no power but merely expresses class powers (modified in his later work); part centers around how the "relative autonomy of the state" should be understood. He says that the state *"institutions or the apparatuses do not 'possess' 'power' proper but do nothing but express and crystallize class powers"* [his emphasis].[45]

Poulantzas also argues that the dominant segments, or fractions, of the bourgeoisie (with perhaps the support of nonbourgeois classes when the former are divided) form a power bloc. These fractions contend for dominance (hegemony) within the power bloc. Even if state policy *appears* to be to the disadvantage of the whole bourgeoisie, however, it is in fact directed toward preserving the bourgeoisie's ultimate interests. He derives much of this from a somewhat superficial exegesis of Marx's *Eighteenth Brumaire of Louis Bonaparte*.

His theory that the "capitalist state" always protects the ultimate interests of the bourgeoisie is—as was pointed out more than thirty years ago by a critic of the same theory that Poulantzas now espouses—either trivial or tautological: "For there is no policy short of exterminating the bourgeoisie that could not be held to serve some economic or extra-economic, short-run or long-run, bourgeois interest, at least in the sense that it wards off still worse things."[46] Nevertheless, a large proportion of the British neo-Marxists writing about South Africa are, to some degree, Poulantzas disciples, many of them self-avowed.[47] The result has been a heavy emphasis on the struggles of "fractions" for "hegemony," which, though the terminology is different,[48] is basically indistinguishable from bourgeois party-political and interest analysis. The neo-Marxists are still heavily influenced by the very view of history that they deride, and their self-conscious rejection of the (liberal) "conventional wisdom" has not yet signalled an ability to cast off the latter's more misleading theoretical legacies.[49]

An exception is the work of Harold Wolpe, a more orthodox and rigorous Marxist who derides the theoretical confusion that allows the neo-Marxists to use terms such as *"white* working class," *"Afrikaner* petty bourgeoisie," and *"national* capital"; but Wolpe, too, sees the state as always an expression of something else (the mode of production) rather than being on occasion an actor with a degree of autonomy.[50]

Liberals, nationalists, and Marxists alike have thus shown the tendency to equate government and the state and, even where this is not done, to see the state as a mere instrument or representative of an interest group or coalition of groups. This manifests itself, *inter alia*, in the tendency to argue the turning-point theory. In rejecting the turning-point theory, this study also rejects the purely instrumental theory of the state; but this is not, of course, to espouse its diametric opposite, the autonomous state. It would be difficult, to put it mildly, to find anywhere in history examples of either purely autonomous or purely instrumental states. The real problem is to locate states sensitively on a conceptual spectrum between the two poles.

The shortcomings of the instrumental view have been dealt with here because they are the major weaknesses of the serious literature on the South African state, and they have tended to cut off some relevant comparative perspectives. The South African state, for example, shares many characteristics of the Latin American "bureaucratic-authoritarian" state, but the general tendency to conceptualize the South African state as instrumental has tended to disguise this. Conceivably, a revision of the so-called turning points of twentieth-century South African history might facilitate both a new periodization and a new conceptualization of the contemporary South African state.

SOURCES OF CONCEPTUAL CONFUSION 2: OVEREMPHASIS ON COLOR DISCRIMINATION

It has already been pointed out that the analysis of South Africa in the twentieth century overemphasizes its unique aspects, such as institutionalized race discrimination, and tends to distort these, first, by considering them in a vacuum and, second, by projecting their contemporary importance into the past.[51] This has taken concrete form in the historians' overly selective quest for the "origins" of South Africa's contemporary racial policy and in their tendency to wrench these origins out of their context by writing "legislative histories" or histories of the development of color-discriminatory legislation.[52]

This is not, of course, to deny that it is legitimate to seek the origins of contemporary racial policy; rather, it suggests that such studies tend to pull race out of context and distort its true significance. An example is the 1911 Mines and Works Act, famous or notorious in the historical literature as the first comprehensive legal color bar. In fact, the color-bar regulations had existed before and were not significantly expanded by the regulations attached to the act: they were hardly debated either in public or in private. The color bar was actually incidental to the Mines and Works Act; the real significance of the act was the marked increase of state intervention in the industry (see Chapter 3).

Yet most of the standard works covering in detail the unique development of color discrimination in South African industrial legislation do not bother to document the important growth of the state's role in determining hours of work, conditions of work, and safety and health regulations.[53] This process of intervention was paralleled in industrial states elsewhere—for example, Australia, which Creswell cited as justification—and was of great significance in understanding the changing situations of the state and industry. The historical overemphasis on race because of present concerns has thus impoverished other aspects of the historiography and has led to an implicit overstatement of South Africa's uniqueness.

In any case, there was a broad, if tacit, consensus among South African whites in the early twentieth century that accepted race discrimination: it was not a question of whether to discriminate, but one of how to discriminate.[54] Because blacks had scarcely any viable economic base, very few political rights, and hardly any access to the state, they had little or no influence on the debate. Partly for that reason, this is a study of white mobilization rather than black exploitation. There is a connection, of course: South African whites had wide divergences of interests and were, at times, united only by their agreement on the necessity to maintain the subordinate position of the blacks. This area of common interest was very important precisely because of the divided nature of the white population: an appeal to the white consensus on color discrimination (the black peril, or *swart gevaar*) was one sure way of mobilizing the support of white groups across the entire political spectrum.

Thus, this study will continually emphasize the political and rhetorical use made of the race issue. This is not to suggest that race was not a "real" issue: clearly, white miners did fear the possibility of replacement by ultra-low-wage black labor. Nevertheless, any analysis should also be sensitive to the political situation of organized white labor, which needed to mobilize the support of other white groups to pressure the state to help in the developing confrontation with the employers. One of the few ways white labor could generalize its support was by appealing to the belief of all white groups that blacks should continue to be subordinated and by overemphasizing the racial content of its differences with the mining capitalists. Conversely, the latter made every effort to underplay the racial issues and generally considered employing blacks at the expense of whites only as a last resort in dire cost crises.

This, it is suggested, is what happened in 1922. A major issue was the color bar, the legal and customary restriction of certain job categories to whites,[55] but the *overriding* issues were whether the increasingly militant white unions were to be conciliated or smashed, and what role the state was to play in the process. Organized labor felt itself under threat from the bosses as well as from black competition. It therefore responded by attempting to recruit outside support, claiming that the basic issue was whether white "civilization" was to survive. Hence the notorious marching slogan of 1922: "Workers of the world unite and fight for a white South Africa." Often cited as an example of fatuous irrationality, it had a logic of its own.

Judging from the lack of support from other white groups in 1922, the appeal to color prejudice was more convincing to today's historians than to yesterday's electorate. In analyzing South Africa, one needs continually to take account of this rhetorical overemphasis on the race issue. During the Rand Revolt, the use of color prejudice as a mobilizing device was particularly pervasive and deceptive.

Historians have been misled into believing that the Rand Revolt marked a frontal attack by the mining capitalists on color discrimination, which at first succeeded (with the crushing of the strike and the rejection by the judiciary in 1923 of the color-bar principle) and then failed (with the election of the Pact and the reinstatement of the principle by the legislature in 1925). They have mistakenly perceived the Rand Revolt as the battle against the color bar, the 1925 Mines and Works Act as the loss of the war against the color bar.

The liberal and nationalist schools have fairly obvious (equal but opposite) reasons for suggesting that the 1922 revolt was primarily about race discrimination—the former to blame working-class racism, the latter to praise the heroic Afrikaner, or white, defense of its identity.

The Marxists are once again something of a special case. They, too, are largely insensitive to the ideological war being waged to mobilize white opinion, but for a different reason: the violent rejection of black miners by white miners greatly perplexes those who are ideologically predisposed to believe in the innate purity and natural unity of the working class. The white miners never showed the remotest desire to link with their black counterparts to form a nonracial common working class. Though the whites occasionally sought and received cooperation from blacks—usually by threats of violence—to make their own strikes effective, they never reciprocated and, in fact, always volunteered freely to serve as "special constables" to help suppress any black working-class militance that arose.

A whole subbranch of South African historiography has developed in response to this problem, which attempts, in essence, to demonstrate that mining capitalists forced white miners to be racists in spite of the miners' valiant attempts to be true to their class.[56] This attempt to whitewash the working class by overstating the role of the mining capitalists[57] is a slavish reaction to the equally ludicrous argument that mining capitalists were forced into discrimination and exploitation by racist white workers. Both extremes[58] fail to take account of the role of the state; moreover, they eschew the simple explanation that both capitalists and white workers were eminently capable of encouraging or harnessing race prejudice, with the aim of transforming it into race discrimination to their respective advantages.

SOURCES OF CONCEPTUAL CONFUSION 3: RHETORIC AND REALITY

The third major conceptual problem one encounters in studies of modern South Africa is the failure to distinguish between the actual process of decision making and the ritualized, or public, process; and the failure to examine the real impact of policy decisions. It has already been mentioned that arguments occasionally are put forward in the text of a work that are contradicted by the statistics in the appendices. But why should this happen? The obvious explanation for the inadequate use of available statistical information is ignorance of its existence, reliability, and significance. This may be true of some, but Wilson, who has written one of the standard works on South African mine labor, specifically points out that "there can be few industries in the world that have published so much statistical information which can be used for purposes of comparison over so long a period of years."[59]

A more important reason for the neglect of the statistics is that they bear very little relationship to what appeared to be actually going on. If one reads the parliamentary debates, the press reports, the public pronouncements of capitalists and organized labor, and the legislation itself, one builds up a picture of an embattled mining capital and a triumphant white working class from the election of the Pact government onward. In fact, this is precisely the picture that both the state and capital were happy to encourage.

This is not to argue that the mining capitalists' early panic over the Pact takeover was not genuine; it was. But these fears can only be put into proper perspective by examining what was actually happening. To do this, one needs to know both the intentions of the state's policy and its consequences. One needs access to both the private deliberations on policy formation and the statistics showing the result of that policy.

They need to be read together; individually, they can be misleading. The statistics, for example, can only describe the *impact* of policy. Clearly, policy can have unintended consequences, especially as it operates in a dynamic context at least partially out of the control of the decision makers. Moreover, it is extremely difficult to break down the process by which decisions are made: to use primarily parliamentary debates, government commissions, and newspapers—as nearly all the accounts of white mine labor have done[60]—is to confine oneself to skewed sources that were intended primarily to mobilize public support. Not only that, but the authors of those sources frequently have every reason to consistently skew their accounts. The Pact government did promise to bring the mining capitalists to heel in order to mobilize and maintain electoral support, but for the historian merely to take it at its word is a gross error.

The three underlying problems in the historiography, it is submitted, explain a whole range of difficulties that are encountered in analyzing the modern South African state. Similar problems are, of course, manifest in the contemporary historiographies of other geographic areas, especially in dealing with issues such as the relationship of affluence and influence or of capitalism and political power in advanced electoral-industrial states. It is not intended to suggest that anyone can completely avoid the pitfalls outlined above,[61] but they are spelled out in some detail in the hope that the need for alternative approaches will be understood.

AN ALTERNATIVE APPROACH: ACCUMULATION AND LEGITIMATION

There is a growing body of literature in social science that analyzes modern capitalist states in terms of the fiscal or legitimation crises they are experiencing.[62] It is hoped that this case study may contribute to the new literature by showing the utility and relevance of its organizing concepts—the accumulation and legitimation imperatives of the state—to more diverse situations than those to which it has been applied. Even more ambitiously, it is hoped that the South African experience may throw some light on the contemporary postindustrial capitalist state. The South African state, it will be shown, faced a crisis of sovereignty arising from the contradictory imperatives of capital accumulation and state legitimation long before the advanced capitalist states of Western Europe, the United States, and Japan. "Colonial societies," it is suggested, would repay more study by academics dealing with "advanced" industrial societies, as they frequently exhibit many social and political tendencies far earlier and in "purer," more recognizable form than their "mother" societies. One striking example of this argues that most of the essentials of Nazi genocidal policies were manifested in the German administration in South-West Africa well before World War I.[63] And students of organized labor in the United Kingdom will be struck by parallels between the general strikes of 1922 (on the Rand) and 1926 (in Britain). For the British, 1926 marked the first general confrontation between state and organized labor;[64] in South Africa, such confrontations began as early as 1913.

The Transvaal state and the newly unified South African state were fledgling capitalist states with enormous problems of raising revenue and providing employment for their white electorate, which was pouring into the urban areas at an accelerating pace. Their most important source of revenue was the gold mining industry, which was also vital as a direct employer of about 10,000 whites and, through its multiplier effect on the economy, was the source of many thousands more jobs in the state bureaucracy (particularly the railways) and in service industries.

For these reasons, it is ultimately impossible to separate the interests of the mining industry from those of the new state. Nevertheless, it is not accurate to see this relationship in terms of domination. A congruence or overlapping of specific interests would characterize the situation far better.[65] To survive, the state necessarily had to commit itself increasingly to ensuring the viability of certain key industries, especially the gold mines; at the same time, it had to do this in a way that would not fundamentally estrange the white electorate. It needed, if possible, to retain the support or complaisance of the white miners. But far more importantly, it needed to prevent the white miners from elevating their particular interests into general issues that might mobilize the white electorate as a whole.

As long as the gold mines remained profitable, the state could maintain a delicate balance between its revenue and employment imperatives. But whenever profits were squeezed, costs had to be cut (because the mining capitalists were not able to lift the price of gold). Since white labor was a very important and highly paid component of costs, by world standards as well as by South African standards, its wages were generally squeezed by any profit reductions. This was the case even though both the state and the industry would always attempt to reduce other costs first (managerial rewards being the sole exception).

The reason for the reluctance to challenge organized labor has already been suggested: the explosive political potential of the white labor issue. A crisis of gold mining profits during the early days of the South African state, therefore, led inevitably to a crisis of the state itself: its legitimacy and economic viability were dependent on white employment and on gold mining revenue. Capital accumulation and state legitimation, then, were the major problems of the fledgling South African state. This is not, of course, to argue that all its problems of legitimation necessarily emerged from problems of accumulation: the 1914 *rural* Afrikaner rebellion, for example, was a nationalist and anti-Imperialist threat to the legitimacy of the state, but it had little, if any, connection to the problems of accumulation or revenue.

When the state's "wealth producing" and mobilizing functions came into conflict, the South African Government increased state intervention in an attempt to ease the contradiction. As the Secretary for Mines and Industries pointed out in 1924 (before the victory of the Pact), this process of state intervention was greatly speeded up by the diversification of the economy inspired by World War I.[66] The process, though uneven, was inexorable.

This, if anything, was the significance of the Rand Revolt: it demonstrated to the government that a far more comprehensive, structured state role in the industrial order was essential. Thus, it will be argued, if any event in 1924 was crucial to the South African state, it was the passing of the Industrial Conciliation Act in 1924 by the S.A. party government, before the Pact took over, supported by a broad party consensus and by a united front of mining, industrial, agricultural, and even organized labor interests.

This legislation, which structured state intervention into collective industrial bargaining, did not mark a departure from previous policy and was not a turning point. But it was an important signpost on the road toward a fully interventionist state with assured sovereignty. The change would have come under any white parliamentary government with vital interests in the stability of *capitalism* (as opposed to specific groups of *capitalists*). The structure of the state and its legitimation and accumulation problems imposed certain imperatives on all potential governments of the time. The extent to which the gold mining industry could be used to solve the revenue (or accumulation) and employment (or legitimation) problems of the state were broadly circumscribed by the nature of the industry and of the South African political economy, not by the policies of the various political parties.

Ironically, it was under the Pact government that the state finally realized and accepted that the mining industry could not be asked both to accept the burden of the employment problem and to continue to be a reliable source of revenue. The Pact, it is true, increased the state's encouragement of local manufacturing industry, a policy that the S.A. party had initiated, but it achieved this partly by compelling the manufacturing industry to employ more white labor at wages higher than those paid to the blacks who were being replaced. Thus, the Pact's "civilized labor policy" was paid for partly by the manufacturing industry. The increased tariff protection provided by the Pact, in other words, had strings attached.

The effect of these strings was that the Pact government formally transferred the burden of providing sheltered employment for whites from the mining to the manufacturing and the state sectors. Previously, during the tenure of the S.A. party government, the mining industry was unofficially obliged to provide jobs for semiskilled and unskilled whites under the so-called Status Quo Agreement. These jobs were either superfluous or were already being done—at a fraction of the wage—by Africans or coloreds (men of mixed racial descent). White jobs under the Status Quo Agreement amounted to a form of subsidy of white labor by the mine con-trollers, given the availability of unorganized, rightless black labor. The Status Quo Agreement was killed by the events of 1922. In-stead of resurrecting it after 1924, however, the Pact government devised a "civilized labor policy," which forced employers in the manufacturing and state sectors to employ whites at a "civilized wage."

This meant that whites would henceforth be employed in jobs previously done at a far lower wage by blacks and that the burden would be borne by the manufacturing industries and the state as a whole. Transferring the burden of sheltered white employment from the mining industry was one of the most important and far-reaching of the Pact's policies, but it has received little or no atten-tion from accounts of the period. In fact, these accounts have almost universally argued that the mining industry suffered as a result of the Pact government's policies, which favored other sec-tors such as the manufacturers or white miners.

Some reasons for this unbalanced interpretation have already been suggested. The Pact did take certain measures to protect both white labor and local manufacturing industries. It is easy to take these at face value—after all, the Pact's electoral constituency did—and to assume a tilt of the state against mining capital. This interpretation is made even more seductive by the mine controllers' propaganda machine, which unremittingly complained about the Pact's reinstatement of the statutory color bar and the protection of local industries by the erection of tariff barriers. It is true that these measures lifted mining costs, but one should not identify the two measures with the Pact's package as a whole.

Both the Pact and mining capital had an interest in portraying the Pact's overall program as an attack on mining capital. Their prop-aganda is still deceiving commentators today, though it is demon-strably untrue. In fact, as has been shown earlier, and will be shown in more detail later, mining costs fell under the Pact and stayed low, and industrial turbulence on the mines virtually disappeared.

This is not to argue that gold mining boomed under the Pact: the static gold price, determined on world markets, precluded that. Rather, it suggests that it did as well as the Pact government could reasonably ensure. Profit margins in the gold mining industry in the 1920s were generally satisfactory to investors, but not nearly tempting enough to encourage large increases of investment, particularly from abroad. Gold mining in the 1920s simply could not afford to finance the diversification of the South African economy; it could not even afford to pay significantly more in taxes. The Pact government—with a little help from the state bureaucracy—quickly came to understand this and acted accordingly.

After devaluation in 1932 and the effective doubling of the gold price in 1933, however, the mining industry could, and in large measure did, finance such a diversification program. The irony of this, particularly for those who see the election of the Pact as a turning point, is that the vastly increased appropriations from the mining industry came from the new Fusion government, a combination of the old S.A. party and the National party from which the Labour party had been purged.[67]

If there is any date that might be chosen as marking a turning point for the modern South African state, then it is 1933. It can be more accurately termed a turning point than the other dates suggested because the doubling of the gold price (over which the South African government and state had no control) brought with it striking effects that were not logically implied by an examination of the trends in South African society.

The doubling of the gold price not only made it possible for the mining industry to finance the diversification of the country's economy; it also made possible the solution (through increased direct employment and through a general multiplier effect) of the white unemployment and the poor white problems. Finally, it gave the state an assured source of direct income. This enabled the state to increase vastly its borrowing powers while simultaneously reducing the proportion of its foreign borrowing. Thus (again through a multiplier effect), the state's degree of autonomy, both national and international, was immeasurably increased.

NOTES

1. The extensive hagiographic literature of Afrikaner nationalism is perceptively reviewed and analyzed in F. A. van Jaarsveld's much underrated *Afrikaner's Interpretation of South African History*, Cape Town, 1964. See also Leonard Thompson, "Afrikaner Nationalist Historiography and the Policy of Apartheid," *Journal of African History*, Vol. 3, No. 1, 1962.

2. A not totally unsympathetic example of the "white tribe" school is

provided by a non-South African Anglophone, Sheila Patterson, in *The Last Trek: A Study of the Boer People and the Afrikaner Nation*, London, 1957. This is probably the best example of its type. One of the worst is provided by another non-South African, W. H. Vatcher, *White Laager*, London, 1965.

3. David Welsh's excellent short overview, "English-speaking Whites and the Racial Problem," in a collection edited by André de Villiers, *English-speaking South Africa Today*, Cape Town, 1976, clearly outlines the decisive Anglophone contribution (p. 226). But Welsh finally accepts the argument that the Anglophone sin has been one of omission rather than of commission, of failing to follow basically "liberal instincts" (p. 236).

4. Anglophones show an uncharacteristic preference for the use of the Afrikaans word in the case of "apartheid" (separateness). This is not unconnected with their desire to avoid the opprobrium generated internationally by that policy. The same preference—and hypocrisy—is to be found elsewhere in the Anglophone world among those anxious to distance themselves from the racist sins of their forefathers and fathers. Another popular Afrikaans word useful for distancing purposes is "laager"; for example, W. H. Vatcher, *White Laager; Christian Science Monitor*; and *New York Times*, passim. The "laager," of course, was not unknown to the American frontier. It was also used in Europe as early as 1420 (Barbara W. Tuchman, *A Distant Mirror: The Calamitous 14th Century*, Harmondsworth, 1979, p. 591).

5. C. M. Tatz's study of the origins of segregation, *Shadow and Substance in South Africa*, Pietermaritzburg, 1962, is a representative example, which, like many such works of liberal historiography, is nevertheless a solid and valuable piece of work.

6. The unusually direct connection between political liberalism and laissez-faire capitalism found in South Africa is discussed in David Yudelman, "Industrialization, Race Relations and Change in South Africa: An Ideological and Academic Debate," *African Affairs*, January 1975.

7. W. K. Hancock, *Survey of British Commonwealth Affairs*, Vol. 2. *Problems of Economic Policy, 1918–1939*, Part 2, London, 1940, p. 64: "The racial-economic system of South Africa is an extraordinary one, but the impulses which have created it are 'natural' . . . the Australians, or . . . the English, if their situation had been a similar one, might have adopted very similar policies." Another exception is C. W. de Kiewiet, *A History of South Africa: Social and Economic*, 1st ed., London, 1941. Both books were written before the era of apartheid and the United Nations; that is, before the uniqueness of South Africa began to be regarded as a difference of kind rather than a difference of degree.

8. Yudelman, "Industrialization, Race Relations and Change in South Africa"; and a neo-Marxist's partial response, accepting that the debate has

reached an impasse: Martin Legassick, "Race, Industrialization and Social Change: The Case of R.F.A. Hoernle," *African Affairs*, April 1976. See also T.R.H. Davenport, *South Africa: A Modern History*, London, 1977, "The Current Debate," pp. 371–76. For a useful Latin American perspective on the general debate on industrialization and social change, see Guillermo A. O'Donnell, *Modernization and Bureaucratic Authoritarianism: Studies in South American Politics*, Berkeley, Calif., 1973.

9. Heribert Adam, *Modernizing Racial Domination: South Africa's Political Dynamics*, Berkeley, Calif., 1971.

10. For an examination of South African state formation in an even earlier period, see Shula Marks and Stanley Trapido, "Lord Milner and the South African State," *History Workshop*, Vol. 8, 1979; and Yudelman, "Capital, Capitalists and Power in South Africa," *Social Dynamics*, Vol. 6, No. 2, December 1980.

11. For example, Jurgen Habermas, *Legitimation Crisis*, Boston, 1973; James O'Connor, *The Fiscal Crisis of the State*, New York, 1973; James Weinstein, *The Corporate Ideal in the Liberal State, 1900–1918*, Boston, 1968.

12. A partial exception is Frederick A. Johnstone, *Class, Race and Gold: A Study of Race Relations and Racial Discrimination in South Africa*, London, 1976. But Johnstone has failed to cover many of the basic sources. For a detailed review of his book, see David Yudelman, "The Quest for a neo-Marxist Approach to Contemporary South Africa," *South African Journal of Economics*, Vol. 45, No. 2, June 1977, pp. 201–205.

13. Ralph Miliband, *The State in Capitalist Society*, New York, 1969, p. 161.

14. Nils Elvander, "The Role of the State in the Settlement of Labor Disputes in the Nordic Countries: A Comparative Analysis," *European Journal of Political Research*, Vol. 2, 1974, p. 364, makes this criticism. Some treatments of the topic in the context of Latin America are, however, emerging. See Kenneth S. Mericle, "Conflict Regulation in the Brazilian Industrial Relations System," Ph.D. diss., University of Wisconsin, 1974.

15. Alfred Stepan, *The State and Society: Peru in Comparative Perspective*, Princeton, N.J., 1978.

16. H. Warington Smyth, "Fostering of Productive Industries: State as Wealth Producer," lecture to the University of Cape Town, April 1924, reprinted in the *Cape Times*, 3, 5, 6 May 1924.

17. To use the terminology of the utilitarian Jeremy Bentham, they were "nonagenda" items. A modern literature on the control of "agendas" is developing: for example, Peter Bachrach and Morton S. Baratz, *Power and Poverty: Theory and Practice*, New York, 1970, p. 44: ". . . nondecision-making is a means by which demands for change in the existing allocation

of benefits and privileges in the community can be suffocated before they are even voiced; or kept cover; or killed before they gain access to the relevant decision-making arena . . ."

18. The best general study is still Sheila van der Horst's classic *Native Labour in South Africa*, London, 1942. See also Alan Jeeves, "The Control of Migratory Labour on the South African Gold Mines in the Era of Kruger and Milner," *Journal of South African Studies*, Vol. 2, No. 1, October 1975, and Alan Jeeves, "Competitive Recruiting and Labour Piracy in South-East Africa, 1900–1921," University of the Witwatersrand History Workshop, February 1981.

19. De Kiewiet, *History of South Africa*, p. 114.

20. Jeeves, "The Control of Migratory Labour."

21. De Kiewiet, *History of South Africa*, pp. 99, 255. Jeeves, "The Control of Migratory Labor," somewhat misleadingly compares the role of gold in South Africa to that of railways in Canada and the United States, saying they were both "perceived as the basic instruments of nation building." In fact, railways performed much the same function in South Africa as in Australia, New Zealand, Canada, and the United States. The degree to which the state underwrote them varied but was vital in all cases; and in each case, they were a service industry to provide for the needs of a profitable primary and exporting industry.

22. A detailed history of the relationship between the state and the gold mining industry in the nineteenth century is being prepared by a Cambridge University doctoral candidate, Richard Mendelsohn. I am indebted to him for many background discussions on the topic. See also Shula Marks and Stanley Trapido, "Lord Milner and the South African State," for a superficial instrumentalist treatment of the topic. Marks subsequently modified her position and was converted to a partially symbiotic view of the state-capital relationship. See Shula Marks, "Scrambling for South Africa," *Journal of African History*, 23, 1982, pp. 106, 113.

23. Two major treatments of the reconstruction, emphasizing the role of the industry, are Donald Denoon, *A Grand Illusion: The Failure of Imperial Policy in the Transvaal Colony During the Period of Reconstruction, 1900–1905*, London, 1973; and Arthur A. Mawby, "The Political Behavior of the British Population of the Transvaal, 1902–1907," Ph.D. diss., University of Witwatersrand, 1969. They have also exchanged articles on the degree of "capitalist influence" exerted on the state and alleged differences between deep-level and outcrop mining groups. Mawby convincingly dismisses the significance of Denoon's distinction, but neither of their explanations of "capitalist influence" or lack thereof is convincing. Both argue the issue in terms of domination and show little understanding of wide-ranging congruences of interests between the state and capital. See

also Denoon, "Capital and Capitalists in the Transvaal in the 1890's and 1900's," *Historical Journal*, Vol. 23, No. 1, 1980; and Yudelman, "Capital, Capitalists and Power."

24. Some accounts of the Rand Revolt are: A. P. Cartwright, *The Gold Miners*, Johannesburg, ca. 1962; Norman Herd, *1922: The Revolt of the Rand*, Johannesburg, 1966; Union of South Africa, *Report of the Martial Law Inquiry Judicial Commission* (UG 35-1922), Pretoria, 1922; Bernard Hessian, "An Investigation into the Causes of the Labour Agitation on the Witwatersrand, January to March 1922," Master's thesis, University of Witwatersrand, 1957; Johnstone, *Class, Race and Gold*; H. J. and R. E. Simons, *Class and Colour in South Africa, 1850-1950*, Harmondsworth, Middlesex, 1969; I. L. Walker and B. Weinbren, *2,000 Casualties: A History of the Trade Unions and the Labour Movement in the Union of South Africa*, Johannesburg, 1961. All of these suffer from being insufficiently based on the primary sources.

25. Secretary for Mines Archives (henceforth MM), MM 1311/22, Vol. 617, "Report on the 1921-1922 Labor Unrest and Rebellion," by the Government Inspector of White Labor, says 219 were killed and 591 wounded.

26. Francis Wilson, *Labour in the South African Gold Mines, 1911-1969*, Cambridge, 1972, p. 11; Johnstone, *Class, Race and Gold*, pp. 145, 167.

27. W. K. Hancock, *Smuts 2: The Fields of Force, 1919-1950*, Cambridge, 1968, p. 68; Hessian, "An Investigation," p. 2; David Kaplan, "The State and Economic Development in South Africa," University of the Witwatersrand, mimeographed, 1975, pp. 16-17; Simons and Simons, *Class and Colour*, p. 321; Davenport, *South Africa*, pp. 199, 200, 361; and Welsh, "English-speaking Whites," p. 232.

28. All this is amply documented in the Annual Reports of the Transvaal Chamber of Mines (ARTCM), in the Annual Reports of the Government Mining Engineer (ARGME), and in the *Official Yearbook* of the Union of South Africa (Yearbook). Tables and graphs extracted from these sources are to be found in the text. The figures were put together and commented on in David Yudelman, "All the King's Men: Reflections on the 1922 Rand Revolt and Its Historiography," Yale University, mimeographed, 1973, p. 17ff. A copy of the paper is lodged with the History Department, Yale University.

29. Recently some neo-Marxists have altered or amplified their earlier positions to make the point that the post-1924 industrial order had disadvantages for white workers and defended "the political interests of capital." But it is still argued that "state interventions" conferred "substantial economic and social benefits on white wage earners . . . ," Robert Davies and David Lewis, "Industrial Relations Legislation: One of Capital's Defences," *Review of African Political Economy*, No. 7, Septem-

ber–December 1976, pp. 58, 60. In an earlier article, "The White Working Class in South Africa," *New Left Review*, No. 82, November–December 1973, p. 45, Davies uncritically lists the benefits of the Pact for the white workers. Finally, in *Capital, State and White Labor in South Africa, 1900–1960: An Historical Materialist Analysis of Class Formation and Class Relations*, New Jersey, 1979, p. 157, Davies has the temerity to criticize Francis Wilson for seeing 1922 as a Pyrrhic victory for the mining industry, without recanting on his own misreading of 1922.

30. Robert Davies, David Kaplan, Mike Morris, Dan O'Meara, "Class Struggle and the Periodization of the State in South Africa," *Review of African Political Economy*, No. 7, September–December 1976 (henceforth Davies et al.), p. 11, argues this while suggesting that the "white workers' state" was a myth. Compare with Kaplan's earlier view that " 'white workers' privilege' was entrenched [by the Pact] in a variety of legislative measures," "The State," pp. 16–17.

31. Stanley Greenberg, "Race and Business Enterprise in South Africa, Part 2," mimeographed, Yale University, 1976, p. 10; Ralph Horwitz, *The Political Economy of South Africa*, London, 1967, p. 217; Kaplan, "The State," p. 12; and Edward Roux, *Time Longer than Rope: A History of the Black Man's Struggle for Freedom in South Africa*, London, 1948, p. 155.

32. Davies, "White Working Class," p. 44; Davies, *Capital, State and White Labor*, p. 169; Davies et al., *Review*, pp. 9–10, 12–13; B. J. Liebenberg, "The Union of South Africa up to the Statute of Westminster, 1910–1931," in *500 Years: A History of South Africa*, edited by C. F. J. Muller, 2nd edition, New York, 1975 p. 399; G. V. Doxey, *The Industrial Color Bar in South Africa*, Cape Town, 1961, p. 126; David E. Kaplan, "Class Conflict, Capital Accumulation and the State: An Historical Analysis of the State in Twentieth-Century South Africa," Ph.D. diss., University of Sussex, December 1977, abstract page, passim. For a more cautious and qualified version of this argument, see Belinda Bozzoli, "The Origins, Development and Ideology of Local Manufacturing in South Africa," *Journal of Southern African Studies*, Vol. 1, No. 2, April 1975, and Belinda Bozzoli, *The Political Nature of a Ruling Class*, London, 1981.

33. Davies et al., *Review*, pp. 9, 13; Davies, *Capital, State and White Labor*, p. 179; Kaplan, "Class Conflict, Capital Accumulation and the State," abstract page, passim.

34. See, for example, S. H. Frankel, *The Railway Policy of South Africa*, Johannesburg, 1928.

35. Kaplan, "The State and Economic Development," passim. Kaplan, for example, tries to prove the theory by showing (p. 9) that the value of total gold output increased from an index base of 100 in 1913 to 220.9 in 1937, dividends to 208, and taxation to 1191. The major point he does not make is that 1922 state receipts from the gold mines more than trebled in

1933, the reason being the doubling of the gold price, which brought enormous windfall profits to the gold mines. Though taxation went up faster, profits remaining were still, in the words of one company history, beyond the dreams of avarice. The government imposing the tax, moreover, was not the Pact, but the new United party government, a fusion of the old S.A. party, which supposedly represented mining capital, and the National party. Kaplan's schematic and dogmatic attempts to impose the revisionist ideas of Nicos Poulantzas, a much-overrated, recently deceased neo-Marxist theorist, on the South African situation has led to a series of half-truths and errors too numerous to detail here. It should be mentioned that Kaplan's work, although largely unpublished, has been most influential among the neo-Marxists writing about South Africa and is frequently cited with approval.

36. Leo Katzen, *Gold and the South African Economy: The Influence of the Gold Mining Industry on Business Cycles and Economic Growth in South Africa, 1886–1961*, Cape Town, 1964, pp. 56–57. (See also Table 11.) The figures, of course, do not alone refute the proposition that the Pact primarily represented nongold-mining interests, but they do suggest that even the opposite may have been true. The figures, incidentally, appear to exclude growing state revenue from the lease mines. Although this might tend to understate total revenue from mines, the lease revenue did not result from any action by the Pact government—the lease concept was introduced before 1920 and was made viable by the S.A. party government. The fact that lease payments increased under the Pact government was due to contingent circumstances (the largest lease mine radically increased profits at this time and lease payments were linked to profits) and had nothing to do with the Pact's program or policy.

37. Davies et al., *Review*, passim; Kaplan, "The State and Economic Development," passim; Kaplan, "Class Conflict, Capital Accumulation and the State," passim; Davies, *Capital, State and White Labor*, passim.

38. For example, Wilson, *Labour*; Horwitz, *Political Economy*.

39. Yudelman, "Industrialization, Race Relations and Change," p. 95; Yudelman, "Quest for a Neo-Marxist Approach," p. 205; Simon Clarke, "Capital, Fractions of Capital and the State: 'Neo-Marxist' Analysis of the South African State," *Capital and Class*, 1978, passim.

40. Stepan, *The State*, p. 3ff.

41. See F. J. van Biljon, *State Interference in South Africa*, London, 1939.

42. For example, J. Albert Coetzee, *Politieke Groepering in die Wording van die Afrikanernasie*, Johannesburg, 1941.

43. J. A. Lombard, *Freedom, Welfare and Order: Thoughts on the Principles of Political Cooperation in the Economy of Southern Africa*, Pretoria, 1978; A. D. Wassenaar, *Assault on Private Enterprise*, Cape Town, 1977.

44. See also *Ideology in Social Science: Readings in Critical Social Theory*, edited by Robin Blackburn, Bungay, U.K., 1973, for an exchange between Poulantzas and Ralph Miliband.

45. Nicos Poulantzas, "Internationalization of Capitalist Relations in the Nation-State," *Economy and Society*, Vol. 3, No. 2, May 1974, p. 164.

46. Joseph A. Schumpeter, *Capitalism, Socialism and Democracy*, 2d ed., New York, 1947, p. 56.

47. For example, Davies et al., *Review*, p. 4. In spite of the frequent recantations that the South African neo-Marxists indulge in (they call them "self-critiques") and that all the above have resorted to, it would still be accurate to characterize them as Poulantzians.

48. Their extreme antipathy to everyday usage and their tendency to create their own terminology would be justified if the new jargon were more precise and less ideological. Unfortunately, the new jargon is frequently just a translation of the old. As the Rev. R. A. Spooner is reported to have once said after leaving the pulpit: "Incidentally, every time I said Aristotle I meant St. Paul." Sometimes the translation not only repeats the problems of the old concept but compounds them: "metropolitan capital" (mining capital) and "national capital" (agricultural and/or secondary industry) are examples of inaccurate, amorphous, and analytically dubious terms on which great weight is placed.

49. See note 39.

50. Harold Wolpe, "The 'White Working Class' in South Africa," *Economy and Society*, Vol. 5, No. 2, May 1976, pp. 197–240. For a polemical attack on the neo-Marxist use of mixed terminology, their view of the state, and the neo-Marxist school in general, see Brian Kantor and Henry Kenny, "The Poverty of Neo-Marxism: The Case of South Africa," *Journal of Southern African Studies*, Vol. 3, No. 1, October 1976.

51. The standard theoretical treatment of this problem is Herbert Butterfield, *The Whig Interpretation of History*, London, 1931. For applications of Butterfield's analysis, see Yudelman, "Slavery and Race Relations," and "Industrialization, Race Relations and Change."

52. Though in some ways misleading, these can, of course, be competent and useful. See, for example, G. V. Doxey, *The Industrial Colour Bar in South Africa*.

53. For example, D. Hobart Houghton, *The South African Economy*, Cape Town, 1973; *The Oxford History of South Africa*, Vol. 2, edited by Leonard H. Thompson and Monica Wilson, Oxford, 1971; Doxey, *The Industrial Colour Bar*; Simons and Simons, *Class and Colour*.

54. This is the real reason for the continual parrot-cry in white South African political circles throughout the twentieth century not to allow the black to become a "political football." To prevent a tactical issue from becoming a strategic issue, it is necessary to keep it out of the arena of public debate.

55. Johnstone, *Race, Class and Gold*, attempts to distinguish between the color bar (which he calls the "job colour bar") and other forms of color discrimination. Yudelman, in "The Quest," argues that Johnstone's categorization, "exploitation colour bars," are not color bars at all, and that it obfuscates the actual structure of discrimination to designate them in that way.

56. Davies had suggested two explanations: the carrot offered by capitalists in sharing the fruits of exploitation of blacks (in "The White Working Class"), and the stick wielded by the capitalists in forcibly dividing the working class and preventing black/white fraternization (in "Mining Capital, the State and Unskilled White Workers in South Africa, 1901–1913," *Journal of Southern African Studies*, Vol. 3, No. 1, October 1976). Both explanations (which are also offered by Johnstone) are unconvincing. Wolpe, "White Working Class," systematically destroys the former argument. Davies produces no convincing evidence to support the latter argument, showing neither that the white miners disapproved of the division of the work force by types of job, nor that white workers *wanted* fraternization. Besides, fraternization was not excluded by separating job categories. The work force was still physically integrated. Wolpe argues that the different functions of jobs done—the difference in the relations of production to capital—divide the working class. He does not attempt to explain why this division is a racial one and even seems open to the idea that the "real" working class is not divided racially.

57. The most extreme example of this is to be found in Greenberg, "Race and Business Enterprise," p. 45. Greenberg, whose theoretical orientation is only partially Marxist, argues that both the "job color bar" and work ratios were introduced at the insistence of various mining houses to prevent competitive advantages from developing among themselves. The only evidence he cites is irrelevant: it refers to ratios and divisions of skills *within* the black labor force, and not *between* black and white labor. See also Greenberg, *Race and State*, p. 183.

58. For a critique of the tendency to attribute most white labor unrest up to 1913 to race discrimination and color bars, see Elaine Katz, "White Workers' Grievances and the Industrial Colour Bar, 1902–1913," *South African Journal of Economics*, Vol. 42, No. 2, 1974.

59. Wilson, *Labour in the South African Gold Mines*, p. xi.

60. Johnstone is a partial exception but, as has been pointed out (Yudelman, "Quest"), concentrates heavily on "public sources." See also note 12.

61. The writer, for one, cannot claim to be immune. See Yudelman, "Quest," p. 204, for an exaggeration of the importance of the color-bar issue in 1922.

62. O'Connor, *The Fiscal Crisis of the State*, and Habermas, *Legitimation Crisis*, use these as central organizing concepts in their analyses.

63. Helmut Bley, *South-West Africa under German Rule, 1894–1914*, London, 1971, p. 282:

> The conflict between the Africans and their European rulers caused a situation in which contemporary ideas developed in a way not relevant to Germany until 1914, or fully until 1933. Methods and attitudes towards the treatment of population groups may even be said to have influenced attitudes within Germany itself. This was possibly not least because the Germans tackled the Colonial disputes in South-West Africa on the basis of their experience of social unrest in contemporary Europe. The division of power in Africa allowed the ideas and methods of modern state control to become obsolete. In SWA conditions crossed over into totalitarianism.

See also Hannah Arendt, *Origins of Totalitarianism*, New York, 1966. I am indebted to Heribert Adam and Hannah Arendt for discussions of this point.

64. Denis Barnes and Eileen Reid, *Governments and Trade Unions: The British Experience, 1964–1979*, London, 1980, p. 6. The 1929 general strike "was denounced as an attempt by the unions to coerce the government by use of industrial power." It is argued below in considerable detail (see especially Chapters 4 and 5) that the 1922 strike was about exactly the same basic issue and that one should not be unduly distracted by the sound and fury of the color bar issue. Naturally there were enormous differences between the South African and British cases; but the central clash on the proper use of industrial power was strikingly similar, as was its results over the following fifteen years.

65. For a useful treatment of congruence of interest as applied to the state and business in Mexico, see Susan Kaufman Purcell, *The Mexican Profit-Sharing Decision: Politics in an Authoritarian Regime*, Berkeley, Calif., 1975, especially pp. 145–47. See also Yudelman, "Capital, Capitalists and Power," on the symbiotic relationship of the state and large-scale business.

66. H. Warington Smyth, "Fostering."

67. The Minister primarily responsible for the massive increases in mining taxation (very strenuously resisted by the industry in public) was Patrick Duncan, one of the "bright young men" who had been brought in by the British after 1902 to restructure the Transvaal bureaucracy. Duncan stayed on after Union, becoming one of the most prominent figures in the Unionist party (which has generally, if mistakenly, been seen by historians as the mere mouthpiece of the gold mining industry) before its absorption into the S.A. party in 1921.

2

The New *Modus Vivendi* Between State and Capital, 1902–1909

> War is all very well as a last resort, but even if . . . a Conservative Government did get back into power with . . . the courage even to take the extreme step of altering the Constitution, the mining industry would be pretty well ground into a powder before all this would happen.
> —Lionel Phillips, mining magnate, 1907[1]

GOLD MINING AND ITS CONTEXT: THE RECONSTRUCTION ERA

Gold mining capital in the Transvaal at the turn of the century was indubitably a big fish in a small pond, almost the only fish in the economic pond. The South African War of 1899–1902 (also known as the "Boer War") between the Transvaal and Britain taught it once and for all, however, that it could not afford turbulence in its small pond. Never again has it been seriously tempted to confront the state directly in a physical trial of strength.

The degree of mining capital's responsibility for the war in the first place is still a moot point,[2] with which this study is not concerned. What is important is the fact that the controllers of the mining industry[3] had come to realize by the time of reconstruction that they needed stability as a prerequisite for development. This meant that they would have to work with any state, however imperfect, that could provide stability.[4] They could still oppose individual governments, and did; but that opposition was to be restricted to electoral politics, and progressively it did not go even that far.

Part of the reason for this restraint is found in the nature of the industry itself: it was a large employer of labor, by far the largest in the Transvaal, and it was remote from its markets (Europe and the

United States) and suppliers. As such, it was totally dependent on the state's transport and policing functions. Since it also imported machinery and stores and exported gold, the level of tariffs was vital.

The ore mined was found in relatively constant reef formations and in large amounts, but it was (and still is) very low grade—that is, it had a low content of gold relative to the amounts of ore that had to be mined and crushed to extract that gold. Moreover, it was becoming necessary to mine deeper as the outcrops of gold reefs were worked out. This, in turn, necessitated more capital, more labor, and more political stability.

In some respects, the gold mining industry is unique, notably in that there has always been (until this decade at least) an almost infinite market for gold at a price that is fixed by factors beyond the control of the industry. This means that companies that mine gold do not have to compete for markets (for they can sell all they produce), and that they can maximize profits only by minimizing costs (as they cannot lift the price of their product) or by increasing their volume.

The companies, then, were not competing with each other for markets, because of the almost infinite demand for their product. They all wanted to minimize costs and would not suffer if their competitors did the same. Hence, technological advances were shared among competing firms to an extent rarely paralleled in industries where technology is a crucial factor. In Australia, by contrast, zinc mining was characterized by intense competition for markets, which resulted, in turn, in ruthless struggles and much litigation over zinc-separation processes.

Competition arose, however, whenever production was threatened by shortages within the partial control of the mine controllers. When black labor was scarce, for example, rifts would start opening up between mine controllers. Enlisting the help of the state, mining capital increasingly managed to suppress its internecine competition for black labor. Its greater long-term need was to collaborate in ensuring the stability of that supply at low wages.[5] The quest for mineral rights also created competition among companies and groups in their quest to maximize output.

There was little competition for white labor, however, largely because supplies of white labor were readily available, except for a short period during World War I when British-born miners enlisted in large numbers. Capital was far less concerned with the supply of white labor than with its cost; therefore, it is generally justifiable to infer a united front of gold mining groups on the issue of white labor.

The lack of competition for markets and the success of the employers in establishing monopsonistic black labor recruiting organizations enable one to suggest further that the substantial congruence of interest among groups generally justifies reference to the Witwatersrand gold mine controllers as a distinct group with common interests.[6]

Above all, the industry was cost-sensitive, and wages were a very large part of total costs, averaging 45–55 percent, with a little over half of that going to whites. Blacks outnumbered whites by between seven and ten to one, but whites earned between ten and twenty times more per capita than blacks. The earnings gap originated because of the initial relative scarcity of white artisan mineworkers, who had to be attracted from Britain, Europe, and Australia, and the relative abundance of unskilled black labor, which was further disadvantaged by its lack of political and economic rights. The gap was reinforced by cultural, racial, and class interests.

The industry was geographically confined at the time to the Witwatersrand Reef, which ran roughly east–west for approximately forty miles. Johannesburg, where the first major discovery had been made, was roughly in the middle. The Reef (also known as the Rand) was clustered with gold mining companies, situated side by side, mining different parts of the same ore body, and generally using the same techniques.

Most gold mines were individual public companies, attached to one of a small number of groups (the number varied over time, but there were usually between six and ten) that dominated the industry. The groups administered the individual mines, though frequently holding only a small percentage of the company's shares. This system of administration enabled the pooling of technical and managerial expertise among companies in the group, thus reducing overhead expenses.

The group system also facilitated the amalgamation of mines into larger units enjoying greater economies of scale and vastly increased the ability of individual companies to raise capital. It suffered from certain drawbacks that have been little commented on by those extolling the system's economic rationality (such as conflicts of interest between shareholders in the controlling group and in the individual company), but these do not concern us here. What is important is that the groups also had extensive cross-holdings in companies administered by other groups—and, therefore, important interests in common. Thus, geographical, technical, administrative, and financial factors combined to accentuate the relatively monolithic nature of mining capital.

The scale and economic importance of the Rand gold mines can be gauged in various ways. It is relatively simple to detail their extremely large and strategically vital significance to the South African economy.[7] In 1914, for example, the British Royal Dominions Commission concluded that of South Africa's general and railway revenue of £27.7 million in 1913–1914, £12 million was traceable to the Witwatersrand mines. The South African Low-Grade Ores Commission of 1932 was more prudent: it quoted, without accepting as definitive, the estimates of a renowned economist and supporter of the industry, S. H. Frankel. Frankel said that fully 50 percent of state finances were derived from the gold mines and that 50 percent of the population obtained its livelihood directly or indirectly from the gold mines. The Commission contented itself with concluding that "the prosperity of the country is largely dependent upon the gold mining industry."

By any criterion, the size of the mines' labor force was a significant policing and political problem for the state. Around 1910, it was a commonplace that "compounded" black labor on the mines actually outnumbered the entire white population on the Witwatersrand. Employment of both whites and blacks on the gold mines in the early days far exceeded employment in secondary industry for the entire country: in 1916, the combined black/white employment in the mines was 238,000 compared to 101,000 in secondary industry; in 1926, the figures were 215,000 and 193,000, respectively. By 1921, the total white population of South Africa's industrial heartland, the Witwatersrand, was 233,420. In the same year, the Rand gold mines employed 172,694 black migrant laborers, quartered in compounds in close proximity to each mine, and 21,036 whites.[8] (See Table 5.)

To sum up, the gold mining industry was very large relative to the South African economy as a whole. Competition within capital was comparatively mild as there was secure access to a large and regular gold-bearing ore body and unlimited markets, but the industry was also intensely cost-[9] and security-sensitive. Its concentration on lowering costs after the South African War took the form of

1. attempting to increase its supply of unskilled labor at reduced wages, and

2. large amalgamations, which turned numerous small contiguous mines[10] into enormous "super mines" in which it was hoped the economies of scale would lower costs.

Lionel Phillips, a prominent mining magnate, wrote to London soon after his return to the Transvaal in 1905: "Increased scale of working wherever possible must be our motto."[11] Large ventures further increased the industry's dependence on the state infrastructure, especially as the electrification of the mines was being introduced and economies of scale were encouraging the mines to purchase power from outside sources.

The Transvaal had an extremely undiversified economy at the time, with mining constituting its only reliable source of revenue. Some of this revenue was direct, but the bulk came from the industry's payments for the use of state facilities, especially the railways. As a Crown Colony under the British umbrella after the South African War, the Transvaal state was more stable and had access to a much greater degree of coercive power than a state of its size and its stage of development would normally command. Largely for this reason, the industry was at first fearful of the prospect of the end of Crown Colony rule.[12]

Those who were destined to take over the government of the Transvaal in 1907 had their own misgivings about the industry. When Jan Smuts, one of the defeated Afrikaner generals in the war, went to Britain in early 1906 to plead for early self-government, he heavily emphasized the danger of the "encroachment of money power." This argument was carefully tailored to appeal to the British Liberals,[13] but Smuts discreetly met two of the leading British-based mineowners on the same trip in an attempt to come to some sort of accommodation. Nevertheless, there is no doubt that

Smuts and his colleagues feared and distrusted the mining capitalists, and he made the same point about the dangers of "money power" in private correspondence with J. X. Merriman, the Cape Prime Minister, later the same year.[14]

Smuts was not, of course, hostile to the existence of the gold mining industry as such; he feared its potential to defy the Transvaal government and was distinctly skeptical that it would willingly help him in resolving the pressing problems of the Transvaal, which was about to regain its sovereignty from Britain. Foremost among these problems was white unemployment; black unemployment was not considered by the government to be a serious problem even when it was chronic because blacks had little or no access to either the government or the state. Whites could, and did, organize in bands of unemployed workers that threatened the state.[15]

White unemployment was a vital issue for the state for a number of reasons. A large proportion of the unemployed Transvaal whites were Afrikaners, the majority of whom had recently moved from farms to the towns in search of work.[16] These Afrikaners, besides being a crucial part of the potential ethnic constituency of the Botha/Smuts Het Volk party, also constituted a policing problem and a potential security threat, both because they were unemployed and because they had a high degree of political consciousness. Many of them wanted to return to farming and to republican government.

Smuts and Merriman frequently exchanged letters in the early part of 1907, blaming the unemployment on the industry that, said Merriman, was producing £25 million of gold per annum but allowing men to starve in the streets or be reliant on a government "dole of work at starvation wages."[17] White unemployment and the "poor white problem" were to continue to engage the attention of the Transvaal government and its successors for many years to come. These problems do not appear to have been finally solved until the post-1932 devaluation boom and the takeoff of secondary industry in World War II. Even then, they were not solved by any direct effort of the mining industry, though the ripple, or "linkage," effects of that industry's prosperity from the 1930s undoubtedly spurred the development of white employment opportunities elsewhere.

A second major issue facing the newly independent state was the need to cultivate reliable sources of both investment capital and revenue. But the maximization of state revenue appeared to be in a certain degree of conflict with the maximization of white employment. The question facing the government was: Is it possible to force the industry to employ significantly more whites without greatly increasing costs and without jeopardizing the state's only reliable source of revenue and only regular source of foreign currency? Moreover, would government intervention not frighten away potential foreign investors generally and cut the struggling new state off from all sources of development capital?

To complicate matters still further, the gold mines were in the grip of a cost crisis precisely when Smuts wanted them to take on more—expensive—white labor. Not surprisingly, then, the first sustained discussion between South African state and capital in the modern era was to be centered around their respective central concerns: white unemployment and working costs on the mines.

At least to begin with, white labor was something of a passive onlooker to this momentous state-capital dialogue. This was not because whites were totally unorganized. Unemployed whites banded together politically on occasion, and employed whites organized into trade unions and conducted strikes.

The scale of this collective action, however, was not sufficient initially to have much impact on the Transvaal state and society. Some welfare was collected and some jobs were found for the unemployed; some notice was taken of trade-union protests. But the conditions of white labor, organized or not, remained a topic that, although it was discussed, was not much discussed with white labor itself.

Even the undoubtedly political issue concerning the importation of indentured Chinese mineworkers in 1904 had failed to elicit any notable response from the weak and divided white workers, partly because the industry promised that the Chinese would only be allowed to undertake a limited and specified number of unskilled jobs.[18] Those trade-union leaders who opposed the importations had too flimsy a hold on their members to risk making it an issue.[19]

The trade-union movement in the beginning of the century was largely confined to skilled white artisans, and wages paid relative to living costs were probably as high or higher than in other mining countries.[20] Relations between capital and organized labor, while not necessarily tranquil, were not an active political issue.

THE DEVELOPING RELATIONSHIP:
FROM FRIEND TO RELATION

Though organized labor was not yet a political force in 1907, it loomed behind the tentative early courtship between the state and mining capital, which focused on the allied issues of white unemployment and working costs on the mines. The takeover of the Botha/Smuts Het Volk government and the withdrawal of colonial rule marked more than a mere change of government: it also marked a change in the form of the state. It was vital that a *modus vivendi* be reached between mining capital and the new state, and the horse-trading over unemployment and costs, paradoxically, speeded up the emergence of the new relationship.

The issue of organized labor was, in a sense, the catalyst that transformed the outer relationship of the state to capital in a remarkably short period. Within two years, they moved from mutual antagonists to fellow conspirators. Within another fifteen years, they had ostensibly become associates bound together by the impersonal operations of law and bureaucracy. This is a process of development—partly genuine, partly obfuscatory—that frequently took centuries in Europe.

The Transvaal had been a Crown Colony in the period of reconstruction after the South African War. The British administration's chief concern was to assure that a state would develop that would be loyal and useful—both politically and economically—to the British Empire. Such a state should preferably be dominated by Anglophones, and the best way to achieve that was to encourage British immigration into South Africa. This, in turn, was to be achieved by encouraging the development of the gold mining industry, the only possible source of prosperity available in the Transvaal at the time.

One of the lasting achievements of the British during the reconstruction period was to create a modern civil service, with controls and an information-gathering capacity sophisticated enough to institutionalize the relationship of the state and industry and make the competence, helpfulness, and honesty of individual state officials relatively less crucial.

Part of the new civil service was a restructured bureaucracy for dealing with the mining industry, which was divided into a

Secretariat and a Government Mining Engineer's Department.[21] The latter was supposed to confine itself largely to technical matters and report to the relevant member of the government or executive through the Secretariat, which, theoretically, would have sole jurisdiction over "policy" issues.

The gold mining industry was (and is) so highly technical, however, that the Government Mining Engineer (henceforth GME) has, over the years, become a far more important shaper or even source of policy than the Secretary for Mines. A traditionally antagonistic relationship developed between the two that was evident in embryonic form almost from the creation of the two offices.

As in Britain, however, the bureaucracy was subordinate to the executive, and the question that largely concerns us here is how the newly elected government used the institutional machinery available to it. In April 1907, government and employer—in the persons, *inter alia*, of Jan Smuts and Lionel Phillips—began to engage in a serious and detailed dialogue about their relationship, with special reference to white labor and its possible use for unskilled, hitherto black, jobs.

The two were undoubtedly the leading figures of the government and mining industry, respectively. Smuts was neither at the head of the government nor its Minister of Mines, but he was already the dominant figure in the Transvaal Cabinet.[22] Whenever an important issue arose concerning the mining industry, Smuts would take personal charge.[23] Lionel Phillips was the senior partner in South Africa of the largest mining finance group, H. Eckstein and Company, representing Wernher Beit and Company and the Central Mining and Investment Corporation Limited of London, and administering Rand Mines Limited. Phillips was earmarked by the senior partner in London, Julius Wernher, to succeed him. Phillips was not mining capital's only spokesman in South Africa, but he was clearly its most authoritative.[24]

The dialogue is of major importance, particularly since it occurred precisely at the formative period of the state-capital relationship and signals the emergence of a pattern that still endures today. Moreover, the dialogue can be traced in some detail because of the extraordinarily rich nature of the source material, in particular, the Smuts Papers and the regular, frank, detailed, and private correspondence Phillips engaged in with his two senior

partners, Julius Wernher and Friedrich Eckstein, who operated
from London.[25]

On April 10, 1907, Smuts began a letter to Merriman complaining about two things, white employment and state revenue:

> That conditions are rotten to the core I grant you; that a town
> of 75,000 whites exporting 26 millions in gold per annum
> should have a threatening unemployed question is a sufficient
> proof of that. I have addressed a strong communication to the
> Chamber of Mines and am to meet a deputation from them
> tomorrow.

He went on to argue that the industry was unlikely to be helpful with
regard to employment and that a policy of agricultural expansion

> seems to me the great desideratum just now. But we are so
> wretchedly poor that such a policy will be enormously dif-
> ficult to carry out. A million sterling now judiciously spent on
> small irrigation works all over the country will not only solve
> some of our most pressing problems, but lead to a new era in
> agricultural development and production in future. But we
> haven't the money.[26]

This lack of investment and loan capital—needed to finance state
projects as well as the expansion of private enterprise—was, in fact,
the Achilles' heel of the fledgling Transvaal state. Lionel Phillips,
the dominant figure in the Chamber of Mines, very quickly got the
message. Immediately after the said deputation from the Chamber
met Smuts, Phillips cabled his senior in London to get Lord
Rothschild to dangle a financial carrot before Louis Botha, the
Transvaal Prime Minister, who was then in Britain. Shortly after,
on April 19, 1907, he wrote a follow-up letter to the partner, Julius
Wernher: "I sent you a cable to ask Lord Rothschild to use his influence with Botha. The Transvaal Government will surely want to
raise some money, and the opinion of Rothschild may therefore
carry some weight."[27]

Phillips was trying to use Rothschild's financial power to delay
the repatriation of the Chinese miners from the Transvaal in this instance. But the question of Chinese labor was indivisible from that

of labor as a whole and from the question of costs, profits, and, finally, the state's power to collect revenue and raise loans. Botha did, in fact, meet a deputation of magnates the following month, and he assured them of his sympathetic cooperation.[28]

Between April 10, when Smuts began his letter to Merriman, and April 22, when he completed it, a great deal of bargaining and friendly persuasion took place. Most of it was conducted on a social and personal level.[29] Individual relationships briefly assumed an importance never again equalled in the relationship of the state and capital. Smuts emerged from a stream of interviews and deputations with a radically different perspective:

> So far I got and then mislaid this letter. The Chamber of Mines told me at above interview that white labour was impossible; too expensive, too inefficient (in fact worse than Kaffir labour) and too intermittent and discontinuous . . . The question is no doubt very difficult, as there is a sound sub-stratum of fact in the contention of the Chamber of Mines.[30]

Thus, Smuts was coming to reject the eventual phasing out of all black labor in favor of white workers. In so doing, he was casting doubt on the argument that the mining industry alone could solve the white unemployment problem. He was not reneging on his commitment to the employment of more Afrikaners on the mines, but he was clearly moving to the realization that the state itself would need to shoulder a greater part of the burden of creating employment. Hence, there was an even more pressing need for loan capital, small irrigation works, general agricultural development, and the employment opportunities these would open up.

Smuts was also becoming increasingly aware of the state's dependence on the mining industry for revenue. He came to understand the essential connection between a viable, profitable mining industry and a reliable source of state revenue. These resurrected state priorities—revenue, foreign investment in the mining industry, and the ability to raise government loans abroad from financiers such as Rothschild—had to be weighed against the possible political benefits of employing only expensive white labor on the mines. The government, therefore, had seriously to consider throwing the might of the state behind capital's drive to cut costs while looking incidentally for less direct methods of increasing Afrikaner employment.

This is not to suggest that international finance capital had taken over the running of the state; the entire situation was far more complex than that. While the *state* urgently needed to raise capital, the *government* urgently needed to create more jobs for Afrikaners, who were its natural electoral constituency and who, unlike most of the other white unemployed, were citizens and therefore voters. The sheer number of unemployed Afrikaners and their potential militance put pressure on the government to intervene and, at the same time, provided it with an excuse to do so.

For its part, mining capital both feared intervention and understood that it could not survive without it. The need for state intervention to secure control of the migratory (black) labor force is well documented;[31] not so well known is the need for state intervention before the control of organized (white) labor could be ensured.

The issue of unemployed Afrikaners, therefore, brought a number of more profound issues to the surface in its wake: in particular, the tension between the needs of the state and those of the government; and the ambivalent attitudes of both government and mining capital to state intervention.

The government and employers considered and debated three possible solutions to the problem of finding jobs for Afrikaners:

(1) The white labor policy—the replacement of all blacks on the mines by whites;

(2) the creation of a new intermediate class of semi-skilled, mainly supervisory, white miners; and

(3) the direct replacement of fractious, organized foreign miners by supposedly docile Afrikaners.

The concept of a white labor policy, keeping all jobs in the mining industry for whites, was mooted shortly after the South African War and was modeled on the "maintenance of a white Australia" policy, which was aimed at preventing those other than whites from migrating to Australia. The Australian influence in this as well as in other respects—such as the formation of the South

African Labour party in 1909, led mainly by trade unionists—was important, though not crucial.[32]

In 1902, white miners on the Village Main Reef Mine struck against the white labor experiments being conducted there by the mine manager, Frederic Hugh Page Creswell. Creswell thought it would be more economical to replace black labor with free (unindentured) white unskilled labor. Skilled white labor regarded this as a threat, and the Transvaal Miners' Association, formed in 1902 as an artisan rather than as an industrial union, opposed the experiment.[33]

The mouthpiece of the mining capitalists, the Transvaal Chamber of Mines (henceforth the TCM), rejected the white labor concept for its own reasons. It argued that unskilled white labor never could be as economical as black, even if it were individually more productive. Moreover, it feared that a large increase in the proportion of whites employed would result in the organization of a much larger proportion of the working class.[34]

Black labor, it felt, was also preferable because it was contract migrant labor, with no political rights. Under the Masters and Servants laws, moreover, a breach of contract by a black was a criminal offense. All these handicaps meant that the black labor force would probably be much more docile. Although the white working force was as yet far from militant, the industry was run by employers with firsthand experience in Europe and Britain of the power of organized labor.

The white labor policy, which continued to be advocated until the 1930s, had some influential backers such as Creswell, who later became the leader of the Labour party, Merriman, and Patrick Duncan, a former member of the Milner kindergarten, which had supervised reconstruction in the Transvaal. Duncan became an influential parliamentarian (for the Unionist and S.A. parties) and, eventually, the Governor-General of South Africa.

But as will be detailed later, even when Creswell became Minister of Labour in 1924, he was wholly unable to enforce a white labor policy, though it was certainly not for want of trying. So, although the state—and even the industry, before the 1913 strike—flirted with the white labor policy, it was never seriously attempted. The government-appointed Transvaal Mining Industry Commission of 1908,[35] headed by Creswell, recommended the policy, but it was ignored by the government. Nor did the white trade unions, for fairly obvious reasons, make an issue of it, particularly after they gained *de facto* recognition from both the state and the employers in 1913.

The white labor policy's main significance, for our purposes, was that it was a potent instrument that the government could use to keep the employers malleable, and it was skillfully used as such. Even more important, it provided the government with a rationale for intervention in organized labor-capital relations. At first, the government was not eager to intervene because the issue could cost it votes and elections, but the potential explosiveness of the question for the state as a whole increasingly forced its hand.

The strategic financial importance of the industry, on the one hand, and the large proportion of unemployed Afrikaners (as well as Afrikaner voters), on the other, meant that increased state intervention was inevitable. Thus, one of the prime purposes of the Mining Industry Commission, appointed on May 4, 1907, was to look into the question of "the means best calculated . . . to increase the employment of white labor in the mines . . ."

When Phillips complained about this and about the appointment of a government watchdog, an Inspector of White Labour, he was reassured by Botha that he would not let the inspector "worry the mining industry" and that the chairman of the Commission would be cautioned about the dangers of a critical report.[36]

Thus, machinery was developed that could be used to worry the employers, making their peace dependent on the goodwill of the government. This "sword of Damocles" technique, involving the accretion of administrative power, which achieves compliance by threat rather than by being exercised, is a worldwide twentieth-century phenomenon. One might go even further and argue that it is characteristic of elected regimes in general and of South African governments in particular.

As Phillips put it in another connection (referring to the 1908 Gold Law): "It leaves great power in the hands of the Government, which we need not be afraid of as long as we remain friends. As you know, the Boers always have left a great deal of authority with their Executive."[37] Phillips apparently did not see the full implications for state-industry relations of the state's accretion of administrative power, and he did not note that the political leverage gained this way would remain with the state even if the government changed. This is surprising because he clearly understood that the residual power vested in the executive made it essential for the industry and the state to "remain friends."

Smuts and Botha were not slow to use Damocles's sword, though they did so with sufficient finesse to keep Phillips trusting in the friendship for two more years. The Mining Industry Commission's report, Botha's promises notwithstanding, was extremely critical of the mine controllers' labor policies. Phillips went immediately to Pretoria to complain to Botha and Smuts, who promised not to implement the report's recommendations, but they once again brought up the question of white unemployment. Phillips rose instantly to the bait: "I told them it was quite unnecessary to legislate; that the industry would be quite ready to agree to take any of the young Afrikaners who are trained. I would sooner make an arrangement, if it was possible . . . than have legislation imposing one man, one drill, and so forth."[38] In his next letter, Phillips talked of the necessity to expand white employment, or else legislation, "justifiable legislation," would be passed. He wanted to employ these additional whites as a new semi-skilled class, earning about half the normal white wage. "And I have no hesitation in saying that, if the Mining Industry and the Government understand each other and work together, the change will probably be accomplished without disadvantage to the mining industry. . . ."[39]

In this way, the government achieved its end without even needing to take the public risk that legislation might have entailed.[40] The white labor policy was also to be used as a sword of Damocles by other South African governments, but it was largely a bluff. The South African state was not set up in such a way that it could actually accommodate a white labor policy; even the archproponent of the policy, Creswell, had come to the conclusion by 1913 that it should be carried out for social rather than for economic reasons—that is, it was economically inefficient.[41] In fact, it was never a serious possibility and was more important for its rhetorical than its actual impact. So, although the issue was the subject of interminable debate until the 1930s, and although the ideology behind it was important in other connections,[42] it is not proposed to deal with it here in any further detail.[43]

Another more feasible method by which it might be possible to employ more Afrikaners was by creating an intermediate class of semi-skilled whites. A very high proportion of the white miners were already in semi-skilled supervisory positions: Phillips, probably exaggerating, said that of 7,000 whites underground, only 2,000 had served a proper apprenticeship.

He hoped that the semi-skilled whites would work for half the wages of the skilled class and be comprised of docile Afrikaners, backed by the government. To that end, he pushed for a government-chartered miners' training school: the suggestion came originally from the Minister of Mines, Japie de Villiers, who wanted to develop a training school for young Afrikaners. Phillips's mining engineers responded with a detailed scheme, but Phillips stipulated that he was agreeable only if the government associated itself directly with the scheme—that is, state intervention was a precondition.

> Smuts expressed himself as absolutely in favour of this being established, and of the Government being identified with it. . . . I was a little surprised to find him so well disposed towards indenturing Afrikaners for 5 years, but he repeated several times 'we must teach the young people of the country to work.'[44]

The plan was to buy a mine for the training school and to discharge all the miners already working there (to avoid "contamination" from trade-unionist ideas and aspirations to high standards of living). Ironically, in view of subsequent events, Phillips thought the Afrikaner workers would be far more docile than were the other whites.

Most of all, however, Phillips wanted the involvement of the state. He already had the state heavily committed to helping the industry find sufficient black labor (through the *Modus Vivendi* Agreement of 1901 and, subsequently, the 1909 Transvaal-Mozambique Convention). Now he wanted the state involved in the white labor supply, too. He wrote to Wernher: "We need to support the miners' training school, not so much for the practical effect in supplying white labour for the mines, as the moral effect of the Government being in the business up to the hilt, with the object of supplying trained labour at cheap rates."[45]

These whites would not, of course, replace unskilled blacks. He expected a maximum of 3,000 men to be trained for this type of job (in 1908, about 150,000 Africans were employed on the gold mines). He saw the miners' training school rather as a lever to encourage the involvement of the state and, if necessary, to buy the allegiance of the government while at the same time preparing to replace expensive and militant foreign white labor. Phillips reported the following year, without a trace of irony, that Smuts was very pleased with the industry for doing what it could to favor white labor and had said, "If you will only go on showing that you will help us as far as you can, you will have nothing to fear."[46]

The training school was established but was never a success. Its major problem was an inability to attract apprentices. White labor was never really that serious about even a watered-down white labor policy, which would have employed more whites on unskilled laboring jobs without totally eliminating blacks. More significantly, however, the government and the employers were beginning to discover that trade-offs between them at the expense of white labor were not only possible but essential.

The final method considered to effect the employment of more Afrikaners was the substitution of Afrikaners for other miners. In normal circumstances, this would have been impossible because of the strong feelings of antagonism and rivalry between white Anglophones and Afrikaners in the Transvaal. When Lord Selborne urged Phillips, before the introduction of responsible government, to import more British miners and their families (Selborne was rightly fearful that the Transvaal British would be outvoted in the Transvaal's first elections), Phillips refused. It was impossible, he said at the beginning of 1906, to import a number of miners and families "in a public way . . . it would cause unrest here, particularly in view of the [forthcoming] public elections."[47]

A little over a year later, in May 1907, Smuts was corresponding with Merriman about the desirability of doing the exact opposite— getting rid of the Cornish miners in the Transvaal. As Merriman put it,

> I agree with you as to your Cornishmen; the sooner they leave South Africa the better for us—overpaid, insolent fellows with their family ties across 6,000 miles of water. If

your Government can carry out the substitution of the South African for the Uitlander miner you will have done much.[48]

By May 1908, Phillips was writing to Friedrich Eckstein that Botha had said he would like to ship away all the unemployed British, though Phillips doubted he would do it. For the mining industry to suggest this, Phillips concluded, would be madness.[49] Apparently, Botha wanted Phillips to take the political heat by making the proposal. Though Botha and Smuts were very adept at manipulating Phillips (using flattery to particular effect), the initiation of such a move by employers was clearly beyond the realm of possibility.

Since Phillips's rapprochement with Smuts and Botha in 1907, he had become very voluble in his expressions, both public and private, of his South African patriotism. One form this expression took was his criticism of the fact that British miners sent money home.[50] The irony of the fact that he repatriated enormous sums from South Africa in an ultimately draining effort to maintain his palatial estate, Tylney Hall, in England, seems to have been lost on Phillips. The mine controllers, in general, were not averse to the repatriation of funds, provided they took the form of dividends. They also introduced deferred-payment schemes for black migrant miners, which forced them to repatriate up to 60 percent of their wages to their home countries.

Phillips's intimacy with Botha and Smuts was not, however, to survive long. By February 1910, and possibly earlier, Phillips was writing of the need to end his policy of neutrality, and by September 19, 1910, he was complaining of the "base ingratitude of Botha and Smuts [which] only proves once again the Boer untrustworthiness."[51] He continued, however, to emphasize the need for close and continuous contact.

The transitory nature of their friendly intercourse underscores the weakness of any attempt to substitute informal friendships between government and capital for a stable, institutionalized state-capital relationship. The major characteristic of the latter relationship, which is also a characteristic of bureaucratized interventionist states generally, is that it does not even require that government and private-sector leaders know each other.

The relationship between the gold mines and the state was important enough to necessitate a permanent institutional framework that would survive changes of regimes and the crumbling of friendships. This institutional framework took another fifteen years to develop in the case of organized white labor. The major reason for the delay was that South African governments were reluctant to intervene between capital and trade unions before they saw it to be absolutely necessary.

This reluctance, furthermore, was eminently rational: the rewards for individual *governments* intervening in such a situation were apt to be small. The risks—as governments were to learn in the political reactions of the electorates to their interventions in the strikes of 1907, 1913, 1914, and 1922—were correspondingly large. This is the major reason why, in spite of the fact that increased state intervention was essential to maintain its own stability and growth, almost two decades of turbulence between capital and organized labor were to pass before a permanent institutional framework was imposed on the participants by the state. The need of the *state* to impose a workable new industrial order for its own security, in other words, was subordinated to the political need of individual governments to avoid unpopular and divisive policy decisions.

THE 1907 STRIKE

When responsible government was granted to the Transvaal, two of the major goals of the state and industry at the time were to find more jobs for the deracinated Afrikaners pouring into the urban areas and to cut costs drastically to make deep-level mining profitable. Various measures, detailed above, were considered, but they were simply not politically or economically feasible.

The government and the mining controllers, however, were to achieve their main objectives without resorting to drastic measures such as replacing all black miners by whites or replacing all foreign-born whites by native-born South Africans, and without even needing to rely on the Government Miners' Training School. The fortunate event that made it possible both to employ more Afrikaners and to cut mining costs was the 1907 strike, the first major strike on the Witwatersrand gold fields. It occurred in May 1907, less than a month after Smuts, Phillips, and others began serious discussions about the need for a new state-capital *modus vivendi.* The first result of the new relationship was a concerted assault on white labor.

This is not necessarily to argue that the mining capitalists were directly responsible for the strike; no employer wants the uncertainty of a strike if he can achieve his ends in some other way. What is certain is that the government and mine controllers had debated whether to "tackle" white labor and had agreed on the necessity of doing so shortly before the strike actually broke out. Furthermore, we know that the employers did nothing to stop the spreading of the dispute: they contemptuously rejected mediation offers, declared a lockout, and took on large numbers of Afrikaners as strikebreakers.

The private correspondence of Smuts and Phillips—augmented by some Chamber of Mines correspondence—provides an illuminating "inner history" of the rapprochement of the state and capital, the explicit sacrifice of white labor on the altar of this new relationship, and the eventual institutionalization of the relationship.[52]

The repatriation of the indentured Chinese miners, which was pending in the early part of 1907, led to increased concern about working costs. Men such as Sir George Albu, Chairman of the General Mining and Finance Corporation, began to talk in public about the need to use proportionately more black miners and to cut white wages. Retrenchments were taking place, and wages were already being cut. The mining regulations were being more honored by mine managers in the breach than in the observance. White labor, in short, was under the whip; moreover, its response to all this pressure was not rendered any more docile by the fact that the ravages of miner's phthisis were just beginning to become obvious in their full horror.[53]

Writing to Wernher on April 19, Phillips expressed the hope that the Mining Industry Commission, which was to be announced publicly the next month, might report that

> the men are capable of supervising a great many more drills than they do now. If that should be the case, Hull [a Cabinet Minister] told King [a mining employer], they intended to urge Directors of mining companies to take the matter up, and see that they get value for the money spent. Nothing of

course could suit us better than that we should take steps to
get efficiency at the instance of the Government. As you
know, Brother Boer has no sympathy with the working man,
quite the reverse.[54]

Wernher might have known this, but the working man did not. The
Het Volk party and its leaders were thought to be well disposed
toward white labor.[55]

Eight days later, Phillips wrote again to Wernher, reiterating that
if the Commission reported that white labor was inefficient, and if
it suggested that the mining industry should take steps to correct this,

we shall lose no time in obeying the Government, and face the
consequences of a possible struggle with our white men with
comparatively light hearts. King lightly counsels an immediate attack upon the white miners, which of course is a
suggestion that emanates from Hull . . .

Phillips was not happy with the idea of the industry doing its own
dirty work without the backing of a favorable Commission report:

If we took the bull by the horns now, and insisted upon the
white men doing all kinds of things which they are not doing
now, but which I admit they ought to do, and a strike followed, we should find ourselves saddled with the whole of the
odium. A vastly different situation would be created if the
Commission reports as indicated: the public is thereby
educated, and we take action under official inspiration![56]

He was not to get his wish. Three days later, on April 30, the
Johannesburg *Rand Daily Mail* reported the announcement that
supervisors of "hammer boys" (African rock-drillers) on Knight's
Deep were to have their wages cut and that white rock-drill miners
should henceforth supervise three machines instead of two. (When
this had previously been tried, on Village Main Reef Mine in 1903,
it had also caused a strike.)

The following day the workers struck, and they sent a deputation to J. de Villiers, the Minister of Mines, a few days later. The

men complained more about the increased supervision than the wage cuts. De Villiers attempted to placate them with the promise of a commission of inquiry into mining regulations. The strike spread rapidly, however, and on May 9, a deputation from the Germiston Chamber of Commerce offered to mediate. It approached Louis Reyersbach, President of the Transvaal Chamber of Mines and Phillips's junior partner in H. Eckstein and Company. Reyersbach contemptuously rejected their offer: "What they want is to bind us to hard and fast rules in exactly the same way the men in Lancashire did eighty years ago . . . It was fought out then, and it will have to be fought out here." Arbitration, he said, was "premature," and the Chamber could not in any case "interfere between employers and the employees." When the delegation expressed fears that violence would spread, he answered flatly: "Then we will have to ask the Government to enforce law and order."[57]

As the strike continued to grow, Phillips turned his efforts increasingly to recruiting the repressive power of the state to squash it. On May 13, he wrote to Wernher to say that the government had first favored the workers but were taking another view "now that they are beginning to know the facts." He boasted again about how friendly he was with Smuts and de Villiers, and about how he had convinced them that anything more than token picketing should be smashed, and arbitration or conciliation eschewed:

> I impressed upon both of them the necessity for taking steps to prevent large bodies of men visiting the various mines, one by one, and "persuading" the men to strike . . . if the strikers are allowed to intimidate the men, we shall very soon have all the underground men out, and the industry paralysed for a time. Both Smuts and De Villiers expressed their determination to avoid anything of this kind. They both spoke to me about arbitration and conciliation boards, but I explained as forcibly as I could the objection to any such proceeding under existing conditions, and I think they saw the point. Smuts has a particularly incisive mind, and catches hold of a point in a second.[58]

Phillips thus made it clear to both Smuts and de Villiers that it was necessary to break up picketing (which, in essence, meant break the strike) by physical force. Though the Transvaal Miners' Association had only 300 members at the time, and though large numbers of Afrikaners were coming forward as strikebreakers[59]— 400 on one mine alone, Robinson Deep—the Government Mining Engineer's figures show that 4,171 men were on strike by May 25.

By May 18, Phillips could report that de Villiers was saying in public that no intimidation of nonstrikers would be permitted. This attacked the strikers' main weapon: picketing.[60] On May 22, the first major outbreak of violence occurred when miners rioted against Afrikaner scabs. Botha told a deputation of strikers that the government did not officially encourage the employment of Afrikaners,[61] which, unless one is seduced by the word "officially," could hardly have been further from the truth. The following day, Smuts called in the British Imperial troops who had been left as a garrison force in the Transvaal. On May 26, using considerable violence, the 2nd Dragoon Guards broke up a meeting of 200 miners. Pickets were withdrawn throughout the Central Rand, open appeals were made to impoverished Afrikaners "to go down the mines and oust the British workers," and mining regulations were bent to allow unqualified men to do certificated work. Finally, as the miners started drifting back to work, a lockout was declared and the strikers were dismissed.[62]

The strikers sent at least five deputations to the government, four of which met Prime Minister Botha. One deputation, on June 6, carried a petition with 3,271 signatures asking for a court of arbitration. Botha did not press the point when the mining houses, which were continuing to tap the flow of Afrikaner strikebreakers, simply refused to negotiate.[63] The state, in other words, had supplied both of capital's major demands: it broke up picketing by force, and it refused to mediate in the dispute by setting up compulsory arbitration or concilation machinery.

On July 15, a meeting of the mining houses discussed whether it was necessary to compromise with the strikers. Reyersbach argued that there was no reason to do so, and that Botha had promised the strikers only that he would ask the individual mine managers to interview the strikers who wanted to return to work.[64] No compromise was offered, and on July 28, 1907, the strike was publicly called off by the Transvaal Miners' Association (TMA). The strike had overturned many notions about natural alliances among groups in Transvaal society. As Phillips pointed out, "the whole position is getting topsy-turvy; a Boer Government calling out British troops to keep English miners in order, while Dutchmen are replacing them in the mines."[65] On the other hand, as he well knew, it all made a good deal of sense. He was able to end "extravagant contract work," get white miners to supervise more than two drilling machines, reduce wages generally, cut the number of whites employed by 10 percent, and reduce the cost of breaking rock by 25 percent.[66] The Government Mining Engineer reported a fall in average working costs per ton milled from 23 shillings to 18 shillings, improvements in efficiency, and reductions in wages.

The government was also able to point to the increased employment of Afrikaners on the mines. The percentage of South African-born whites employed on the mines increased from 17.5 percent just before the strike to 24.6 percent during it—an increase of about 1,250 men. The numbers fell back slightly afterward, with the Afrikaners blaming the "clannishness" of the British miners. The employers suggested that some of the Afrikaners had simply found themselves unsuited for this kind of work and that they had left. But the proportion of South African-born whites stayed steady at 23 percent—about 4,600—and grew uninterruptedly at a rapid pace each year from then on until the present, with the sole exception of 1922, the year of the Rand Revolt.[67] (See Table 2.)

Government actions also put capital in debt to the state and gave the state greater leverage. A year later, Phillips was still acutely aware of this: "Decreasing cost is due to decreasing the amount of supervision, and unquestionably it adds to the unemployed."[68] For this reason, he said, the mining houses should attempt to create white jobs by opening up new mines or reopening old ones. He went so far as to write to Friedrich Eckstein that legislation against the industry would be "justifiable" if the industry was "expanding output and profits considerably, and at the same time decreasing the number of white men employed . . . [we should] meet the Government in this matter and not put our heads in the sand."[69] Phillips, somewhat naively, had found it difficult to understand why the government did not make public its alliance with capital. In spite of its conservative and aristocratic instincts, he wrote, its utterances indicated an intention to side with labor against capital: "The *action* they took during the strike was all in the opposite direction, so the truckling to the TMA, appointment of Raitt [as Inspector of White Labor] and general deference to working men may be merely a blind."[70]

As a blind, it worked better on Phillips than on the white workers. After the strike, trade unions throughout South Africa gained members: the TMA had 300 members at the start of the strike in May; there were 4,000 by September 1907.[71] Trade unionists formed the Labour party in 1909, and with only a short time to organize and prepare for the 1910 election, it won 5 seats. The state-capital alliance over the 1907 strike was very successful in that it achieved what it set out to do, but it was also to have far-reaching, unintended consequences in that it shaped and accentuated the politicization of white labor.

There was, of course, far more behind the government's action in breaking the strike than the pressure of Phillips's logic, more even than the desire to employ more Afrikaners. As Smuts said in the letter to Merriman begun April 10 and completed April 22, 1907, not only white employment but also state revenue was vital. The Transvaal government, to quote Smuts again, desperately needed to raise money—even £1 million sterling would "not only solve some of our most pressing problems, but lead to a new era in agricultural development and production in future. But we haven't the money."

And money, of course, is where Lord Rothschild comes into the picture. It would be easy to overstate the power of international capital and to suggest that it ultimately ran the Transvaal, but it would be equally easy to overlook the real needs of the Transvaal state and the constraints imposed on it by its very nature. The white parliamentary government needed to provide employment for its electorate; while the developing capitalist state had to achieve this and other ends by coaxing investment and loan capital—private and public—from abroad to expand and diversify the economy.

This does not mean, of course, that Lord Rothschild and others ran the Transvaal. Finance capital offers its suitors a choice: either create a favorable context for the seeking of profits or forego the chance of significant loans and investments. Finance capital would be bored with the very idea of running a country: it is blind to race, ethnicity, and personality; blind to everything, in fact, other than security and percentage return. The remote-control nature of finance capital's power is neatly conveyed by Trotsky, if a little overstated: "The strength of finance capital does not reside in its ability to establish a government of any kind at any time, according to its wish; it does not possess this faculty. Its strength resides in the fact that every nonproletarian government is forced to serve finance capital. . . ."[72]

To a large extent, this was how the Transvaal (and shortly after, the South African) state experienced the demands of finance capital: they provided an extremely powerful incentive to create a favorable context for the seeking of profits. Thus, to justify the importance of Lord Rothschild in the events surrounding the 1907 strike, it is not necessary to produce personalized evidence of the "smoking gun" variety. It is by no means certain that Lord Rothschild ever talked to Botha about Afrikaners and white labor. Nor is it important, in view of the structural relationship of international finance capital and the Transvaal state. What we do know, from the private correspondence files of both Smuts and Phillips, *inter alia*, is that the Transvaal government was delicately but deliberately made aware of the connection between the raising of finance capital and the lowering of working costs on the mines. In trying to decide between the respective claims of white miners and mining capitalists, this connection could not fail to be of some relevance.

It is not clear what happened to Louis Botha's application for a loan from Rothschild or even whether he formally applied for one. What is known, however, is that Botha managed to obtain a £5 million loan from the British government. Private foreign investment returned to the gold fields; the year 1908 was the gold mining industry's best since the South African War, and prosperity gradually returned to the Transvaal as a whole.[73]

The breaking of the 1907 strike led to a substantial, immediate drop in mining costs and was, therefore, an important direct cause of the revival; its long-term effects were even important. It signalled to financiers and capital in general (nearly all of whom had been extremely nervous about how the government would harness state power) that the state was committing itself to the establishment and maintenance of an environment in which profits would be reasonably assured over the long term. That commitment takes precedence over a commitment to white employment or even—one is tempted to suggest—to any other commitment of the South African state. Rhetoric aside, it has never been broken to this day.

NOTES

1. Barlow Rand Archives (henceforth BRA), HE 152, Lionel Phillips to Julius Wernher, 19.04.1907. The importance of Wernher, Phillips, and the companies they represent is discussed in the text.

2. The literature is voluminous, but the debate is still inconclusive. J. A. Hobson developed his theory of imperialism from this basic case study. For a concise summary of the debate, see *The Oxford History of South Africa*, edited by Leonard Thompson and Monica Wilson, Vol. 2, Oxford 1971, pp. 313–24.

3. Robert V. Kubicek, in *Economic Imperialism in Theory and Practice: The Case of South African Gold Mining Finance, 1886–1914*, Durham, N.C., 1979, p. 16, suggests that "mine controller" is more accurate than "mineowner" because owners frequently delegated control. Kubicek's term is useful on occasion but should not be allowed to obscure the fact that owners continued to exercise ultimate control, albeit occasionally at two or three removes. The most important managers, moreover, were also significant shareholders. Therefore, the situation was not the same as the one (dubiously) characterized by James Burnham, John Kenneth Galbraith, and others in the 1950s and 1960s as the separation of ownership and control (by a new class of managers or technocrats).

4. Shula Marks and Stanley Trapido, "Lord Milner and the South African State," suggest that the reconstruction state was far from "imperfect," that it was, in fact, custom-built to mining capital's specifications. From this, they draw the implicit conclusion that the state increasingly developed into the mere instrument of capital. There is something in the first part of their argument, but it should be remembered that an administratively more efficient state is not only better equipped to fulfill the needs of capital; it is also better able to look after its own interests, as will be shown.

5. Jeeves gives a good account of this process in "The Control of Migratory Labour."

6. There were, it is true, divisions within the industry, but they have been exaggerated. See Donald Denoon, " 'Capitalist Influence' and the Transvaal Government During the Crown Colony Period, 1900–1906," *Historical Journal*, Vol. 11, No. 2, 1968; the rejoinder of Arthur A. Mawby, "Capital, Government and Politics in the Transvaal, 1900–1907: A Revision and a Reversion," *Historical Journal*, Vol. 17, No. 2, 1974; and Yudelman, "Capital, Capitalists and Power in South Africa."

7. Leo Katzen, *Gold and the South African Economy*, passim. The industry remains vital still, as is shown by J. A. Lombard and J. J. Stadler, *The Role of Mining in the South African Economy*, Pretoria, 1980. The study was commissioned by the Chamber of Mines of South Africa for political reasons, but it nevertheless backs this conclusion with overwhelmingly convincing evidence.

8. Katzen, *Gold*, p. 53; *Union Statistics for Fifty Years, 1910–1960*, Jubilee issue, compiled by the Government Bureau of Census and Statistics, Pretoria, 1960 (henceforth *Union Statistics*).

9. For a detailed account of its cost-sensitivity, see Frederick Johnstone, *Class, Race and Gold*.

10. On amalgamations and technical developments in the industry after the war, see Pieter Cornelius Grey, "The Development of the Gold Mining Industry of the Witwatersrand, 1902–1910," Ph.D. diss., University of South Africa, 1969.

11. BRA, HE 152, Phillips to Wernher, Vol. 152, 4.12.1905.

12. BRA, HE 152, Phillips to Lord Selborne, Governor of the Transvaal, 24.1.1906.

13. W. K. Hancock, *Smuts 1: The Sanguine Years, 1870–1919*, Cambridge, 1962, pp. 207–10.

14. W. K. Hancock and J. van der Poel, *Selections from the Smuts Papers* (henceforth *Smuts Papers*), Cambridge, 1966, 1973, 7 Vols., Vol. 2, p. 299.

15. Charles van Onselen, "The Main Reef Road into the Working Class: Proletarianization, Unemployment and Class Consciousness Amongst Johannesburg's Afrikaner Poor, 1890–1914," University of the Witwatersrand History Workshop, 1981. Van Onselen does not really attempt to explain why whites succeeded in organizing in this way and blacks did not. The answer was surely the differential access to government and the state enjoyed by the two groups.

16. Though they included non-Afrikaners as well, see *Smuts Papers*, Vol. 2, p. 399. See also Van Onselen, "The Main Reef Road," pp. 23–28.

17. *Smuts Papers*, Vol. 2, p. 336.

18. Donald Denoon, *A Grand Illusion*, pp. 139–46.

19. This was so much so that, in 1906, when the British Liberal government stopped the importation of Chinese laborers, effigies of Winston Churchill and Campbell-Bannerman were burnt by white miners in the market square in Boksburg: Deryk Humphriss and David G. Thomas, *Benoni, Son of My Sorrow: The Social, Political and Economic History of a South African Gold Mining Town*, Benoni, 1968, p. 147.

20. MM 3431/20, Vol. 548, R. H. Miller, Inspector of White Labour, to Superintendent and Chief Inspector of White Labour, Pretoria. Miller, generally sympathetic to white labor, states this categorically in his long historical review, written in 1920. The relatively high wages commanded

by white artisans was a standard complaint of employers throughout the first two decades of the twentieth century.

21. For an exhaustive account, see Grey, "The Development." Jeeves, "The Control of Migratory Labour," provides an account of the growing bureaucratic structures dealing with the recruitment of black migrant labor. See also Marks and Trapido, "Lord Milner and the South African State."

22. L. M. Thompson, *The Unification of South Africa, 1902–1910*, Oxford, 1960, pp. 31–32.

23. Smuts continued to do this in the period 1910–1924, when F. S. Malan was Minister of Mines. See Hancock, *Smuts Papers*, Vol. 1, p. 64.

24. Some of Phillips's colleagues, including three of the most senior of the mining capitalists in South Africa, Sir George Farrar, Sir Percy Fitzpatrick, and Drummond Chaplin, felt that he was far too amenable to Smuts and Prime Minister Louis Botha. They went into party political opposition at an early stage and took little part in the early formative debate. See B. K. Long, *Drummond Chaplin: His Life and Times in Africa*, London, 1941, p. 126; A. H. Duminy and W. R. Guest, eds., *Fitzpatrick: Selected Papers, 1888–1906*, Johannesburg, 1976, passim. For an evaluation of Phillips's importance and that of the group he led in South Africa, see A. P. Cartwright, *Golden Age*, pp. 12, 16–19. The budget of the group of companies, he says, was bigger than that of either Natal or the Orange Free State.

25. Maryna Fraser and Alan Jeeves, eds., *All that Glittered: Selected Correspondence of Lionel Phillips, 1890–1924*, Cape Town, 1977.

26. *Smuts Papers*, Vol. 2, p. 338.

27. BRA, HE 152, Phillips to Wernher, 19.4.07.

28. Johannesburg *Star* 10.5.07, and HE 253/148/24, both cited in Jeeves, "The Control of Migratory Labour."

29. D. Yudelman, "From Laissez-Faire to Interventionist State: Subjugation and Co-optation of Organized Labour on the South African Gold Mines, 1902–1939," Ph.D. diss., Yale University, 1977, pp. 63–64.

30. *Smuts Papers*, Vol. 2, p. 339.

31. Jeeves, "The Control of Migratory Labour."

32. The Australian influence is traced in detail by Elaine N. Katz, especially in "Early South African Trade Unions and the White Labour Policy," mimeographed, University of the Witwatersrand, 1976. See also her "Origins and Early Development of Trade Unionism in the Transvaal, 1902–13," Master's thesis, University of the Witwatersrand, 1973. This was published under the title *A Trade Union Aristocracy*, Johannesburg, 1977.

33. Katz, "Origins," p. iv; Denoon, *Grand Illusion*, p. 140.

34. Grey, "The Development," p. 232 ff.; Mawby, "The Political Behaviour," Chapter 4.

35. *Report of the Transvaal Mining Industry Commission, 1907–08,* Pretoria, 1908.

36. BRA, HE 154, Phillips to Wernher, 17.10.07; BRA, HE 154, Phillips to Wernher, 12.11.07.

37. BRA, HE 154, Phillips to Eckstein, 13.4.08.

38. BRA, HE 154, Phillips to Wernher, 16.3.08.

39. BRA, HE 154, Phillips to Eckstein, 13.4.08.

40. This is not, of course, to argue that the Mining Industry Commission was specifically formed for this purpose: the Botha/Smuts government had other political reasons for appearing to be sympathetic to the white labor policy.

41. R. Davies, "Mining Capital," p. 36.

42. For example, in the debate on whether to ban foreign migrant labor.

43. For discussions of the white labor question, see P. C. Grey, "Development of the Gold Mining Industry of the Witwatersrand," and E. Katz, "Origins."

44. BRA, HE 153, Phillips to Wernher, 25.5.07.

45. BRA, HE 154, Phillips to Wernher, 17.10.07.

46. BRA, HE 154, Phillips to Wernher, 4.5.08.

47. BRA, HE 152, Phillips to Selborne, 24.1.06.

48. *Smuts Papers,* Vol. 2, p. 344; 22.5.07.

49. BRA, HE 154, Phillips to Wernher, 4.5.08.

50. For example, BRA, HE 153, 3.6.07.

51. BRA, HE 155, 7.2.1910 and 19.9.1910.

52. Grey, "Development," provides a detailed "public" account (pp. 250–93), which will be drawn on here; see also Walker and Weinbren, *2,000 Casualties.*

53. Miner's phthisis is a lung disease brought on by prolonged exposure to dust in underground conditions. It affected a high proportion of the early underground workers and was very frequently fatal.

54. BRA, HE 152, Phillips to Wernher, 19.4.1907.

55. Walker and Weinbren, *2,000 Casualties,* p. 23. See also D. Denoon " 'Capitalist Influence' and the Transvaal Government," p. 301, for a description of Louis Botha's "ardent" courtship of white labor. R. Davies, "Mining Capital," p. 64, interprets the switch of government favor from white labor to mining capital as a sign that Phillips had been successful "in bringing the reigning classes 'to heel' . . ." This mistakenly implies that the "reigning classes" were being forced to act against their own interests, and fails to take into account the overlapping interests operating here.

56. BRA, HE 152, Phillips to Wernher, 27.4.1907.

57. Transvaal Chamber of Mines Archives (henceforth TCM) 1899–1910 Series, File W.9.

58. BRA, HE 153, Phillips to Wernher, 13.5.1907.

59. Jeeves, "Control of Migratory Labour," p. 18, gives a government estimate at 2,000 in early June, and the TCM estimate at 2,500 to 3,000. The Government Mining Engineer estimated about 1,250, and is likely to be the most reliable source.

60. BRA, HE 153, Phillip to Wernher, 13.5.1907, 18.5.1907.

61. Grey, "The Development," p. 272.

62. Walker and Weinbren, *2,000 Casualties*, p. 24; *Annual Report of the Government Mining Engineer* (henceforth ARGME), 1907, p. 11; Grey, "The Development"; TCM 1899–1910 Series, File W.9.

63. Grey, "The Development," p. 278; *Annual Report of the Transvaal Chamber of Mines* (henceforth ARTCM), 1907, p. 33.

64. TCM, File W.9.

65. BRA, HE 153, Phillips to Wernher, 3.6.1907.

66. Walker and Weinbren, *2,000 Casualties*, p. 24.

67. ARGMEs.

68. BRA, HE 154.

69. Ibid., 13.4.1908.

70, Ibid., 14.10.1907.

71. Grey, "The Development," p. 293.

72. Leon Trotsky, "Bonapartism and Fascism," July 15, 1934, quoted in *The Struggle Against Fascism in Germany*, New York, 1971, p. 440.

73. A. P. Cartwright, *Golden Age: The Story of the Industrialization of South Africa and the Part Played in It by the Corner House Group of Companies, 1910–1967*, Cape Town, 1968, p. 7.

3

The Center Holds: Sovereignty and Violence, 1907–1914

If you wish to marry suitably,
marry your equal.

—Ovid

The symbiotic relationship of the state and capital established in 1907 resulted in a degree of complacency on both sides, and they tended to ignore the susceptibilities of Afrikaner poor whites and organized white labor more than they might otherwise have done. This resulted in a ground swell of opposition that rapidly grew more radical as it became clearer that the interests of the center were paramount in determining policy. The opposition came to a head in 1914, when two of the most significant events in twentieth-century South African history occurred: the general strike and the rebellion. The state and capital were challenged in these two events, first, by organized white labor and its syndicalist leadership and, second, by disaffected republican nationalist Afrikaners.

It is not proposed here to deal with the rebellion in any detail other than to suggest that it was radical in that it aimed at a basic change in the status quo, and that the rank and file of the rebels perceived themselves as alienated from both the state and Imperialist capital.[1] The importance of the rebellion for this study is primarily negative: the forces resulting in the rebellion remained completely distinct from the labor unrest that culminated in the general strike. Thus, there were two powerful forces looking for an outlet in South Africa between 1910 and 1914, but there was no meeting ground between them. When they faced the state and capital, they did so on separate occasions, and alone. In fact, the

1914 strike was put down by rural Afrikaner commandos led by two men who later that year led the rebellion.

This chapter will analyze the second significant event in the holding of the center, the 1914 general strike, and the events leading up to it. The period is marked by a rapid increase of state intervention into the economy, despite the government's reluctance, for political reasons, to become fully involved. The naked subjugation of the 1907 strike was followed by a half-hearted attempt at co-optation of organized labor, which failed so miserably that it necessitated an even greater degree of coercion as the expectations of labor contrasted ever more starkly with its achievements. A pattern was established in this period: violence followed by partial conciliation, followed by rising expectations of labor and rising indifference of capital and state, followed by more violence. The pattern was to recur in the period after 1914 on the Rand and, of course, is not atypical of industrializing countries generally.

Though the government achieved most of its ends in the 1907 strike, it was not as successful as were the mining capitalists, who had managed to harness the state's power to the task of slashing working costs. But the government had to face the unintended consequences of its actions in the political arena: the growth of labor militancy, the estrangement of voters sympathetic to white labor, and the questioning by some of the very legitimacy of the state. Clearly, any popularly elected government—albeit elected by only a section of the population—that might ally itself too publicly with as concentrated and visible an interest as the Transvaal gold mining industry would be taking large political risks. Equally clearly, any state that visibly excluded the interests of a socially and politically coherent group such as the white miners risked sustained challenges to its legitimacy.

What was badly needed, then, was to create some kind of machinery that would enable governments to deal administratively rather than politically with organized white labor. Such machinery was sought after each major outbreak of violence involving white labor, and even the mining capitalists agreed, especially after 1913, on its desirability. The main question, then, was not whether organized white labor should be incorporated into the state, but when and on what terms. The escalation of state intervention was seen to be unavoidable, both to set limits on political radicalism arising from labor organizations and to ensure the economic viability of the industry. Legitimation and accumulation, in other words, continued to be two of the state's top priorities.

When a strikers' deputation went to Botha during the 1907 strike and handed him a petition with 3,271 signatures asking for an arbitration court, he told them there was no legislation to provide for one. Later he met another deputation and told them he had failed to get the mining capitalists to agree to arbitration. On June 10—as the strike petered out—a motion was introduced in the Transvaal Legislative Assembly asking for legislation to deal with labor disputes. De Villiers, the Minister of Mines, replied that the government had sent commissioners to New Zealand and Canada to see if a version of their labor legislation was suitable for South African conditions.[2]

Less than a year later, de Villiers sent Phillips a draft of a new bill, the Industrial Disputes Prevention Bill. The bill was drafted by H. Warington Smyth, who became Secretary for Mines after Union, and was based on what he called the Canadian principle. As Warington Smyth later explained, legislation throughout the world to prevent "industrial war" was at an "experimental stage" but could be roughly grouped into "voluntary" (United States and United Kingdom) and "compulsory" systems (New Zealand). The "voluntary" system laid down machinery for appointing conciliation boards "on the initiative of the parties concerned"; it generally provided that no strike or lockout should take place during the currency of the agreement, and that these agreements were binding on both parties. The "compulsory" system repressed strikes and lockouts by making them illegal; disputes were settled by industrial boards or courts whose decision was binding.

The Canadian Lemieux Act of 1907, which was the model for the Transvaal act, tried to compromise between the voluntary and compulsory systems by recognizing "the rights of employees to strike or employers to declare lockouts, but lays down certain courses which have to be followed before it is legal to strike or declare a lockout."[3] It also gave the state the power to refuse to allow strikes or lockouts in public-utility services "until they have done their utmost to come to terms and until the State and the public have had the time to know what the trouble is all about."[4] Furthermore, Warington Smyth conceded that there was "some

truth" in the view that "to deprive the workmen in any industry of
the right to strike when and where he likes is to blunt the sharp-
est weapon at his command and is altogether in favour of the
employer . . ."[5]

Phillips approved of the bill, especially the fact that strikes and
lockouts were illegal until a board was appointed to report on the
dispute. The report of the board, he observed, would then be
published to educate public opinion: "The essential difference between this Act and the English procedure is the rendering of a lockout or a strike illegal until after the report, instead of allowing the
intervention of the conciliation board to be a purely voluntary
affair."[6]

The Transvaal Industrial Disputes Prevention Act was passed in
July 1909. It formally continued to govern practice on the Transvaal gold fields after Union in 1910, though it was honored more in
the breach than in the observance. Although this original act was to
go through a myriad of aborted redrafts and changes in detail
before it was transformed into the South African Industrial Conciliation Act (I.C. Act) of 1924, it is important to remember that the
basic principles of the I.C. Act were almost identical to those of the
Transvaal Industrial Disputes Prevention Act, and still apply today. This is not to minimize the importance of the technical and
administrative differences, which made a basically unworkable act
workable, but merely to point out that all South African governments have aimed to preside over a similar basic relationship between employer and organized labor. Even the organization of
black labor that occurred gradually in the 1970s and continues in
the 1980s with the (wary) blessing of the government is merely
attempting to extend formally to all races the compromise between the compulsory and voluntary systems initiated before
Union in 1910.

It is also important to note that the 1909 act covered only whites
(blacks were already, in effect, forbidden to strike by the nine-
teenth-century Masters and Servants acts), and excluded those
employed in the public (civil) service.[7] Moreover, it had been
preceded in 1908 by the Railway Regulation Act, which prohibited
strikes by railway workers and which was extended over the whole
of South Africa in 1912 by the Railways and Harbours Service Act.

This differential legislation for sections of the labor force—defined not by occupational category or color, but by sector of the economy—began what has been referred to as "the decomposition of white labour solidarity by statutory means." The effect was to separate white railway workers from other sections of labor, destroying all possibility "of a repetition in South Africa of the powerful British 'Triple Alliance' of mines, railway workers, dockers and transport workers."[8]

The 1909 act had been supported in the Transvaal Legislative Assembly debates by the Progressive party, which represented largely the mining capitalists, and opposed by labor sympathizers on details rather than on principles. The Progressives were particularly pleased that the government "has learnt progress is absolutely essential in this country . . ."[9] For various reasons, however, the law never worked effectively. The government and the Chamber of Mines bear the brunt of the blame for exploiting loopholes to avoid the spirit of the act, not the least of which was the categorical refusal of the Chamber to recognize the unions. By 1913, the act was a dead letter.[10]

In 1911, another labor law was passed, the Native Labour Regulation Act, which standardized the recruitment and treatment of Africans, in particular, the contract migrant mineworkers. This act affected white labor in that it streamlined the separate and unequal position of the bulk of the black labor force; by making such workers cheaper to recruit and retain, they became more accessible to the mines, thus accentuating the threat to the white miners of very low-wage black competition. The law largely consolidated existing regulations and regularized procedures that had been developing since the formation of the Government Native Labour Bureau in 1907.

Once again, the bill was supported by the mining industry spokesmen, by the agricultural members (with an equal interest in a poorly paid, well-controlled black labor force), and by the government; again the labor spokesmen "praised with faint damns." These two bills "laid the groundwork for two discrete systems of industrial relations"[11]: the "archaic" system, affecting the mobility of (black/ African) labor, especially from country to urban areas; and the "modern" system, affecting work conditions in industrial society.[12]

STATE REGULATION OF WORKING CONDITIONS: THE 1911 MINES AND WORKS ACT

Another important piece of mining legislation regularizing the relationship of the state, capital, and labor—the 1911 Mines and Works Act was carried through as a result of the 1907 strike. Remembered today mainly as the first comprehensive codification of the color bar on the mines, the color-bar regulations received scant attention at the time relative to other issues arising from the bill. This is not to argue that they were unimportant to the industry as a whole, but merely that they were not the major issue of dispute between capital, labor, and the government at the time.

Of far more importance at the time than the color bar were the issues of Sunday work and the eight-hour day, which, like the provision of industrial conciliation machinery, were also being debated between the state and industry in Europe and America. The eight-hour day on mines had been made compulsory by legislation in the United Kingdom in 1908, after more than twenty years of political and industrial pressure by miners.[13] "State interference" on the British mines in the nineteenth century had been only mildly resisted by laissez-faire Victorians because "in return there was the prospect of fewer accidents and fewer strikes . . ."[14] State intervention in the United Kingdom can be dated to the 1840 prohibition of the underground employment of females and of boys under ten years old and the provision at the same time of strict safety regulations.

The South African 1911 Mines and Works Act dealt with similar issues. A limited eight-hour day was introduced for most underground workers, though it was hedged with loopholes of which the employers could and did take advantage.[15] A prohibition on underground work for females or for boys under fourteen years old was introduced; the age was lowered from sixteen to fourteen when it was protested that it was difficult to tell the age of illiterate Africans who had no birth certificates.[16] And Sunday milling was prohibited, though existing installations were allowed to continue milling, and Smuts probably even agreed privately to allow mills already planned to go ahead on the basis of Sunday milling.[17]

The Chamber of Mines opposed the color bar, which was introduced in the attached regulations but not mentioned in the body of the bill. But it did so very circumspectly. In a letter dated

November 17, 1911, to the Secretary for Mines, following a deputation to Smuts, as Minister of Mines, the Transvaal Chamber of Mines (henceforth TCM) argued that "competency" should be the standard for working at any job rather than color and that "differential legislation of this nature is most undesirable."

It also softened its protest by leaving out a significant paragraph that had been included in the draft of the letter:

> There is the further question of the validity of such regulations. From the consideration of Section 4 of the Mines and Works Act, under which these regulations are framed, there appears to the Chamber to be no power to make legislation prohibiting the anomalies referred to. This, however, is more a matter for the Government and Courts to decide.[18]

In other words, the color-bar provisions were *ultra vires*. The TCM need not have bothered to remove the paragraph since the government was well aware of this.[19] But the issue was highly charged politically, and neither party cared to challenge the color-bar regulations until 1923, when the government forced a test case and the regulations were, as expected, found to go beyond the powers accorded by the legislation.[20]

PARLIAMENT, PRESS, AND PUBLIC OPINION: A CASE STUDY

The internal debate about the Mines and Works Act is even more important for our purposes than are its actual provisions because it vividly illuminates the decision-making process and the symbiotic relationship of the state and capital. It is also striking that the state, labor, and capital all shared little interest in the color bar in their private deliberations. Finally, it provides a revealing example of the skillful use of public institutions and publicity to obfuscate the private clash of minority interests.

Several influential mining capitalists were elected to the first South African Parliament in 1910; among them were Phillips, Sir George Farrar, Drummond Chaplin (all representing the Unionist party), and J.W.S. Langerman (S.A. party). Phillips had refined his doctrine of "friendly intercourse" with the government. He continued to stress the importance of close contact and of influencing policy before it became a public issue, but he now felt that the mining employers were also needed to mobilize outside support through the press and effective participation in party politics.

He saw it as his job to counteract publicly the "glibness and apparent earnestness" of a critic like Creswell, given that Parliament and the public were ignorant of the true problems of the industry.[21] He also wanted to retain and strengthen the hold of his firm over various English-language newspapers, the bulk of which, in the Transvaal at least, were originally established by mining money. In this matter he had a sharp exchange with the head of his firm, Julius Wernher, who was quite happy to have them taken over by others because they earned such poor profits.

Phillips fought a running battle with his colleagues over the issue of the press for many years: even after he became the London-based chairman of his firm, the Central Mining and Investment Corporation, he could not mobilize enough internal support to regain the former position of press preeminence for his mining group. Phillips made the point to Wernher that the group should not be seen from a "purely commercial standpoint" in "discussing association with politics":

> It is not true of an immense organisation like ours, which has had to bear the brunt of a leading part in a country where politics and business are so intimately linked. If our party were not as strong as it is I think you would see a much greater disposition to tax it even more highly than at present.[22]

Phillips and his Unionist colleagues in Parliament lived up to this doctrine of wider responsibility (that is, wider than the industry's immediate interests) by supporting the eight-hour day, much to the fury of the Executive Committee of the Chamber of Mines. The Executive Committee cabled Smuts denying that the mining members, all of whom supported the eight-hour day in Parliament, represented their views. The TCM President-elect, J. G. Hamilton, was so angry that he considered dissolving the Chamber by moving a motion in the Executive Committee "that in view of the position created by the actions of members of parliament claiming to represent the mining industry, that steps be taken to ascertain whether under the circumstances it is desirable to continue the existence of the chamber."[23]

When Farrar got wind of the motion, he resigned from the TCM, but he was mollified when the Executive Committee hurriedly reconsidered and wrote to him saying it understood the special problems of "certain members of the Unionist Party, whose Parliamentary constituencies are largely represented by employees of various mining groups" and that it did not question his right to express opinions that differed from those of the TCM.[24]

The government, too, had its internal problems, particularly with its caucus. A rather bizarre and comic situation arose, for example, in regard to Sunday milling. Anticipating the restriction, a TCM subcommittee studied its possible effects on the industry and, in July 1910, concluded that, with the exception of some acceptable additional capital expenditure, the restriction "should not result in material loss to the Industry . . ."[25] In October, the Secretary for Mines wrote to the TCM saying that his Minister (Smuts) thought it an appropriate time to restrict Sunday work. The employers continued their vehement public opposition to the abolition of Sunday work but hinted that they might withdraw opposition to it if there were a *quid pro quo.* On March 3, 1911, employer opposition was weakened even further when the mining members of Parliament recommended to the TCM not to press the Sunday milling issue as it would arouse "further hostility" (in Parliament).[26]

In the meantime, Smuts was approached by an S.A. party member, J.W.S. Langerman, who was also a mining employer, and asked to block the Sunday provision. Langerman was second in command to J. B. Robinson, a mining magnate who was known to have contributed generously to S.A. party funds and who was himself later to become an S.A. party member of Parliament. Robinson was far more emphatically opposed to stoppage of Sunday work than was the rest of the industry,[27] because his mills could not crush a week's worth of mined ore in six days. He was also a maverick in a conformist industry and was thoroughly despised by the mining establishment.

Thus, Langerman approached Smuts directly, bypassing the TCM. Smuts then cabled Langerman, suggesting that he get the TCM Executive Committee on March 11 to pass a "strong resolution as to serious effects Sabbath stoppage milling, emphasising loss of employment and shaking of credit. Would like telegraphed Prime Minister and Minister of Mines. Strengthen Prime Minister at Party meeting Monday."[28] This was only a week after the mining members of Parliament had privately recommended the dropping of the issue. So the TCM was obliged—because of its previous use of the Sunday work issue as a bargaining chip—to send a strong resolution requesting something it did not particularly want in order to provide a way for Smuts to manipulate his own party caucus largely on behalf of someone the TCM almost unanimously disliked.

The net result was that the Sunday milling prohibition still went through, but all mills already operating were to be allowed to continue operating. Edward L. R. Kelsey, the TCM legal advisor and parliamentary lobbyist, then wrote to the TCM from Cape Town to say that the bill probably would not become law for six months. He wrote on March 18 that he hoped to see Smuts the next week: "Wire some idea of time required to complete erection [of new mills]. Would like some instances." Kelsey, who by then was cabling in a crude code (an old industry custom that became a regular TCM practice), very probably received some generous concession. On March 24, the TCM President called a meeting of the Executive Committee "for the purpose of seeing a private letter from Mr. Kelsey." Needless to say, the letter referred to is nowhere on file. One hesitates to guess what it contained, given that none of the other information divulged above was regarded as sensitive enough to merit exclusion from the file.

The contortions of the TCM throw some interesting light on the parliamentary process, which is frequently a "strife of interests masquerading as a contest of principles" and is equally frequently irrelevant to the decision-making process. The Sunday work saga has been described in some detail to demonstrate the difficulty of attempting to trace and analyze the decision-making process merely from public, published sources. These sources give the impression of a monolithic body of employers, united in favor of Sunday work but resisted by a government determined to guard the sanctity of the Sabbath. The actual horse-trading behind the scenes and the manipulation and mobilization of "public opinion" are entirely different, and they indicate far better the real nature of the political process and the interests predominating in it. These machinations show graphically the symbiotic nature of the relationship of the state and capital as well as the systematic need to conceal this relationship.

The mills that were running or planned before the legislation came into effect were allowed to continue running on Sundays. Some of them have continued to do so until this day.

THE 1913 STRIKE

> . . . the art of Government consists largely in appeasing
> the proletariat when they are in the wrong . . .
> —Robert Kotze,
> Government Mining Engineer, 1914[29]

The 1907 strike had started the government thinking about industrial relations and about the state's role in regulating the clash of labor and capital. In general, however, its approach was piecemeal and overly cautious. Though attempts were made to improve miners' conditions, the government was out of touch and did not face the basic problems.[30] The white workers had many genuine grievances, some of which concerned the threat posed to their position by the black miners, and others that were standard industrial grievances occurring throughout the industrial world at the time: high-handed managements refusing to recognize unions, let alone closed-shop situations; puny workmen's compensation and medical benefits; and terrible working conditions.[31]

Central to their grievances was a feeling of extreme insecurity. The turnover of jobs was staggering: in 1911, 13.3 percent of white mine employees changed employment every month, an annual turnover of 163 percent.[32] A union leader, J. T. Bain, claimed that the white miner averaged eight months' employment per year. Wages were high, but not excessively so considering the risks, especially from miners' phthisis, that cut the life expectancy of white underground workers drastically—fourteen of the eighteen members of the 1907 strike committee had died of phthisis before the 1913 strike began.[33]

Finally, the 1909 Transvaal Industrial Disputes Prevention Act simply did not work to protect the security of the mineworker and, in fact, came increasingly to undermine it. F. S. Malan, the Minister of Mines, knew of the opposition arising from the law but did nothing about it, even as late as the 1913 parliamentary session.[34] Malan's own account of the situation, written two decades later, tries to put all the blame on the mining capitalists:

> . . . The industrial upheavals on the Rand of 1913 and subsequently, made me realise that there was something radically wrong in the relationship between the State and the gold mines. The mining companies' refusal to recognise trade unions was exercising a disturbing and sinister influence on the whole of our community. And yet I had no say in the matter, though I was the Minister concerned.[35]

It is fairly clear, however, that while Malan had little or no say, it was not because of his impotence in the face of the mining capitalists' recalcitrance, but because of his own lack of competence and drive. Smuts and Botha seldom, if ever, left any decision of principle to him, and they usually left him out of the negotiations with labor and capital even when he was readily available. He was not generally taken seriously on mining matters by labor and capital, by Smuts, or even by his own bureaucrats.[36] Smuts and the GME, Robert Kotze, were old friends, and they completely overshadowed Malan and his Secretary for Mines, Warington Smyth, in policy making for the gold mines.[37]

If it is true that the white miners had many genuine grievances by 1913, it is also true that the mineowners were under growing pressure to keep costs down and productivity up, as the better grades of ore became progressively mined out on the central Witwatersrand gold fields. Many of the mines, particularly those of the Gold Fields and Goerz (later, Union Corporation) companies, were making little or no profit.[38] The problem of the low-grade mines—which are ultrasensitive to changes in costs because of the extremely small margin between revenue and costs—began to assume far greater importance around this time and has continued periodically to be vital until the present.

To fight the cost crisis, the employers put intense pressure on both black and white workers to increase productivity. Between

1911 and 1915, the number of white employees at work per 1,000 tons hoisted showed a continual decline; for a good part of that same time, black employees per 1,000 tons hoisted also declined. So productivity clearly did improve.[39]

The improvement was achieved in various ways, but the most important was probably the accelerating fragmentation of skilled jobs into semi-skilled jobs that could be performed by blacks cursorily supervised by whites. ("Job fragmentation" is sometimes also referred to as "deskilling," a somewhat less accurate description.) The 1907 strike had been partly caused by the attempt to get whites to supervise three drilling machines: by 1913, it was not unusual for whites to oversee six to ten machines. In 1907, there were 2,234 whites supervising 1,890 black-operated rock-drills; by 1913, there were 2,207 supervising 4,781 machines.[40] Job fragmentation undoubtedly added to the insecurity of the white workers, but its importance, and that of the color bar, as issues of contention between white labor and capital at the time should not be exaggerated. The new Afrikaner miners, in particular, had fewer skills to protect and were more content than were the foreign-trained miners merely to supervise blacks.[41]

To sum up the prestrike position in 1913, then, the white miners had many genuine grievances. The state was beginning to intervene in industrial relations, but only sporadically, and on an *ad hoc* basis. The employers were preoccupied with cutting costs and increasing productivity; their general feeling was that the miners were well paid and should not also expect to be well treated. For their part, the miners resented the fact that their grievances of 1907 had not been significantly alleviated by 1913.

The strike began characteristically at a mine called New Kleinfontein, on a technical question that merely affected the working hours of five men. The mine management quickly backed down, but the issue had sparked a series of general grievances, and a strike committee had already formed by that time (May 29). The committee comprised eight trade unionists, each from a different union, and it demanded an eight-hour day bank-to-bank (that is, from time of going underground to return to the surface).[42] The issue quickly escalated to one of recognition of trade unions for the purposes of collective bargaining, which the mining groups refused to do. They offered to reinstate the strikers but set a deadline (June 11) that was ignored. On June 17, a deputation of Kleinfontein strikers met the management of the mine and settled all the issues except for reinstatement.

The strike began to spread. On June 22, Smuts met the representatives of the mining groups; that afternoon, the groups refused a strike deputation's request to reinstate the strikers. By June 29, there were resolutions at a large meeting at Benoni—which defied a government prohibition under an 1894 anti-sedition law—calling for a general strike. The leaders were arrested under the 1909 Industrial Disputes Prevention Act and later released on bail. But the strikers appeared ready to back down. As G. McKneight wrote in his "Diary of the Kleinfontein Strike": "The position today [June 29] appears to be that if all the Kleinfontein hands were taken back the strike would end, this is the only demand that the Strikers are now insisting upon . . ."[43]

In spite of this, Smuts did not intervene. On the contrary, he cabled the TCM the next day, suggesting that it begin to prepare confidential lists of men who might be suitable to be sworn in as special police to protect mine property.[44] The employers tried but could not get him to ask for volunteers on behalf of the government; nevertheless, Smuts did promise to arm the mines' volunteers and have a magistrate swear them in.

The same day, June 30, Phillips wrote to London, blaming the government for the spread of the strike (in not preventing strikers' meetings), but he was not particularly worried about the prospect of a general strike. As in 1907 (and, later, in 1922), he was more impressed by the opportunities presented by such a strike:

> A general strike would of course be a serious matter from a dividend-paying standpoint. I do not think, however, that it could last very long and, if it does happen, we must make up our minds once and for all to break the Unions here, and the men will certainly not be permitted to come back to work upon the same high rates of pay they hitherto enjoyed.[45]

Unlike Smuts, who was in daily contact with the Chamber of Mines to impress on it the dangers to property posed by the spreading strike, Phillips was confident that the power of the state would crush the strikers:

> I do not feel very apprehensive about damage to property, as although the Government has been so dilatory in handling the strike up to the present, they will certainly not allow themselves to be played with if any serious situation arises. We had an example of their attitude upon matters of this kind in the strike of 1907.[46]

Phillips was assuming that because the government's spirit was willing, the state's flesh would not be weak. Smuts knew better. Legislation had recently been passed to reconstitute the army completely: the old forces had been disbanded, and the new ones were only in the process of formation. The volunteers for the active citizen force numbered only about 4,000, and they were scattered throughout the union.[47]

Not only was the state far short of possessing the coercive power needed to contain any violent general strike, but the Witwatersrand gold fields were an exceptionally difficult area to police: the Reef was forty miles long, which would spread the government forces thin; and it was totally dependent on its railway and tramway service, especially as there was only a three-day supply of food on hand. It was feared that the explosives stored on the mines might be captured. Above all, there was the fear of an uprising by the 250,000 black miners who were observing the unrest from their compounds.[48] This group was far larger than the total white population in the area; it had every reason to be equally dissatisfied with its treatment; and it was almost totally dependent for food on its employers.

On June 30, the same day that Phillips was expressing confidence that property would be protected, Smuts was cabling Lord Gladstone, the Governor-General, asking his permission to use Imperial troops to protect the mine properties. Before Union, Phillips claimed that these Imperial troops had been left in South Africa at his (Phillips's) suggestion, and it was for occasions such as these that Phillips had intended them to be used. He had written to Eckstein on January 11, 1909, that both Botha and Lord Selborne liked his suggestion of subsidizing the Imperial Government

> to maintain a few thousand troops always in South Africa. . . . In any active outbreak of course the first

measures are undertaken by the police, but in the event of any
petty disaster it is of the highest importance to have a force of
3,000 to 4,000 men able at least to hold their own, if not to
deliver a crushing blow, while burgher forces are organised. I
look upon this suggestion [sic] also as a step in the right direction from the imperial standpoint.[49]

Deep-level gold mines, of course, are peculiarly vulnerable to attack. One of Phillips's (and the employers') nightmares was the
possibility of planned sabotage: "Nothing of course is easier than
for the miners to steal and conceal dynamite. I recommend some
heavy penalties for being in illegal possession of explosives, as if the
men ever resorted to systematic damage of property, immense
damage could be done in a very short time."[50] Smuts shared this
nightmare, with the additional fear that the power stations might
be taken over or their coal supplies cut by industrial action.
Gladstone was sympathetic and quickly agreed to the use of Imperial troops. The day after Smuts's request 550 Royal Scots
Fusiliers were helping police and the S.A. Mounted Riflemen on the
East Rand.[51]

The next day, July 2, the executives of the Federation of Trades
and the Transvaal Miners' Association met separately and decided
on a general strike from July 4. A union leader, Tom Matthews,
threw down the gauntlet to the state as well as to the employers:
"The Government has practically called Martial Law in coming to
the assistance of the Mine Owners. Now we have called the Martial
Law of the Strikers—the General Strike."[52] About 5,000 of the Witwatersrand's 22,000 miners were already on strike. On July 3,
troops poured into the Rand from Pretoria and Potchefstroom.
Some miners who had been sworn in as special constables left to
join the strike. After a sharp tussle, the police and military dis-
persed strikers who were attacking the Kleinfontein power station.
At the request of the Coal Owners' Association, twenty mounted
police were assigned to protect the Witbank coal supply and
railway line to the east of the Witwatersrand.

By July 4, sixty-three of sixty-seven mines were out, with 18,000
men on strike, though pumping was continued because it was vital
to avoid flooding of the mines. Assemblies of more than six people
were forbidden, but a large gathering at Market Square, Johan-

nesburg, resulted in serious rioting and in the burning of Park Station and the offices of the *Star* newspaper. The police and military fired on the crowd several times, and there were many casualties on both sides.

Rioting continued throughout the next day in Johannesburg and on other parts of the Reef. Just how unprepared government forces were for an occurrence of this nature is indicated in the urgent request of the Under Secretary for Defense to the Secretary for Mines asking for maps of Benoni and the rest of the Reef. The request came through on July 1, and a draft of the map, called the "Industrial Disputes Map—Witwatersrand," was only completed on July 4, after the violent confrontation had already started.[53]

The climax of the strike came on July 5. All sixty-seven mines were out, and 19,000 men were on strike. As rioting continued throughout the Reef, Smuts and Botha came from Pretoria and met a strikers' deputation, which included J. T. Bain. The two generals then met the three most important mining employers (who were also all members of Parliament), Phillips, Chaplin, and Farrar, "who agreed to leave the question of the settlement of the strike entirely in the hands of the Government."[54]

The police and the army, even with the aid of the Imperial garrison—British troops alone killed over 100 strikers and bystanders[55]—had lost control of the situation, and it seemed that J. T. Bain's boast (in a pamphlet on June 24 calling for an illegal mass meeting) was well founded:

> . . . come armed if you can in order to resist any unlawful force which may be used against you. If unlawful force is used, we are ready to meet such unlawful force with lawful force, and 20,000 men cannot be beaten by all the forces of the Mining Industry and the Government as well.[56]

The generals had little choice, then, but to meet the strikers' leaders and negotiate a settlement. The meeting was held at the old Carlton Hotel in Johannesburg, under humiliating and dangerous circumstances for Botha and Smuts. It is unlikely, however, that (as has been claimed) the agreement was signed at gunpoint.[57] Smuts denied that he had seen any guns at the signing, but he conceded that the actual signing was one of the hardest things he ever had to do.

Smuts signed because he feared the possible sacking of the Reef towns and permanent damage to the mines, but he made up his mind that the government would never again be put in such a position.[58] It was not merely a defeat for the government, moreover, but also one for the fledgling South African state, which had failed to enforce public order even after its draconian treatment of the massed opposition.

The fact that the mining representatives had allowed the government to negotiate settlement terms has been interpreted as an indication of their power: ". . . they were in a position to obtain the services of the Prime Minister [Botha] and the most influential minister in the Government [Smuts] to do what they themselves persistently refused to do—negotiate with Federation representatives."[59] A more credible interpretation, however, is that the incident showed the weakness of the employers, who had to leave their fate completely to the discretion of the government. Nevertheless, although the agreement was forced on both the government and the employers, the union leaders failed to take full advantage of the situation at the height of the strikers' militance. They missed a clear opportunity to seize control of the state, by wavering between purely industrial demands and radical political goals.

The victory of the strikers was therefore Pyrrhic: the only concrete gain was the government's guarantee that the New Kleinfontein strikers would be reinstated. The radical socialists denounced the agreement, but the Federation leaders recommended its acceptance.[60] Unrest and riots continued, but on a smaller scale, and when another union delegation met Smuts and Botha on July 7—this time, in Pretoria, the capital of government—it achieved little. On July 9, charges against strike leaders under the Industrial Disputes Prevention Act were withdrawn, as had been promised earlier.

In addition, the state footed part of the employers' strike costs, by giving financial compensation to strikebreakers, who had been promised permanent employment but who were now being discharged at the insistence of the strikers. The compensation came from public funds. The Minister of Mines, F. S. Malan, for the first time playing a part in the events of 1913, paid out £45,590 to 168 strikebreakers on July 11. Men who had been employed before the strike and who had stayed on at work received no government compensation, though they were equally unpopular with the strikers.

An indication of how high feelings were running is provided by the fact that the government also supplied the strikebreakers with police protection from the mine "and a free railway ticket to any station within the Union."[61] The state made no effort to regain the money from the industry employers, and thus the taxpayers subsidized the employers' strike costs. The strike ended on July 12.

Threats of another strike—a general strike—continued, however. Such threats did not unduly bother Phillips, who wrote to Eckstein on July 28:

> Bad as the effects of a general strike would be today . . . I am not sure that in the end, if the men went to extremes now, from the purely industrial standpoint it would not be the best thing. From the humanitarian standpoint, of course, it would be a deplorable thing, because the suffering would unquestionably be great.[62]

He saw such a strike as likely to result in the breakdown of the color bar, and he noted that the concessions agreed to by the employers as a result of the 1913 strike were "not very important."[63] Phillips's attitude in this respect was not shared by the government, which interpreted the threat of the unions and the general strike to be a threat to the very security of the state. The Federation of Trades was established in South Africa in 1911 precisely because general strikes had been seen to be so effective in Britain, the United States, Australia, and Europe.[64]

A panic-stricken memorandum on the topic was sent by the Inspector of Mines in Pretoria to the Government Mining Engineer, and it was passed in turn to the Secretary for Mines and the Minister of Mines. The Inspector, Tudor Trevor, argued that the miners were prepared to obey their respective trade-union executives absolutely:

> . . . loyalty to their Union has quite taken the place of loyalty to their Government . . . and . . . should the order of the Union and the orders of the Government clash, they would not hesitate in obeying the former and treating the latter with contempt . . . they regard the Union as more powerful than the Government . . . treason to a Union entails far heavier and more certain consequences than treason to the Government.[65]

One of the safeguards for the state suggested by Trevor was a new act against sedition making it treason to the state and drastically increasing the penalty for "attempts to terrorize the State by organized general strikes or mob violence." Annotations by Warington Smyth, the Secretary for Mines, and Robert Kotze, the Government Mining Engineer, make it clear that they heartily agreed.

The threat to the state also worried various other groups that had a vested interest in stability—the center rapidly began to gird itself. On August 30, the Chamber of Commerce and the Master Builders' Association sent a deputation to tell F. S. Malan that he could rely on their support in "a definite line of legislation for dealing with industrial agitation and disputes."[66] Merriman crisply summed up bourgeois phobias when he complained in writing to Smuts about the general mortification felt because "the Government of the Union should have proved itself incapable of protecting persons and property or of keeping law and order without the aid of Imperial forces."[67] The Imperial forces, moreover, were unlikely to be unleashed by the British Government again. Enormous indignation arose in Britain over the idea of Imperial troops shooting British workers who, it was said, were merely exercising their freedom to gather in public and express their grievances.[68]

The state responded in two ways: it moved to consolidate and augment its coercive powers, and (as in 1907, but with more urgency) it moved toward establishing an institutional framework that would formally co-opt organized white labor into the state's administrative structure. In a plan for a comprehensive solution to the industrial disputes, the policy was succinctly stated by Lord Gladstone, the Governor-General. He wrote a private note to Botha, apparently unsolicited, saying how disastrous a general strike would be for the country as a whole:

> . . . the duty of the Government is plain. They [sic] make it known that they are fully prepared to deal with disorder and to repress it by force if unhappily the occasion arises—but they are of the opinion that disagreement between employers and employed in the vast industry of the Rand which threatens disaster to South Africa can no longer be tolerated.[69]

What Gladstone wanted above all was to depoliticize disputes between employer and employee in such a way that "if disputes develop even so far as an industrial strike, the dispute can be conducted without menace to the public peace."[70] The best way to achieve this, in his opinion, was by state intervention. It was necessary to guarantee the "financial stability" of the industry, and he recommended that the government announce that it was "prepared to consider what steps to take to secure this."[71] He also recommended that a similar "sound basis" be established to deal with railways disputes.

Gladstone had taken an active interest in labor relations and in the mining industry generally from his arrival in 1910. He approached the Chamber of Mines in 1911 with a request (which was granted) to meet its Executive Committee.[72] After the 1913 strike, he cabled the Home Office in the United Kingdom for advice on how to deal with strikes and what to do if the strikers were represented by several different unions. The reply, in September 1913, suggested that anyone who represented a substantial body of workers be interviewed.[73]

It should be mentioned here that Gladstone's concern, and the British concern over the use of Imperial troops, was very largely confined to white worker disputes. Black miners, it was taken for granted, could be treated very differently. A notable example of the fact that it was not thought necessary to conciliate or co-opt black miners is provided by the putting down of their strike in 1913, soon after the white miners' strike. During the white miners' strike many blacks had provided support by refusing to work, which had far less to do with working class solidarity than with threats that they would be blown up if they worked with strikebreakers.[74]

After the settlement for whites, the black miners struck for a wage increase from two shillings and three pence to five shillings a day. Imperial troops drove them back to work with bayonets and rifle butts.[75] White miners showed little sympathy, and there was no British outcry about the use of Imperial troops comparable to that accompanying the white miners' strike. Racial prejudice of both the British and South African states no doubt played a part in the discriminatory treatment of black and white strikes. Probably more important, however, is the (related) fact that the black miners were only marginally accepted as part of society because of both their color and their status as indentured migrant workers on time-limited contracts. Nor were they seen as a group that the state would ordinarily represent. They were housed in compounds that were physically located in such a way that the violence of the Imperial troops toward the black miners provided no threat to bystanders and nonstrikers generally—that is, the violent breaking of their strike posed no unacceptable threat to middle-class whites or to society as a whole. By contrast, the white miners' strike seemed to Gladstone, to the Chamber of Commerce, and to others to posit a very definite threat to the state and society overall, a "disagreement between employers and employed . . . which threatened disaster to South Africa and can no longer be tolerated."[76]

A copy of Gladstone's "plan" of July 30, 1913, has ended up in the F. S. Malan personal papers, possibly passed on to him by Botha with instructions to implement it.[77] On September 6, Malan told the press that legislation would be prepared on various aspects of industrial legislation. Two days later, Merriman wrote derisively to Smuts: "Surely legislation of that nature is not committed to the tender mercies of Malan and the Yachtsman?"[78] The "Yachtsman" was Warington Smyth, the Secretary for Mines and Industries, who was not ashamed to add to his profile in the South African *Who's Who* that he was a member of the Royal Thames Yacht Club, among others.

While this legislation was being prepared, Malan and Phillips exchanged several letters, with Malan pressing for trade-union recognition by the employers and Phillips agreeing to do so on certain conditions, such as: no recognition of federated unions; no closed-shop agreements; the recognition to be temporary, pending government legislation requiring the incorporation and registration of unions to make them liable for the acts of their officials and agents. On October 29, Phillips wrote to Malan grudgingly agreeing to "a measure of recognition" for the Transvaal Miners' Association on condition that the government guarantees that it (the TMA) would not attempt "to cause dissension or interfere in matters of internal management."[79]

Warington Smyth clearly recognized the need to incorporate the unions, to formally co-opt them into the state apparatus, and was contemptuous of his mining inspectors who objected to the recognition of trade unions because their power posed a threat to the state. One annotation in his handwriting to such an objection reads: "Writer forgets that recognition implies regulation also."[80] This was not, of course, an original insight, and Smyth was well aware of the use made elsewhere of the possibilities of taming worker militancy through state-chartered trade unions. On August 25, he sent a coded cable to the S.A. High Commissioner in the United Kingdom asking for all available material on the recognition and registration of and conditions for the conduct of trade unions. By September 18, he had received eight bluebooks on the subject.[81] Smyth was friendly with Lord Gladstone, and it is possible that Gladstone's "plan" had been worked out in advance with him before being sent on to Botha.

Warington Smyth also attacked the contract system by which white miners received no guaranteed wage but were paid according to their results. This sometimes resulted in high wages, but if contracted work targets were not achieved, it could also result in no wage at all or even debt for the contractor (who had to pay for explosives, equipment, and the labor that worked under him). It was one of the major causes of the chronic instability and mobility of the white mine labor force. In a draft letter, marked "not sent," he urged F. S. Malan to "insist" on the abolition of contract work even if the TCM should refuse to do so voluntarily. On November 5, 1913, the TCM wrote to say that it was investigating the underground contract system. After several more letters were exchanged, the TCM finally wrote, on May 27, 1915, that it was abolishing the "flat contract" system and replacing it with a system of a definite daily wage plus incentives.[82] The issue of contract work subsequently became a very important cause of the 1922 strike, when the mining employers sought to abolish the very system they had been so reluctant to do without in 1913.

In addition to seeking employer recognition of unions, Warington Smyth was also hard at work on legislation to provide for industrial conciliation. The latter was based on the 1909 Transvaal Industrial Disputes Act, which was probably drafted largely by Smyth himself and which he continued to defend.[83] Smyth wrote to the Secretary for Justice on September 19 that he had been instructed "by the government" to make certain amendments and he detailed them. The bill proposed to establish a Department of Industries and Labour and an Inspector of White Labour (a resurrection of the Het Volk government provision). It gave the government the power to investigate employer-employee relations even when it was not requested to do so; and it made unions liable for wrongful acts of their officials *and* members. This drastic measure, he noted, "may be going rather far," but it was being enforced by other countries at the time and was seen to be "the only way of preventing the Unions from sending out members to threaten and influence people in the direction of a strike for whose actions they would otherwise disclaim all responsibility."[84]

This went too far for the Cabinet, however, and on October 1, Smyth once again wrote to the Secretary for Justice that after further "discussion and consultation it has been thought that the trade unions should be reasonably defended from this class of attack"[85] and that it was decided merely to make the unions responsible for their own breaches of the law and to prevent them from paying benefits to members who broke the law.

The reason for the slightly more lenient attitude to the unions, Smyth explained, was that "unless the Government is frankly to go in for repressive legislation, it is desirable to hold out some benefits to trade unions in return for registration. . . ."[86] The idea, he said, was to drive a wedge between the "extremists" and the "ordinary working men." This made a good deal of sense from the point of view of both the state and the employer: if the white worker was to be co-opted in some way, it would have to be through the unions; and the policy of co-optation could only work as long as the unions, to some extent at least, could represent and articulate the interests of their members. The bill, before amendment, would have opened the way for a continual attack by employers on the unions' finances by damage suits on issues in which union members (but not the union) had been involved.

In general, however, the post-1913 strike industrial legislation can be fairly characterized to a significant degree as "repressive": it forbade "pulling out" (coercing men by force or threats), and refused bail to inciters of strikes. The latter provision emerged directly from the 1913 New Kleinfontein events, when strike leaders on bail "pulled out" other mines and accumulated enough backing to force the government to drop charges against them. Smyth was ordered to add amendments to his old Transvaal law, and their repressive nature was most clear in the provision that attempted "to confine an industrial dispute to the original parties to it and to enable them to fight it out on its merits without interference from outside."[87] There were also provisions to prevent the simultaneous use of strikebreakers and the institution of picketing—again, to isolate the strike or lockout and minimize the likelihood of violence that might threaten public order. In general, there was a strong emphasis on provisions that would prevent the dreaded "general strike" and the disruption of essential services by syndicalist strike tactics.

These two bills—on industrial conciliation and the recognition of trade unions—were published soon after the 1913 strike. After the 1914 strike, they were overtaken by a combined measure, the Industrial Disputes and Trade Unions Bill, which passed the House of Assembly but failed, through lack of time, to pass the Senate. It was not reintroduced after the beginning of World War I.[88] Not surprisingly, the TCM was disappointed that the bill had not passed,[89] while the labor leaders did not lament the fact. Creswell, the leader of the S.A. Labour party, denounced the bill for attempting to get the unions "in such a position that they could be brought under the grip of law and prevented from expanding."[90] It took another large and violent strike, in 1922, to provide the final impetus for the reintroduction and passage of a similar law.

One law resulting directly from the 1913 strike did, however, pass. This law was one of the major steps to achieve the other half of government strategy—to consolidate and augment the state's coercive powers—and was called the Riotous Assemblies and Criminal Law Amendment Act No. 27 of 1914.[91] As has been pointed out, the power of the unions (especially the federated unions, with their power to organize general strikes) was seen as a distinct political threat that fell under the category of "radical syndicalism." They were a threat to the state's power as well as to that of the employers.

The 1913 strike created a precedent by which white labor resorted to extraconstitutional means—and achieved its ends that way. Those leaders who had broken the law were released precisely because their followers had mobilized enough power to flout the law. Even the Labour party leader, the usually conservative Creswell, accepted the use of nonconstitutional means if the goals of the white workers could not be achieved by constitutional protest, in marked contrast to his actions in 1922.[92]

The Riotous Assemblies Act was meant to help the government

keep industrial turbulence under control, enabling state authorities to ban gatherings if they were deemed by a magistrate to constitute a threat to public peace. One entire chapter of the law's three chapters applied only to strike situations. It forbade forceful picketing, forbade even the verbal haranguing of workers, and made it a criminal offense for a worker in a local authority or public utility to break his contract in a way that threatened light, power, or water services.[93] The law has been described as an attack on both civil liberties and working-class rights, marking the transition from a colonial to an industrialized economy.[94] The act was passed in July 1914 and was supported by white middle-class professionals, farmers, and small businessmen because a prime goal of all these groups was stability, and the strikes of 1913 and 1914 had seemed to threaten the stability of the state itself.

THE 1914 STRIKE

The settlement of the 1913 strike had cheated the white workers of a victory they might easily have achieved by virtue of the temporarily weak position of the government and the state. The period after the 1913 strike was characterized by the bitterness of organized labor and their open defiance of the existing order. The radical nature of their demands, however, alienated much of the centrist public support for the miners' cause that had resulted from the state's violence during the 1913 strike. The six months of demands and threats reduced even an avowed enemy of the mining capitalists such as Merriman to impotent rage. He wrote to Smuts on January 10, 1914, after the 1914 strike had already begun, that it was necessary to act against "labour agitators," not merely threaten them: "Surely under the common law of any civilized country these men are liable to arrest for using language calculated (even intended) to provoke a breach of the peace, and arrested they should be unless the law is a farce."[95]

The 1914 general strike[96] started with government retrenchments on the railways on Christmas Eve, 1913. A fairly strong case has been made that the government wanted to force a strike.[97] Lionel Phillips, who was lying in hospital after an (apparently nonpolitical) attempt on his life, reported in his *Reminiscences*:

General Smuts came to see me and . . . told me another strike was impending and timed to break out about the New Year. I asked him whether the Government had benefited by the experience of the previous strike, and he said there need be no apprehensions on that account, and so it proved.[98]

On January 6, a mass meeting of railwaymen in Pretoria decided to strike, and by January 8, the railway strike had spread to Johannesburg and Germiston. A Committee of Public Safety was formed in Johannesburg, and special constables were enrolled both there and in Pretoria.[99] On January 9, the Active Citizens Force (ACF) began to be called up. The railway strike spread, but most trains continued to run. The engine of the Cape mail train was blown up near Johannesburg. Bars were ordered closed. Finally, a wave of arrests of union leaders began, and the Federation of Trades threatened to retaliate with a general strike.[100]

On January 12, after balloting among its members, the Federation of Trades called a general strike. The mining unions only narrowly decided to join the strike, the required two-thirds majority being exceeded by a mere 166 votes. The less skill-orientated "industrial" mining unions were far more heavily in favor of a strike than were the artisan miners' unions.[101] Nevertheless, for a sympathy strike, the strike on the mines was very successful. The Government Mining Engineer's figures show 5,301 fewer men working on January 21 than at the end of the previous year; that peak rapidly decreased from then on as the miners returned to work.[102] According to TCM figures, the number of gold mines that came out was 53 (July 1913 : 55), men on strike totalled 9,059 (14,555), and shifts lost totalled 43,957 (69,665).[103]

Before the 1914 miners' strike had been started, Smuts had brought 10,000 troops to the Rand. By January 14, the day he proclaimed martial law, he had called up 70,000 men throughout South Africa. The rural Afrikaner commandos were led into Johannesburg by Generals Beyers and de la Rey (who, later in the same year, were to lead the armed rebellion against the state and its participation in World War I).[104] The Johannesburg Trades Hall was besieged, the entire Federation of Trades Executive Committee was arrested on January 15, and the strike began to disintegrate. On

January 17, Creswell and Boydell, both members of Parliament and subsequently Cabinet Ministers, were arrested. A week later, the acting executive of the Federation called off the strike.

A few salient points should be noted. The gold miners' part in the 1914 strike was largely confined to sympathy striking, which may account as much for their relative lack of physical resistance and violence as for the rapid mobilization of state military power (which is usually given credit). Only one violent incident is noted by McKneight: the throwing of a bomb at the police, which resulted in the arrest of 200 miners.[105] McKneight does not mention any casualties, and Hancock notes only two deaths[106]—although at least eleven black miners, in a concurrent but unrelated strike, were killed by a vigilante force of white miners.[107]

Smuts has generally been given credit for reorganizing the army between July 1913 and January 1914 into "an efficient military organization."[108] Possibly of equal importance in the success of the rapid mobilization, however, was Smuts's personal relationship to the generals who put the strike down, bringing their own personal followers with them, and the fact that Smuts had orchestrated the timing of the strike. Many of the soldiers were housed and fed at the mines during the strike, and in most cases, the costs were borne by the mining companies. On February 9, the TCM sent an effusive cable of thanks to the government for "defeating the recent attempts to paralyse the industries of the Union [of South Africa]." Botha cabled back: "Much appreciated."[109]

Finally, and most important from the point of view of the relationship of the state's power to organized labor and industry, the impact of the civil-rights issue on the middle classes must be noted. The strike was characterized by the rapid and widespread arrest of leaders, with at least fifteen arrested before the declaration of martial law.[110] Parliamentary labor leaders and the entire Federation Executive Committee were arrested soon after. Normally, these arrests would probably have created little political reaction; after all, the arrest of leaders has subsequently become a standard method of the South African state for preempting threats of insurrection, with a notable absence of protest from the center.

Smuts, however, went further, and late in January, long after all "clear and present danger" had disappeared, he illegally deported nine of the union leaders.[111] The strikers were all foreign-born and included several of the leaders who had been prominent in the government's humiliation in 1913: J. T. Bain, George Mason, Andrew Watson, Robert Waterston, and Archie Crawford, as well as W. Livingstone, Dave McKerrill, W. H. Morgan, and J. H. Poutsma. Why the leaders were deported after the strike had already been broken is still something of a mystery. The explanation given was deterrence and the threat to the state of general strikes, aggravated by the parallel threat of black risings. In Smuts's case, revenge and retribution were probably as important. The deportations were temperamentally consistent with his reaction to crisis situations. President Kruger was supposed to have said to him: "Smuts, you crack your whip too loud."[112]

Whatever the government's rationale, the deportations were very widely criticized. Even Smuts's best friends wrote him letters condemning the move, and Merriman, who had so strongly urged him to come down hard on the strikers, rejected his methods.[113] It is interesting to ask why the deportations should have aroused passions that the killing of numerous strikers and bystanders in 1913 had not. The most convincing explanation seems to be that Smuts had infringed civil liberties and the "rule of law" by the surreptitious deportations. If he could violate the rule of law, the centrist argument went, who was he to demand that strikers should stick to it? As his friend H. J. Wolstenholme, a Cambridge don, put it,

> . . . the use of force and the suspension of law will tempt even many moderate men to think it fair policy to retaliate with defiance and circumvention of law, and the assertion of their own right to ruthless use of their own power and force. And the more the struggle is shifted on to this plane the worse it will be for all parties, and the civilisation.[114]

Flouting the rule of law, then, was dangerous and threatened "civilization" itself; in particular, Wolstenholme claimed, it threatened "law and order" and the classes most bent on preserving it: the "strong capitalist and burgher elements."[115] Merriman made the same point somewhat less precisely, echoing Burke's famous distinction between the rights of men and the rights of Englishmen. He accused Smuts of justifying his action by advocating "a Latin American doctrine and not the doctrine of a free country where

Englishmen and Dutchmen live."[116] The Act of Indemnity, excusing the illegal actions of the government, was nevertheless passed by a large majority in Parliament. Criticism of the deportations by the parliamentary opposition and public support of that criticism did, however, contribute toward the attainment of the Labour party's zenith: a majority of seats in the Transvaal provincial administration in 1915.[117]

SOVEREIGNTY AND CO-OPTATION

Behind the controversy over the deportations lay the crucial issues of legitimation and co-optation. Both Smuts's allies and the opposition National party strongly supported the declaration of martial law to protect the stability of the state. They also felt, however, that the rights of the propertied classes would be best protected by a not-too-explicit alliance and by taking care to leave, ostensibly, some access to the state for the white workers. But it became difficult to convince white workers that they should support the "rule of law" when the state ignored it in their case. The deportations threatened the credibility of the "rule of law"—a system that supposedly applied equally to all and usually successfully concealed its built-in bias toward the propertied classes—as a legitimating device. The deportations, therefore, weakened the state's overall quest for legitimation.

Wolstenholme put this point to Smuts very perceptively and succinctly. On the necessity for a loose alliance of the propertied classes, he said, after condemning the deportations:

> In South Africa, with its strong capitalist and burgher elements, bent on preserving the "order" which protects their interests, there ought to be little difficulty on the part of the Government in securing sufficient authority and support for a firm maintenance of "law and order," through constitutional forms and administration. Indeed the danger would seem to be rather the temptation to follow too far the policy of the "high hand."[118]

The necessity for some sort of alliance of property owners was recognized even by such a partisan defender of the mining industry's specific interests as Lionel Phillips. From 1907 onward, he had advocated "best man government," and continued to do so privately after joining the Unionist party. He wrote to Wernher that South Africa and the industry really needed a government of progressives from both sides (alias "best men," alias "strong capitalist and burgher elements"):

> What is really needed in my opinion in this country (and of course I give you this confidentially, because it is sound reason but not good politics!) is not a defeat of the Boers by our side and the replacement of Botha's government by a Unionist Government, but a union of the best men of both sides, and I still believe this will be accomplished in time.[119]

Phillips was acute enough, then, to recognize a community of interest between his predominantly Anglophone, mining-capitalist party and the Afrikaner, rural South African party. Compared to Botha and Smuts, however, he was politically naive: they, too, saw the community of interests, of course, but tried extremely hard throughout the period 1910–1920 not to formalize it in an electoral pact or fusion of political parties. Quite correctly, they saw little gain in such a move and considerable loss,[120] for the South African party drew considerable support from several groups directly hostile to mining capital and to urban Anglophones, though these groups were already beginning to drift away. The smaller Afrikaner farmers, *bywoners* (squatters), and urban poor whites would increasingly move toward the National party, and white workers and small shopkeepers would move to the Labour party, especially after the 1913 strike. A formal alliance or amalgamation with the Unionist party, which was finally forced on Smuts in 1920, could only hasten the drift and narrow the South African party's political base. Besides, Botha and Smuts knew that the Unionists would inevitably support the South African party on issues affecting property owners in general, whether there was a formal alliance or not.

The dangers of alienating organized labor, then, were obvious; on the other hand, syndicalist industrial strife, especially on the Reef, threatened the fundamental stability of the state, which had to insist absolutely on its exclusive right to the legitimate use of force. The breaking up of the 1907 and 1914 strikes by state force was rationalized at the time (partly justifiably) as protection of the rule of law. Hence, Smuts's deportations—an openly admitted violation of the law—put the state in the decidedly tenuous position of appearing to be selective about its enforcement of the rule of law.

Such violations also threatened the middle classes generally, for whom the rule of law and property rights are intimately bound up. That this was perceived as a threat is shown by the outcry that followed the 1914 Peace Preservation Bill, which would have given the state the right by proclamation to, *inter alia*, enter homes, read mail, prohibit free speech and public assembly, prohibit strikes, and banish citizens for life without accountability to a court of law. The bill was withdrawn after even South African party members of Parliament opposed it.[121]

In addition to attempting to maintain its legitimacy and exclusive right to the use of force, the state also embarked upon a program of direct co-optation of organized labor. This was to be achieved by the means cited above: the state regulation of industry in general; the state chartering of bodies such as trade unions; and the opening of day-by-day channels of communication between the state bureaucracy and organized labor, through the reappointment of the government Inspector of White Labour.

Wolstenholme, somewhat euphemistically but nevertheless acutely, wrote to Smuts justifying the increasingly interventionist role of the state generally. This, he pointed out, was necessitated by the altered situation of the modern industrial world:

> Modern conditions, in the industrial world and elsewhere, are not met by our traditional machinery of government . . . and some reorganization of our legal and administrative institutions is necessary. . . . But every Government must so renew and reform itself as to make itself adequate to the control of, and the even distribution of justice among, whatever elements of population its history and its own policy have gathered within its limits.[122]

It has already been pointed out that the major issue was not whether organized white labor should be incorporated into the state, but when and on what terms. What the state needed was an institutional framework to enable it to distance itself from the conflict of labor and capital and to deal with it administratively; in short, it needed to depoliticize organized labor and labor-capital relations. It needed to create a structure that would put the state in the ostensible role of neutral arbiter while leaving it with sufficient control both to ensure the continued viability of the industry and to abort any attempt by labor to achieve its ends by prolonged strikes or insurrectionary violence. The state, in short, needed to co-opt organized labor.

Co-option had been described in another connection as "the process of absorbing new elements into the leadership or policy-determining structure of an organization as a means of averting threats to its stability or existence."[123] An organization (such as a state) will embark on formal co-optation to win itself public legitimacy. It does this by drawing in groups that are quantitatively or strategically important in society, "elements which in some way reflect the sentiment or possess the confidence of the relevant public or mass . . ." It might also formally co-opt such a group when "the need to invite participation is essentially administrative," making "it advisable to establish the forms of self-government."[124]

Co-optation, thus, neatly describes the aim of the South African state in attempting to incorporate the trade unions: it required acceptance of its legitimacy by all sections of the white electorate and the use of the institutions of organized labor to govern organized labor. Organized labor had to be co-opted precisely because it had a relatively independent power base that the state wanted to neutralize and/or utilize.

The major point of formal co-optation is "that what is shared is responsibility for power rather than power itself."[125] The recognition of trade unions for the purposes of collective bargaining under the state umbrella makes them responsible for their contractual undertakings and legally liable for the breaking of agreements. This means that organized labor barters the unconditional right to strike for conditional access to the state structure and the decision-making process.

Naturally, this can lead to considerable economic advantages in some circumstances. Organized labor, moreover, frequently finds its options for direct industrial action circumscribed to some extent by society as a whole: strikes cause inconvenience to various groups, not only to employers. These are two of the factors that might justifiably motivate organized labor to impose or accept restrictions on its most potent weapon. But it is important to emphasize that the extent to which organized labor agrees to operate under the state umbrella is directly related to the extent to which its own autonomy and power can be maintained. When it forsakes the relatively autonomous source of its power, it also largely forfeits control of its own destiny. A corollary of this is that it becomes powerless to effect radical changes in either the form or priorities of the state and society.

Conversely, state power can actually be augmented by the nominal rights of recognition and access that it bestows on trade unions though co-optation. This is largely true because formal co-optation shifts the responsibility for the actions of organized labor to the trade unions without granting them any corresponding autonomy. Furthermore, recognition of unions, in Warington Smyth's phrase, implies regulation.

While formal co-optation accurately describes the state-labor relationship, *informal* co-optation is a useful (though partial) concept for characterizing the state's relationship with capital. Such co-optation occurs when it is necessary to meet

> the pressure of specific individuals or interest groups which are in a position to enforce demands. The latter are interested in the substance of power and not necessarily its forms. Moreover, an open acknowledgement of capitulation to specific interests may itself undermine the sense of legitimacy of the formal authority within the community. Consequently there is a positive pressure to refrain from explicit recognition of the relationship established. . . . Co-optation reflects a state of tension between formal authority and social power.[126]

Mining capital fits the above example in that it could enforce certain demands—which is not to say that the state is run merely in the employer's interest—and was concerned more about the reality of power than with its prestige. Moreover, explicit recognition of its relationship to the state could weaken the state's power to legitimate policy.

The violence of the 1907 and 1913 strikes threatened civil society and moved the South African state to lay down a rudimentary and therefore abortive framework for the "formal" co-optation of organized labor. The overlapping of interests and the agreement between the state and mining capital about the threat posed by organized labor strikes led, on the other hand, to the "informal" co-optation of the gold mining capitalists. The events of 1914 marked the further cementing of the symbiotic relationship of mining capital and the state and the growth of a more sophisticated, institutionalized format for the relationship. Their respective bureaucracies cooled and formalized their relationship into an ostensibly "arms-length" situation that allowed—and even encouraged—differences between the two to emerge in public (for example, on the issue of recognition of trade unions). This did not in any way weaken their basic commitment to each other; rather, it strengthened their ability to pursue that commitment.

It is also worth noting that the events of 1914 marked the defeat of both potential class revolutionaries and nationalist revolutionaries, a defeat from which they never recovered. In Wolstenholme's terms, the "burgher and capitalist elements" at the center had decisively vanquished radical challenges to their hegemony. No alliance between the two radical groups was even seriously considered, and each actively opposed the other in their respective struggles with the state. Similarly, the white miners rejected the advances of black miners, who could have been a powerful force for class revolution. Even the 1924 Pact between the National and Labour parties was to "succeed" only as an entirely different type of alliance: they were establishment parties from which radicals of both groups had been largely purged or reeducated. Creswell, the Labour party leader, and Archie Crawford, the trade-union leader, might have been radicals in some ways in 1914; by 1924, they had become—rhetoric notwithstanding—pillars of the establishment.

The next chapter will examine the third and culminating round of violence and the events leading up to it, and the third and culminating attempt at formal co-optation and depoliticization of organized labor. The state, of course, played a crucial role in shaping these events and was, itself, radically changed by them.

NOTES

1. S. B. Spies, "The Rebellion in South Africa, 1914–1915," Master's thesis, University of the Witwatersrand, 1962, pp. 89–118, 224.

2. P. C. Grey, "The Development of the Gold Mining Industry of the Witwatersrand, 1902–1910," pp. 276–78; *Debates of Transvaal Legislative Assembly*, 10.7.07, pp. 797–800.

3. MM 4256/13, Vol. 217, "Industrial Disputes Prevention Bill."

4. Ibid.

5. Ibid.

6. BRA, HE 154, Phillips to Eckstein, 11.5.08.

7. Ellison Kahn, "The Right to Strike in South Africa: An Historical Analysis," *South African Journal of Economics*, Vol. 11, No. 1, March 1943, pp. 25–27.

8. W. K. Hancock, *Smuts 2: The Fields of Force 1919–1950*, Cambridge, 1968, p. 67; Jeffrey Lever, "Creating the Institutional Order: The Passage of the Industrial Conciliation Act, 1924," chapter of forthcoming Ph.D. diss., University of Stellenbosch, p. 3.

9. Lever, "Creating the Institutional Order," p. 5.

10. Katz, "The Origins," pp. 129–31.

11. Lever, "Creating the Institutional Order," p. 9.

12. Guy Routh, *Industrial Relations and Race Relations*, Johannesburg, 1952. The migrant labor system is mentioned here to illustrate how the denial of rights to blacks made them more attractive as workers to potential employers and, therefore, a greater threat to white labor.

13. Roy Gregory, *The Miners and British Politics, 1906–1914*, Oxford, 1968, p. 14.

14. Ibid.

15. TCM M 41: Smuts overruled his Government Mining Engineer's apparently accurate ruling that underground work should be restricted to eight hours in twenty-four, and said that the restriction to forty-eight hours a week was sufficient—subverting the rationale for the provision as a health measure.

16. The agricultural interests in Parliament had earlier attempted to have the recruiting of Africans under eighteen for the mines prohibited by law, as they were competing for labor with the mines, TCM 1911–1922 Series, N 11.

17. MM 2570/10, Vol. 27; MM 275/11, Vol. 43; TCM M 5(g), 1899–1910 Series; TCM M 41.

18. TCM M 41.

19. MM 2081/14. On 1.4.1914, the new Minister of Mines, F. S. Malan, told a deputation protesting the exclusion of coloreds from skilled work that this was the case. He appeared to have been hinting to them that they should challenge the regulations in court.

20. F. A. Johnstone, *Class, Race and Gold*, p. 147.

21. BRA, HE 155, 8.2.11. In BRA 155, 7.2.10, Phillips explained that his decision to go into politics resulted from the failure of the proposed coalition between the Botha/Smuts S.A. party and the mining-dominated

Unionist party. The final end of the honeymoon with Botha and Smuts came when Smuts attacked Phillips at an election meeting held for Phillips's party opponent. Phillips commented: "The base ingratitude of Botha and Smuts proves once again the Boer untrustworthiness." Phillips won the election comfortably.

22. BRA, HE 155, Phillips to Wernher, 1.3.1911.

23. TCM Executive Minutes, 2.3.1911.

24. TCM Executive Minutes, 15.3.11, 1.4.1911.

25. TCM M 5g, 1899–1910 Series.

26. TCM M 41.

27. MM 2570/10, J. B. Robinson to Smuts, 14.12.1910.

28. TCM M 41, 11.3.1911.

29. MM 3220/15, Vol. 530, 17.11.1914, referring to a dispute on the remission of diggers' license fees.

30. Katz, "Origins," p. 313; C. R. Ould, "General Smuts' Attitude to White Labour Disputes Between 1907 and 1922," Master's thesis, University of the Witwatersrand, 1964, p.36.

31. Katz, "White Workers' Grievances," provides an excellent account; see also Davies, "Mining Capital."

32. *Report of the Economic Commission*, UG 12–1914, paragraph 39.

33. Katz, "White Workers' Grievances," p. 155. Of the other four, one died in an accident and three were phthisis sufferers; Walker and Weinbren, *2,000 Casualties*, p. 23.

34. Katz, "White Workers' Grievances," pp. 130–31.

35. F. S. Malan, "Autobiography," Chapter 20, unpublished manuscript in the F. S. Malan Collection, Cape Archives. I should like to thank Peter Kallaway for drawing it to my attention.

36. For an alternative view, stressing the importance of Malan's administrative functions and role in introducing industrial legislation, see Lever, "Creating the Institutional Order," and Peter Kallaway, "F. S. Malan, the Cape Liberal Tradition, and South African Politics, 1908–1924," *Journal of African History*, Vol. 15, No. 1, 1974. Cartwright, *Golden Age*, pp. 30–31, graphically conveys Malan's ignorance of the mining industry, his lack of a sense of the state's growing role, and the way Smuts was relied upon to deal with mining crises.

37. See Chapter 4 for a further account of the Smuts-Kotze relationship.

38. BRA, Phillips to Chairman, Central Mining and Investment Corporation, 30.6.1913.

39. ARGMEs, *Economic Aspects of the Gold Mining Industry*, UG 32–1948, Report No. 11 of the Social and Economic Planning Council; see also Figure 1, Chapter 6.

40. Katz, "White Workers' Grievances," p. 151; Davies, "Mining Capital."

41. Katz, "White Workers' Grievances," p. 146. Martin Legassick, in an

unpublished paper presented at the 1976 University of Witwatersrand Conference on Southern African Labour History, "The Mining Economy and the White Working Class," has suggested a far too mechanistic connection between job fragmentation and strikes (p. 8). Katz, whose work he relies on, provides a more perceptive analysis.

42. The following account of the strike is drawn largely from "Diary of the Kleinfontein Strike," compiled by a Department of Mines clerk, G. McKneight. It is to be found in MM 1779/13, which is attached to MM 1295/14, Vol. 238. Henceforth referred to as the McKneight Diary.

43. Ibid.

44. TCM S 44, "Strikes on the Mines."

45. BRA, 30.6.1913.

46. Ibid.

47. Lewis Harcourt, U. K. Secretary of State for the Colonies, in the *Times* (London), 8.7.1913, 10.7.1913. The Police Act, No. 14 of 1912, came into effect on April Fool's Day 1913, creating a permanent force, but only on paper.

48. See the *Manchester Guardian*, 10.7.1913.

49. BRA, HE 155, Phillips to Eckstein, 11.1.1909.

50. BRA, HE 154, Phillips to Wernher, 24.2.1908.

51. McKneight Diary.

52. Ibid.

53. MM 2266/13, Vol. 187, "Witwatersrand Disturbance Maps."

54. MM 1779/13, McKneight Diary.

55. *Manchester Guardian*, 10.7.1913.

56. Quoted in full in Walker and Weinbren, *2,000 Casualties*, p. 340.

57. R. K. Cope, *Comrade Bill: The Life and Times of W. H. Andrews*, Cape Town, n.d., p. 135; Walker and Weinbren, *2,000 Casualties*, pp. 36–37; Katz, "The Origins," p. 316.

58. Simons and Simons, *Class and Colour in South Africa*, p. 158; McKneight Diary.

59. Walker and Weinbren, *2,000 Casualties*, p. 36.

60. Simons and Simons, p. 159, say that "the right-wing [union] leaders killed the strike."

61. MM 1779/13; McKneight Diary; F. S. Malan, "Autobiography," Chapter 19, pp. 4–6.

62. BRA, 28.7.1913.

63. Ibid., and BRA, 30.6.1913.

64. Katz, "The Origins," pp. 312–13. She says that the principle of the general strike was the only feature of syndicalism that had any impact on the South African unions.

65. MM 1074/14, Vol. 234, 9.9.1913.

66. MM 1350/14, Vol. 239, "Notes of Interview."

67. Hancock and van der Poel, *Smuts Papers*, Vol. 3, 8.9.1913, p. 133.

68. C.D. 6941 and C.D. 6942, reports containing correspondence relating to "Recent Disorders on the Witwatersrand and the Employment of Regular Troops"; TCM, S 44, 1911–1922 Series, "Strikes of the Mines"; British *Daily News*, 4.7.1913; *Manchester Guardian*, 10.7.1913.

69. F. S. Malan Papers, Acc. 583, 30.7.1913.

70. Ibid.

71. Ibid.

72. TCM Executive Committee Minutes, 21.12.1911.

73. MM 1344/14, Vol. 239.

74. Cope, *Comrade Bill*, p. 135.

75. Ibid., p. 142.

76. It was also a very uncomfortable situation for mining magnates. Sir George Albu, head of the General Mining and Finance Corporation group, applied urgently for £5,000 insurance on his home during the 1913 strike. The financial agents did not effect the insurance, saying they had been "ordered closed" for the day (5.7.1913). See General Mining and Finance Corporation miscellaneous correspondence, located in the Strange Africana Library, Johannesburg.

77. F. S. Malan Papers, Acc. 583, 30.7.1913, Gladstone to Botha.

78. *Smuts Papers*, Vol. 3, p. 133.

79. TCM File T 12, "Transvaal Miners' Association 1913," especially Malan to Phillips, 2.9.1913; Phillips to Malan, 10.9.1913 and 29.10.1913. These negotiations were not, however, carried on through the TCM. The groups bypassed the TCM and negotiated directly (see Phillips to Malan, 17.11.1913) and only subsequently gave copies of their correspondence to the TCM. This unusual procedure could have had something to do with the feud between the mining members of Parliament and the TCM that had surfaced in 1911.

80. MM 1073/14.

81. MM 2896/13, Vol. 196.

82. MM 1074/14.

83. MM 4256/13, Vol. 217.

84. Ibid.

85. MM 4253/13, Vol. 216.

86. Ibid.

87. MM 4256/13.

88. Lever, "Creating Institutional Order," pp. 10–11.

89. ARTCM, 1914, p. lxxi. The TCM induced further amendments favorable to the employers in a select committee after the original publication of the bills.

90. House Assembly Debates, 1914, col. 1974, cited in Lever, p. 11.

91. *Statutes of the Union of South Africa*, Cape Town, 1914, pp. 240–59.

92. H. J. and R. E. Simons, *Class and Colour in South Africa*, p. 160.

93. *Statutes*, p. 248.

94. Simons and Simons, p. 171.

95. *Smuts Papers*, Vol. 3, p. 157.

96. For a detailed account, see MM 1295/14, McKneight's 1914 strike diary, compiled at the request of the Secretary for Mines. See also Walker and Weinbren, *2,000 Casualties*, p. 46 ff.; Simons and Simons, *Class and Colour*, pp. 166–70.

97. Walker and Weinbren, *2,000 Casualties*, pp. 47, 51.

98. Lionel Phillips, *Some Reminiscences*, London, n.d. [1925?], p. 225.

99. MM 1295/14, Vol. 238.

100. Ibid.

101. See ibid. for a partial voting breakdown.

102. MM 1296/14, Vol. 238.

103. TCM 1911–1922 Series, File I-12, "Industrial Unrest."

104. Simons and Simons, *Class and Colour*, p. 168.

105. MM 1295/14, January 15.

106. Hancock, *Smuts*, Vol. 1, p. 368.

107. Simons and Simons, *Class and Colour*, p. 168.

108. Hancock, *Smuts*, Vol. 1, p. 369.

109. TCM I-12, 1911–1922 Series, File I-12.

110. MM 1296/14.

111. Simons and Simons give the date as January 30 (p. 170); Hancock, *Smuts*, Vol. 1, gives January 27 (p. 368).

112. Hancock, *Smuts*, Vol. 1, p. 373. See Chapter 5 for Smuts's similar reaction to the Rand Revolt in 1922.

113. *Smuts Papers*, Vol. 3, pp. 164, 166–67.

114. Ibid., p. 166.

115. Ibid., p. 167.

116. Hancock, *Smuts*, Vol. 1, p. 370.

117. D. W. Kruger, *The Age of the Generals*, Johannesburg, 1961, pp. 76–77.

118. *Smuts Papers*, Vol. 3, p. 167, 26.2.1914.

119. BRA, HE 155, Phillips to Wernher, 10.10.1910.

120. For example, *Smuts, Papers*, Vol. 3, p. 298, Smuts to Sir David de Villiers Graaff, 14.6.1915, talking about a "very difficult" matter—how to "avoid the fatal impression (fatal to us) that there is a secret agreement" [between the S.A. party and the Unionists]. See also ibid., pp. 170–71. N. G. Garson, in "South Africa and World War I," *Journal of Imperial and Commonwealth History*, Vol. 8, No. 1, October 1979, p. 83, shows that Botha was seriously considering "best-man" government in private as early as 1914.

121. Walker and Weinbren, *2,000 Casualties*, p. 56.

122. *Smuts Papers*, Vol. 3, p. 167, 26.2.1914.

123. Phillip Selznick, *TVA and the Grass Roots: A Study in the Sociology of Formal Organization*, Berkeley, Calif., 1949, p. 13.

124. Ibid., p. 14.

125. Ibid.

126. Ibid.

4

The Struggle Broadens: Legitimation and Accumulation, 1914–1921

In a country where the people have votes it is, of course, necessary to cultivate friendly relations with them. The mining industry is not like a big retail business where you have only to think of profit and loss. Its fortunes are a great deal dependent upon popular goodwill.

—Lionel Phillips, 1915[1]

THE DEVELOPING CRISIS: AN OVERVIEW

The 1913 and 1914 strikes demonstrated conclusively that quarrels between employers and unionized employees on the gold mines were national issues that could not be ignored by the rest of South African society. Nor could the protagonists ignore South African society. The government's handling of the 1913 and 1914 strikes created dissatisfaction within both the white working class and the middle class, which was probably the major cause of the sweeping Labour party victory in the Transvaal provincial council election of 1914 that gave it control of the council and victories in two parliamentary by-elections. The illegal deportation of labor leaders, as we have seen, was probably the major cause of middle-class disaffection with the government,[2] and the continuing move of Afrikaners into jobs on the mines also played its part.[3]

In general, it was becoming clearer that mining capitalists, organized labor, and the government itself would have increasingly to seek outside support on the issue of the relationship of the state and industry. The balance between these groups was sufficiently delicate to necessitate the recruitment of noncombatant social groups as allies. It was thought necessary, in short, to win what was then referred to as "the public," particularly as the public had shown, by its response to the deportations, *inter alia*, that it was vitally interested in the relationship between the state and mining capital.

The mobilization of support from groups not directly concerned with the capital-labor clash is a vital theme throughout the period 1914–1921. One has the acute sense of the protagonists continually glancing over their shoulders, justifying their actions to a much larger audience. This struggle for legitimation was exacerbated by the relatively undeveloped nature of the state. The police and the army, for example, could not easily control even a small sector of the population such as the white miners. Moreover, a large part of the electorate simply rejected the validity of the state, as was shown by the rural Afrikaner Rebellion resulting from the government's decision to support Britain actively at the outbreak of World War I.

Besides having problems in its legitimation role, the state was also faced with a developing crisis in its accumulation role. The growing cost crisis on the gold mines threatened its major source of revenue: if the profits of mining capital dried up, so did the state's revenue. State action to help the mines cut costs was generally unpopular with the white electorate, who would portray the government as the lackey of foreign capitalists and even of black migrant labor, much of which was also foreign.

Thus, individual governments were afraid to intervene in the escalating capital-labor clash: they feared the short-term danger to their popularity and worried about the next election. By contrast, the state was inexorably pushed into intervention by the growing tension between its legitimation and accumulation roles. It needed to establish financial stability and its own legitimacy, and to do this, it had to intervene progressively more in the economy. The government needed to convince the electorate that state intervention was necessary because of the threats to the interests of broader white society posed by organized white labor's radical militance. To a large extent, the government succeeded in doing this during the seven years after 1914; meanwhile, white labor was failing to weld into one coherent force the republican radicalism of many of its Afrikaners and the syndicalist/unionist radicalism of many of the Anglophones. In the period 1914–1921, organized labor lost a great deal of support from other groups in the electorate. The first major setback occurred as early as August 1914, with the outbreak of World War I. The response to the war also illustrates the complexity of the economic and political aspects of the capital-labor conflict, and the way they frequently clash.

Politically the war dealt the Labour party a blow from which it never recovered. In the October 1915 general election, it won only 1 of 15 Rand seats. Never again could it dream of gaining support outside of the urban areas.[4] The main reason for this was that the war split the organized white working class into jingoistic Imperialists, who formed "labour legions" to enlist, and a sullen republican proletariat, which stayed at home. *Economically*, however, the war weakened the mining employers, partly by severely depleting their supply of skilled labor, and resulted in a "swing of the pendulum" in favor of organized labor.[5]

The salient issues of the state-capital-labor relationship between the "wars" of the 1914 and 1922 strikes can be reduced to four:

1. The (largely political) issue of the "Afrikanerization" of the mining labor force;
2. the (largely economic) issue of the low-grade mines and the cost and profitability crisis surrounding them;
3. the highly contentious color-bar issue, which emerged from the problem of the low-grade mines. The struggle over the color bar rapidly made the low-grade mines as much a political as an economic issue;[6] and
4. the struggle over the proper relationship between industrial and political action.

The final issue was brought to a head and fought out in the open as a result of the cumulative effect of the first three: the rapidly changing composition of the labor force, the attempted reorganization of the industry to meet its cost crisis, and the consequent surfacing of the race issue in the political arena. The significance of the 1922 upheaval and its aftermath is largely to be found in its effect on the relationship of industrial and political action. Worker racism and capitalist greed, or economic "rationality"—which are usually said to be the central issues—were actually subsidiary themes.[7]

THE AFRIKANERIZATION OF THE WHITE
WORKING CLASS

The state's role in encouraging the increasing employment of Afrikaners after the 1907 strike has already been discussed. White unemployment constituted a problem that governments elected by white voters could hardly ignore, and most of the unemployed were Afrikaners. British immigration could be (and was)[8] cut because of the shortage of jobs, but there was no stopping the flow of Afrikaners from the rural to the urban areas.[9]

British artisan immigrants had, up to about 1905, provided the bulk of new white miners. From then until 1910 there was a net outflow of British settlers. British immigration picked up from 1910–1914, but at the beginning of the war, it dwindled from an annual 10,000 to 1,500 and, with the exception of one brief flurry from 1918 to 1920, continued to lag throughout the interwar years. Moreover, what immigration there was tended to be middle class.[10]

It is not clear to what extent the state's action affected the dwindling numbers of British artisan immigrants. Clearly, other factors, such as the very high death rate from miner's phthisis (which both decimated the existing work force and discouraged others from leaving Britain to join it), kept the British out. Where the state did act, however, it was to discourage British miners. The deportation of the nine union leaders to Britain in 1914 was a strikingly symbolic example.

There were other less dramatic but equally effective measures. One that was particularly effective was the South African Government's anti-phthisis stipulation that miners had to pass a medical examination in South Africa before being allowed underground. Therefore, British immigrant artisans stood the chance of being rejected before starting work and were understandably reluctant to embark on the trip. The authorities would not accept a medical examination that was conducted in Britain before the prospective immigrant left. The criticism of this measure by a parliamentary commission was to no avail.[11]

Equally important was the active support given to Afrikanerization by the mining employers. Part of the explanation has been given in reference to the pre-Union period: the employment of Afrikaners was a *quid pro quo* offered for the state's participation in breaking up strikes and for help in other areas; it was also felt Afrikaners would be more docile, less susceptible to trade unionism, and cheaper to employ.

Another factor, however, was becoming increasingly important: the drive by mining capital to change the actual structure of the white working force by fragmenting its jobs—turning whites into supervisors of black labor rather than skilled artisans working with the help of unskilled labor. The implication of this policy for the industry's cost structure will be discussed in the next section. What needs to be noted here is that increasing mechanization, particularly through the introduction of the hand machine drills, opened the way for the profitable employment of semi-skilled supervisors, and that most of the people in this category were Afrikaners.

Afrikaners preferred to supervise several drills, while British artisan miners wanted to keep their "touch" by personally undertaking work.[12] The phasing out of the highly paid artisans and their replacement by Afrikaner supervisers and black migrants made good economic and technical sense from the point of view of the industry, in addition to the other benefits already specified. Because of the nature of mining (which made clear definitions of skilled, semi-skilled, and unskilled work virtually impossible), it was extremely difficult for the artisan miners to protect themselves from this job fragmentation.

In 1913, therefore, the Transvaal Miners' Association formally accepted its transition from an artisan union to an industrial union by allowing white miners to receive blasting certificates (their "license" to work) after only nine months' training.[13] This move was crucial. Not only was it a capitulation to the employers on the fragmentation of the skilled labor force, but it also marked the formal acceptance by the skilled (largely British) miners that their fate would henceforth be allied with those of the semi-skilled (largely Afrikaner) miners.

Intensive efforts by mining capital to open up a rift between the two groups in 1921–1922, by proposing to abolish only the customary color bar (which affected semi-skilled workers) rather than the statutory color bar (which protected mainly skilled workers), were to fail. Paradoxically, the main reason for the failure was the success of job fragmentation, which meant the blurring of the distinction between skilled and semi-skilled and which resulted in a common front against wage cuts or the threat of black competition.

Lionel Phillips's hope of keeping the new Afrikaner miners quarantined from trade-union influences and similar "contamination" proved to be illusory. The very changes in the structure of white jobs in fact united Anglophone and Afrikaner miners into a strongly coherent group. However, the coherence was, as we shall see, fatefully limited to industrial action. Political coherence was another matter. Nor was Phillips correct in predicting that the Afrikaner would prove less susceptible to unions, less politicized, and less likely to strike.

A radical socialist strain of thought was brought to the miners' unions by leaders with British and Australian experience.[14] But it is not clear to what extent the average non-Afrikaner miner shared these radical views. Certainly, their jingoistic sympathies were as strong as was their labor militance. Even the use of the British troops in 1913, which aroused violent expressions of anti-imperialism,[15] did not stop British miners from flocking to join in the World War.

The militance of the Afrikaner miners, on the other hand, developed a distinctly nationalist, revolutionary strain because of the fervent desire among a large number of them for the restoration of a Boer republic. It should be emphasized that the South African state had only very recently been formed at that time and that even "respectable" leaders like the head of the Labour party, Creswell, talked in revolutionary terms at times. Such talk was perhaps taken more seriously by the Afrikaners—a group, by and large, less than a generation away from a defeated struggle for independence— than by the predominantly Anglophone trade-union and Labour party leaders. One manifestation of this Afrikaner militance was the fairly regular appearances of the old republican *Vierkleur* flag at trade-union conferences. The Anglophone miners were totally unsympathetic to these republican ideals, but there was sufficient common ground between the groups for such important differences to be papered over. The different nature of the radicalism of two major groups that comprised organized labor was crucial and vitiated its impact very considerably.

The South African police were emphatic about the threat posed to the state by Afrikaner miners. A report by the District Commandant of the Boksburg police on a 1917 strike stresses the fact that about 2,500 Afrikaners, largely from the Orange Free State, had replaced war volunteers on the East Rand mines and were outspoken in supporting the strike, being particularly opposed to the use of black labor. Most of them, the report claimed, belonged to the National party rather than to the Labour party:

> And it is there that the danger lies for they would seize any pretext to jeopardize the position of the Government and with it the British regime in South Africa. For this reason, should there be a Strike, I believe that "race hatred" [used here to denote English-Afrikaner conflict] will replace "class" making a rebellion possible. Should it not reach this point, there is little doubt that any industrial trouble will have the support of an element with less respect for Law and Order than was the case in Strikes of July, 1913 and January, 1914.[16]

Thus, the Afrikaner miner was seen as a greater threat to the state because of his nationalist radicalism than because of his working-class radicalism. The report correctly judged the revolutionary threat from the Afrikaner miners as being as important as the industrial threat. Another point made in the report was that Afrikaner miners feared replacement by returning soldiers and were "bound to come into conflict with the Labour Party, who get very little monetary support from them and are therefore anxious to have their old members back." The weakness of the Labour party was not, of course, caused by the increasing proportion of Afrikaner miners *per se*, but by the fact that the war issue had caused the party to lose the allegiance of the greater part of the Afrikaner miners.[17] Between the 1914 strike and the outbreak of World War I, in fact, the political and industrial arms of white labor, the Labour party and the unions, had worked closely together—more closely than ever before or since. A political observer even pointed out to Smuts in March 1914 that the Afrikaners' trek to the mines had encouraged them to join the unions, and this, in turn, had pushed them into the Labour party.[18]

The withdrawal of Afrikaner allegiance from the Labour party after 1914 emasculated it, for the loss of the miners constituted the loss of the largest and most coherent block of white workers in

South Africa. The party also split internally on the war issue into pacifists (the forerunners of the South African Communist party) and Creswellite Imperialists. The subsequent "revival" of the Labour party in the 1920 general election was largely due to split votes between the South African party and the Unionist party in the urban areas. The loss of the Afrikaner miners' vote was reconfirmed in 1920, when Creswell fought to retain the Imperial connection.[19] If the National party had contested the urban seats more aggressively, the Labour party would probably have been far less successful.

The Afrikanerization of the white mine labor force did not, of course, in itself break the Labour party. It would be fair to argue that Afrikanerization, allied to the Imperial issue (whether to be loyal to the Empire in war and in peace), split the white working class politically and gave the rural National party a toehold in urban constituencies. The implications of this rift for mining capital and the state will become clear later.

It has been pointed out with some justification that the process of Afrikanerization is difficult "to document precisely,"[20] but it is possible to chart the changing composition of the white mine labor force fairly accurately by nationality. Statistics available in the Annual Reports of the Government Mining Engineer and in the Official Yearbooks of the Union of South Africa give a breakdown of South African-born mine employees over time (see Table 2). The statistics show an almost inexorable expansion over several decades of the South African complement in mines throughout the union, including the Transvaal gold mines, by far the largest employer.

The statistics show very clearly the accelerating indigenization of the mine labor force. They do not distinguish between Anglophone and Afrikaner South Africans, but contemporary reports suggest that the vast majority of the new South African miners were Afrikaners. The new miners tended to be drawn from the poor whites, who were being forced off the land into the cities without any skills that might have enabled them to compete for employment with established urban dwellers. As the Carnegie Commission was to point out in its exhaustive survey fifteen years later, the "poor white" problem was essentially a "poor Afrikaner" problem.

South African-born whites increased from 17.5 percent of the organized labor force in 1907 to 23 percent by the end of the 1907

Table 2 The Indigenization of Organized Labor on the Gold Mines, 1907–1945

Year	% Born in South Africa	Total number of white miners
1907 (before strike)	17.5	18,600[a]
1907 (during strike)	24.6	17,631[a]
1907 (after strike)	23.0	18,687[b]
1910	27.2	26,791
1913	36.2	29,710
1915	41.0	26,329
1918	50.2	28,722
1920	50.8	28,055
1922	48.6	22,099
1923	52.2	23,457
1925	55.9	25,312
1930	64.6	27,880
1935	73.2	38,774
1936	75.1	42,231
1940	81.2	51,994
1945	85.8	47,634

Sources: ARGMEs; Union of South Africa Official Yearbooks.

[a]These figures are for the Transvaal gold mines only, before and during the strike.
[b]These figures are for all Transvaal mines, including nongold mines.

strike and to 36.2 percent in 1913. For the first time, in 1918, more than half the white mine employees were South African-born, and by 1936, they represented 75 percent. The figures confirm the trend commented on elsewhere, though they show a somewhat slower growth than estimated by most commentators, several of whom seem to have misread the *Report of the Martial Law Inquiry Commission.*[21] The report says, without attributing a source, that at the beginning of the 1922 strike, 75 percent of *all* Rand labor, not just on the mines, were Afrikaners.[22] The figures reproduced in Table 2, however, are probably a more accurate representation of the trend to indigenization and, by extension, Afrikanerization.[23]

It is interesting to note that the process of Afrikanerization continued unabated for over forty years. The only two setbacks occurred in 1907 and in 1922, and these were both minor and short-lived. The drop of South African-born miners from 51.5 percent to 48.6 percent in 1922 tends to contradict the suggestion that "many British workers left the Rand, and Afrikaners from the Platteland, potential Hertzog-supporters, took their places."[24] It is, of course, possible that some British workers left the Rand, but, clearly, more Afrikaners left their jobs as miners. The explanation is probably that a higher proportion of semi-skilled and unskilled whites (who would tend to be Afrikaners) were laid off in the wake of the 1922 strike than were the skilled workers. In any case, by 1923 the proportion of South African-born miners was once again climbing (to 52.2 percent), not to be reversed to the present day.

Afrikanerization of the mine labor force was significant for the state-industry relationship in a number of ways. Politically, it supplied a transfusion of revolutionary blood to the aging militance carried over by the British and Australian trade unionists (who still dominated the leadership of the trade unions), though Afrikaners were more inclined to be republican than proletarian revolutionaries. In terms of the occupational structure of the mine labor force, the influx of unskilled Afrikaners allowed mining capitalists increasingly to fragment jobs and mechanize: the Afrikaners generally received no extended artisan training and were far more willing than were their predecessors to be mere supervisors.

The increasing predominance of semi-skilled and unskilled white labor changed the nature of the major mining union, with the artisan-dominated Transvaal Miners' Association being transformed into an industrial union, the South African Mine Workers' Union (henceforth the SAMWU), in 1913. The umbrella body, the Federation of Trades, became the South African Industrial Federation (henceforth the SAIF) at about the same time. In effect, then, Afrikanerization created a new work force of a more "industrial" type, with job fragmentation and mechanization enabling far fewer skilled workers to achieve the same results or better in an increasingly supervisory capacity.

This process, in turn, opened up the possibility of the increased use of unskilled and semi-skilled blacks, who were paid only a fraction of the white wage; it also opened the way for mining capital to foster a new class of senior worker-supervisors, the "officials," who identified more with management than with the working class. The officials, it was hoped, would be the organizers of the new industrial work force, able to run the mines without white workers should it prove necessary. With the reorganization of the work force, they were to prove quite capable of doing so. Even more important, they have been consistently willing to and have destroyed many embryonic white miners' strikes by their mere presence. By the late 1970s, there were as many officials on the mines as there were trade-union members. (See also Chapter 5.)

THE PRODUCTIVITY AND COST CRISIS

Another important feature of the deepening crisis after 1914 was the contrary movement of productivity and costs. From 1914, working costs started rising on the Witwatersrand gold mines, while working profits continued the downward trend started in 1912. A cost crisis on the gold mines is necessarily a profitability crisis since the gold producers do not control the price of their product and cannot, as other producers might, raise prices to cover increased costs. Thus, working profits declined from 1912 to 1919 (when the gold price increased temporarily), corresponding roughly to the increase in working costs.

Gold mines were also peculiarly vulnerable to inflation because, as long as there was no free market for gold (that is, until the 1970s), the price tended to remain static while the price of producing it increased. The inflation accompanying World War I, therefore, seriously affected the mines by pushing up the cost of equipment and stores and by exerting upward pressure on wages as their purchasing power diminished. Between 1914 and 1920, the cost of stores increased from £10.2m to £14.3m (39.8 percent), the cost of black labor increased from £5.4m to £6m (12.2 percent), and the cost of white labor increased from £7.2m to £11.4m (58.4 percent).[25] Even the ostensibly large increase in white wages actually constitutes a 10 percent drop in per capita real wages compared to 1911 wages. (See Table 8, Chapter 7.)

This means that white workers' wages and stores were not responsible for the profitability crisis because, in real terms, their prices did not increase. The real culprits were world inflation and the fixed price of gold, which had the effect of cutting the purchasing power of gold. In terms of its purchasing power, gold was being sold at a far lower price in 1919 than before 1914. (See Table 3.)

The price of gold in pounds sterling in 1920 was the highest ever, and remained a record until 1933. But in "real" terms—calculating its purchasing power after allowing for inflation—it was the lowest price in the twentieth century.

The costs on the mines rose rapidly during the period 1914–1921, but not as fast as the cost of living. Other factors, however, emerged to exacerbate the crisis: steep declines in productivity for black and white workers in 1914 and 1915, respectively[26]; and an actual decline in tons of ore treated in 1917,[27] when a severe black labor shortage set in. (See Figure 1, Chapter 6).

The decline of productivity has been attributed to the reduction of working hours secured by whites as a result of their strengthened wartime bargaining position. This decline in white productivity directly affected black productivity because, under the mining regulations, blacks had to be supervised by whites.[28] Black productivity started declining in 1914, two years before white productivity slumped. There were more blacks employed on the Rand gold mines in 1916—201,873—than at any year up until 1931. By contrast, there was only an average number of white miners—22,085. This shortage of white supervisors meant that blacks frequently

Table 3   The Effect of Inflation on the "Real" Gold Price, 1910–1938

Year	Index of real prices on the Witwatersrand (all items, 1938=100)	Gold price £ Sterling per fine ounce	"Real" price of gold (deflated by index of real prices)
1910	78.3	4.247	5.424
1914	82.4	4.247	5.154
1918	105.6	4.247	4.022
1919	116.5	4.715	4.047
1920	144.0	5.590	3.882
1921	130.8	5.342	4.084
1922	109.6	4.614	4.210
1923	105.9	4.544	4.291
1924	107.2	4.673	4.360
1925	106.4	4.247	3.992
1931	97.6	4.247	4.351
1932	91.3	6.237	6.831
1938	100.00	7.172	7.127

Source: ARTCMs; *Union Statistics for Fifty Years, 1910–1960*, Pretoria, 1960.

worked only five hours a day underground, though they spent almost the same amount of time underground waiting for the supervisors to set up the work place and blast the stope face.[29]

The importance of the cost and productivity crisis, for the purposes of this study, is that it forced the initially reluctant state to take a far more direct role in the problems of the industry in general and in the low-grade mines in particular. As more and more mines came under the imminent threat of permanent closure, the government became acutely aware of the role of the mines as employers and as generators of revenue.

THE LOW-GRADE MINES

It should be emphasized at the outset that the low-grade mines (LGM) concept is as much a political concept as a genuine economic problem.[30] The LGM were developed into a symbol by mining capital to mobilize public support for its cost-cutting campaign. Before the South African War, technological changes made deep-level mining economically possible, largely by permitting the extraction of a much greater proportion of gold from crushed ore. The decision to pursue deep-level mining was taken in the 1890s, and thus mining capital determined that the industry would henceforth be a low-grade industry.

Mining capitalists embarked quite deliberately on projects to exploit the deep-level ore. Though this ore had a low gold content, it was found in relatively consistent reef formations of immense size. These projects were financed because it was expected that they would be very profitable if costs could be reduced sufficiently. Capital's strategy after 1902 was to lower costs, particularly by lowering wages generally or by amalgamating small mines in an attempt to benefit from the economies of scale. Massive super mines resulted, like East Rand Proprietary Mines, which is still in operation, and Crown Mines.

Capital had decided—without any pressure from the state at that stage—to exploit as much as possible of the massive but low-grade ore body of the Witwatersrand. This plan entailed very stringent cost control and, of course, in itself created many of the low-grade mines (others started off as richer mines but found grades tailing off as mining progressed). Lionel Phillips clearly showed the employers' financial motive in creating and fostering the LGM. Writing to Eckstein in 1909, before the concept became a political tool to extract various forms of aid from the state, he justified the reopening of such a mine by saying that cheaper working costs meant that "low grade mines, . . . concerns like Bantjes, have *great possibilities . . . 20 shillings—22 shillings and 6 pence yield on a big scale means large* profits."[31] Even more potentially profitable was the financial gearing that operated when dealing in shares of marginal mines: because such mines were more cost-sensitive than others, small reductions in costs could vastly increase their values. Phillips thus instructed Eckstein not to sell Bantjes shares because they were likely to double in value.[32] Share-dealing profits were considered capital gains and were not taxed.

The converse of this was that if costs *rose*, profits and share values of the LGM would plummet far quicker than those of the less marginal mines. In fact, this was exactly what happened: capital's gamble that it would be able to cut costs failed. Part of the failure was due to circumstances beyond the employers' control such as inflation from 1914 onward, white labor unrest, and the war-induced shortage of skilled labor.[33] But a large part of the failure was capital's own; it failed to secure a stable black labor supply. Even the ban on importing "tropical labor" from north of latitude 22° south was in large measure the fault of the industry because it failed to act quickly to correct a scandalously high pneumonia rate among that group. It failed, at least temporarily, in its attempt to cut costs by employing bigger operating units because of teething and managerial problems.[34] Phillips had considered closing down his group's LGM in 1911, when the failure to contain costs started to become evident, but he had decided against doing anything, even though he was convinced that the government would not oppose such liquidations.[35]

Thus, when mining capital sought state aid, it was asking for help in a dilemma that was at least partly of its own creation, though the major culprit was undoubtedly world inflation and the static gold price. This was the first time, in fact, that mining capital had thrown itself on the mercy of the state by asking for direct subsidies. The TCM slid skillfully past its members' own shortcomings and made a strong general case for state support on the usual grounds: the mines employed a large number of whites, and they supplied a large proportion of the state's revenue. The TCM also added that the gold output was vital to the wartime needs of the Empire. The claim was that fourteen LGM, constituting 25 percent of industry output, were "barely paying their way" in 1917—mines that employed 6,000 whites and 48,000 blacks, spent £6.6m in working costs (mainly in South Africa), and produced about £7m of gold per annum.[36]

On July 13, 1917, Evelyn Wallers, President of the TCM, wrote to the press about the danger to the LGM. The letter was directed at the white miners who were in the process of demanding better conditions; it pointed out the difficulties of the industry and the dangers of unemployment and of shutting down the mines. But it was also directed at "educating" public opinion. On November 16, 1917, Wallers sent the government a letter drafted by the TCM Joint-Secretary and Actuary, William Gemmill.[37] Gemmill was to become one of the most important figures in the industry, especially in labor matters. Wallers's letter pointed out that probably "50 percent of the total revenue of the Union may be attributed to the Gold Mining Industry." He particularly asked for state help in securing a better black labor supply and reauthorization of the importation of "tropical labor."

Gemmill followed this up a few days later with another letter in which he made several concrete suggestions. It is not proposed to deal with the general issue of state revenue from the LGM here, but it is notable that no state help was asked for at that stage to deal with organized white labor. The danger of white unemployment posed by the threat of closing down the LGM is mentioned, but the employers simply did not raise the issue of reducing the largest component of increased costs: white wages. They planned to crack the hardest nut last, and even then, only if it became absolutely necessary.

At about the same time, Lionel Phillips renewed his old acquaintanceship with Smuts in London and, on December 4, 1917, wrote him a long memorandum on the LGM repeating Wallers's arguments.[38] On December 11, 1917, the Secretary for Mines and Industries, Warington Smyth, wrote to the TCM asking if it would give evidence on the LGM issue to a parliamentary Select Committee (it agreed with alacrity). On January 4, 1918, Wallers wrote to the Minister of Mines, F. S. Malan, proposing the closing of four or five of the poorer mines. Warington Smyth's reply asked for the closure to be delayed until after the Select Committee's enquiry, which, he suggested, would educate the public *before* any action was taken.[39] Mining capital again agreed since it was as concerned with educating public opinion as was the state, and it was no simple matter for the biggest, richest, most hated industry in South Africa to mobilize general support for closures or for subsidization by the taxpayer. Nor is it certain that the TCM wanted to close the four or five marginal mines; threatening to do so might itself have had the desired effect on public opinion and on mining costs.

The Select Committee, chaired by F. S. Malan, turned down sub-sidization[40] and took up a hard-line posture toward the employers; but, in fact, Malan wanted to avoid involvement with the industry's problems while appearing to be taking decisive mea-sures. This politicking infuriated Wallers and Gemmill, who wrote increasingly threatening letters about unemployment and the closure of mines. Finally, on May 9, 1919, Wallers wrote to F. S. Malan:

> We have frequently been told, on placing our views before the Government on particular aspects of the position, that the matter in question has a political aspect, affecting this or that political party. The Mining Industry is outside of politics and is not concerned with any Political Party . . . however, . . . when a large number of European employees are out of work, and when the Witwatersrand, with all the other parts of the country, is in a state of depression, *all* Political Parties will find themselves to be concerned in the Mining Industry and in the causes of its decline.[41]

Wallers threatened to publish the letter. Warington Smyth blandly suggested in reply that a small commission be appointed to report on each proposed mine closure, to "keep public opinion informed. . . ." But a month later, after a continued barrage of letters and cables from the TCM (and the drafting of a "public petition" by the TCM, calling on the government to make tax concessions and direct sub-sidies to the industry as well as restoring tropical recruitment), the Low-Grade Mines Commission was appointed. It was chaired by the Government Mining Engineer, Sir Robert Kotze, and included both Wallers and Gemmill.[42]

The two reports of the Low-Grade Mines Commission were extremely sympathetic to the employers, although they were against direct subsidies in most cases. They made a number of suggestions about possible state help to the LGM, but they also brought up the sensitive issue of white labor as an element in escalating costs. The TCM, in its evidence, equivocated about the color bar, saying that it had no intention of abolishing it as long as the majority of Rand whites supported it. It also said that it was unjust "and public opinion always, sooner or later, discovers and denounces injustice."[43] Translated, this meant that the employers dared not attack the color bar, though they sincerely wished someone else would.

The final report of the LGM Commission on May 5, 1920, duly obliged by recommending the abolition of the legal color bar. Impressed by the large-scale strike of black miners in February 1920, it suggested that black aspirations could not be permanently held in check. There was also a pious recommendation of greater cooperation between labor and capital and the suggestion that underground work be rearranged to get a longer working period from blacks (in effect, by decreasing white supervision).

Capital was not to follow up on these recommendations for another year. It had done all it could to keep the black/white labor issue from surfacing after 1914, largely because it realized that challenging the color bar was a certain way to politicize the white labor issue—and mining capital felt extremely isolated politically and unable to generate outside support from the electorate. As Smuts pointed out privately in 1920 to the President of the TCM, H. O. Buckle: "Nothing in the interests of the mines ever got any support from the Rand members [of Parliament], which made it very difficult for the Government to do anything."[44]

The cost crisis was, therefore, fought by the employers in other areas: government subsidies, loans, tax cuts, and help in recruiting black labor were sought, though with very little success. The government had little revenue to spare, and Parliament rejected its efforts to reintroduce the influenza-prone tropical laborers from central and east Africa. Before attempting a frontal assault on organized labor, mining capital preferred even to attack other sectors of capital. One of the cost-cutting methods attempted by the state and the mining capitalists, for example, was an attack on the profit margins of commercial capital. Mining capital attempted to

keep white labor costs down by supporting trade-union cooperatives, which bought items like food and clothes in bulk for union
members: the idea was to keep the cost of living down for white
workers in the hope of keeping their wage demands down. Similar
schemes also mushroomed in the Australian mining centers during
and after World War I.

It is difficult to gauge the success of these measures, but, as has
already been mentioned, real white wages were considerably higher
in 1911 than in 1920. Such success as was enjoyed by the cooperatives was achieved with the help of state cash subsidies and at the expense of the merchandising wholesalers and importers, who lost
sales to the mining industry-financed trade-union cooperatives.[45] In
this way, both the state and mining capital actively supported a
limited transfer of wealth from the "commercial community" to the
white workers (and possibly to mining capital itself).

A government commission explicitly justified state aid to the
cooperatives at the expense of commercial capital:

> The urgent matter today . . . is to preserve industrial peace,
> and the commercial community in their turn should be willing
> to make some sacrifice to attain this end. It should also be
> remembered that if trouble arises the commercial community
> will suffer as much as any other section in the Union [of South
> Africa].[46]

Clearly, a significant part of the South African white population,
including segments of labor (for example, Tommy Boydell in the
Labour party, and Archie Crawford, Secretary of the South African Industrial Federation, in the trade unions), was beginning, as
early as 1917, to accept the fact that the LGM needed help from outside the industry itself.

In 1919, the state and mining capital combined to impose a new
method of disposing of South African gold through the United
Kingdom, which enabled the mineowners to get a considerably
higher price per ounce. This alliance of so-called Imperial, or
metropolitan, capital (British-dominated mining capital) with the
colonial state (South Africa) against the Imperial power (Britain) is
by no means unusual and illustrates the need to distinguish carefully between the different types of imperialism. The higher price

was forced upon Britain because, though the British and South African currencies had become considerably inflated against gold, the U.S. currency had not. The differential between the U.S. and U.K. currencies became particularly marked in 1919, and the South African Government made it clear that gold would be sold on the U.S. market if British buyers did not pay a rate equivalent to the dollar price of gold. The British quickly agreed to pay the U.S. rate. This meant a substantial premium for mining capital on the 1919 sterling price for gold: 24 percent for the last five months of 1919.

The premium, then, was the equivalent of a temporary increase in the price of gold, and it substantially aided the gold mines. In 1918, 261.8 kilograms of gold fetched £36.8 million; in 1920, 253.8 kilograms earned £45.6 million. The premium sharply increased working profits between 1919 and 1921 and delayed the final cost crunch in the industry until 1921; but it was only temporary and disappeared, as expected, with currency deflation in the United Kingdom. Even though it was recognized as only a temporary alleviation of the cost crisis in the industry, the higher price and apparently improved results forced the state and capital to delay tackling organized white labor because public opinion was no longer unequivocally behind them.

The employers, by seeking direct state aid and subsidies, also sought to avoid a confrontation with organized labor. But the direct help it received was minimal, on the principle that if such aid were to be granted to the industry, it could not be refused to other industries, including agriculture.[47] There are, however, definite indications that an important change of state policy on direct aid to the mines was imminent by mid-1921, as the cost crisis deepened.

The Government Mining Engineer, Sir Robert Kotze, the Chairman of the LGM Commission, was a close friend of Smuts. They had gone to university together and had been keen competitors for the position of top student. In 1908, Kotze became the GME at Smuts's recommendation.[48] There is a good deal of evidence that Kotze was the major architect of the state's policy toward the mines, though he almost always deferred to Smuts's strategic goals. His intelligence and indifference to personal gain were matched only by Smuts's. On June 11, 1921, Kotze wrote to the Minister of Mines, reversing his earlier stand on subsidization after having "given further thought to the question."

His reasoning, he wrote, had been faulty. Other industries were being protected by the state through import duties—a form of subsidy. There was no real difference between this and direct subsidies: the public paid both ways, and more in the case of import duties. The state, he estimated, probably earned 8 shillings a ton from the gold mines in 1918 (1 shilling and four pence in direct revenues, 2 shillings and 9 pence in indirect revenues, and the balance from railway revenue). So it was "good business for the state to spend as much as 2 shillings or 3 shillings per ton on a gold mine, for the sake of the amounts accruing to it in various ways owing to the productive activities of the mine."[49] Underlining this point, he said that the South African gold mines "have always been looked upon as milch cows for State revenue," but that the state attitude to them had to change: ". . . The time is coming when it will be as necessary in the national interest to support and stimulate mining as any other industry . . ."[50] This is an extremely important admission, which Kotze would never have made in public. It was, in fact, precisely the argument of mining capital, which Kotze had rejected countless times both in public and in private. His change of opinion was not illogical: he had always seen the state's policy toward the mining industry as the maximization of revenue to the limits "which the traffic could bear," to the limits compatible with continued growth. The limits had now contracted, and so the extraction of revenue had to do likewise. In other words, the government did not feel—even privately—that the state was in any way the instrument of mining capital; rather, it saw the industry as the state's instrument: a "milch cow," or golden goose, whose survival had to be ensured in crisis situations. Kotze's view is important, not because it is correct (it is argued throughout this study that analyzing either the state or capital purely as instrument is inadequate and fails to take into account the independent and overlapping interests of each), but because he believed it, and he represented the most intelligent and knowledgeable part of the state bureaucracy.

Smuts and Kotze later discussed the memorandum and the need for direct subsidies. On September 14, 1921, Kotze submitted, on Smuts's instructions, a ".bare outline" of a scheme to assist the LGM that would have involved the state in providing direct compensation for capital's revenue shortfalls caused by higher white wages, up to 20 percent of the wage bill at the 1913–1914 levels. The outline was forwarded to Smuts on September 15. It was never acted on, and does not appear ever to have been made public or even leaked to the employers.

Instead, Smuts made a crucial decision at about that time to embark on an alternative course: to support a direct onslaught on the unions by the mining employers. He probably felt at that stage that he could mobilize as much support for that course of action as for Kotze's plan, and at less cost to state revenues. It was a gamble that might well have succeeded because the TCM's skillful handling of the LGM issue to mobilize public support for an attack on *all* mining costs had had considerable success. Labor, however, had its own mobilizing symbol, the color bar, which it proceeded to use with equal skill.

THE COLOR BAR AND THE STATUS QUO AGREEMENT

To understand the development of the color-bar issue between 1914 and 1921 and its connection to the changing nature of the state, it is necessary at the outset to distinguish three distinct aspects of the color bar,[51] the third of which has not commonly been noted to date.

First, there was the statutory, or legislative, color bar, which reserved certain jobs for whites through government regulations. The enabling power for these regulations came from the Mines and Works Act of 1911, though there was the suspicion from the time the legislation was passed that these regulations were *ultra vires.*

Second, there was the "customary color bar," a purely informal agreement between capital and labor, which reserved jobs for whites on the grounds that they had always done these jobs. There was no statutory color bar on the Kimberley diamond fields at this time, but custom imposed a job-reservation policy as strict as any on the Witwatersrand. The diamond mines were not generally as cost-sensitive as were the gold mines, and organized diamond labor did not feel the same need for direct state protection.

Finally, there was the status quo color bar, which attempted to arrive at new job reservations by written agreement between capital and organized labor. This applied particularly where job fragmentation and mechanization had created new jobs never covered by either the statutory or the customary color bar.

There is no doubt that white miners saw blacks as a threat to both their jobs and their wage rates, and they genuinely felt the need for the various restrictions on the employment of black labor that cumulatively came to make up the color bar. Besides being a genuine issue, however, the color bar was an extremely potent political symbol that could be used to mobilize support from all sections of white society, if it was argued that the security of whites *per se* was being threatened by black encroachment.

Thus, industrial disputes were frequently obfuscated by an exaggerated trade-union emphasis on the color bar. Even when the immediate cause of a dispute was color-bar related, as in the case of the 1907 strike, it usually had as much to do with other grievances.[52] Clearly, labor needed to broaden its basis of support. South Africa was not primarily an industrial country at the time, and in addition, labor was internally divided because white labor never showed any signs of accepting black miners as allies in a common struggle. As Merriman put it, speaking in Parliament in 1914,

> When he heard the hon. member for Jeppe [Creswell] . . . talking some balderdash about shifting the basis of society— Good Heavens! a small minority of this country was going to shift the basis of society [laughter]. . . . The workers who the hon. member said secured the greatest resources of this country, what were they compared to 200,000 men who did labour at the resources in this country and got precious little consideration?[53]

One of the aspirations of organized labor, particularly the South African Industrial Federation (SAIF), was to broaden its own support by strongly advocating the employment of more whites in semi-skilled jobs. This period is often portrayed as evidencing a rearguard action by the unions, who were fighting increasing infiltration of white jobs by Africans and Cape coloreds. The picture, in fact, is far more confused, and an equally impressive (but also only partially accurate) argument can be made that white labor actually embarked on a plan during the war, not only to open up new jobs for whites, but also to seize unskilled and semi-skilled jobs previously held by blacks. These, it was proposed, should become "white jobs," and at far higher wages.

Broadly, however, it appears that the early years of the war were marked by black advances in job opportunities, many of them replacing whites who had gone to war or moving into new jobs created by the shortage of skilled labor. During the later years of the war, when production and productivity fell as costs and strikes escalated, the white workers staged a counteroffensive and attempted to expand job opportunities for semi-skilled and unskilled whites. By mid-1916, Lionel Phillips, now London-based Chairman of the Central Mining and Investment Corporation, was writing to Evelyn Wallers (who headed the firm's South African operations) sympathizing with the "harassing time" he was having with white labor, and counselling "a stiff upper lip" and "friendly cooperation where possible."[54] Wallers was also President of the TCM from 1914 to 1919, and in 1924, and was mining capital's senior spokesman in South Africa at the time.

One of the areas where "friendly cooperation" was attempted was the color bar. In September 1916, and again in November, the unions brought up the question of extending the range of jobs available only to whites.[55] Wallers, at a TCM Executive Committee meeting, said that there were very few cases of blacks working in the suggested jobs: "I mean, if there was any idea of substituting colored for white, then you might have a deal more trouble." The next day, the TCM replied, turning down the SAIF request on the grounds that the mining regulations (the statutory color bar) already protected whites.[56]

The unions persisted, however, and on February 14, 1917, representatives of the TCM and the South African Mine Workers' Union (SAMWU) met to discuss the color bar. The TCM spokesmen denied that a deliberate attempt was being made to substitute "colored" (a usage that at the time included African, Indian, and Cape colored) for white workers. That denial, of course, was untrue: months before, for example, Phillips had authorized Wallers's increase in the numbers of "Cape boys" (Afrikaans-speaking men of mixed descent, also known as Cape coloreds), as long as the increase was not "on such a scale as to cause an upheaval."[57] By 1920, there were 1,100 Cape coloreds and Indians employed on TCM-affiliated mines compared to 22,400 whites.[58]

A week after meeting the SAMWU, Wallers lectured the TCM Executive Committee at length about the necessity of compromising with the unions. The address is remarkably revealing. Talking in private, he then admitted candidly that the substitution of colored for white workers was taking place "on a considerable scale along the Reef, very steady and consistent . . ." and that the mining regulations offered the whites only limited protection. "Because, as I tell you, the mining regulations do not protect certain types of white workmen who have hitherto been employed on jobs getting skilled rates of pay, it does not protect them, won't protect them in future either."[59] Moreover, he added candidly, "wherever the mining regulations do not protect the white man, the coloured man is being gradually substituted."[60]

For that reason, he said, it was not enough to continue to say that the industry would go along with the mining regulations. The unions had asked if the employers would abide by the schedule of reserved jobs that was introduced when Chinese labor had been imported. An examination of the schedule showed that it did not protect the whites in some areas where they sought protection. The fragmentation of skilled work had created new jobs, which the schedule could not cover because they had not existed at the time it was drawn up (this has been, and still is today, a major way around job reservation and statutory color bars). Thus, jobs that had become accepted as "white" were not protected by regulation: jobs performed by stope timbermen, tracklayers, pump lifters, and waste packers were being increasingly taken over, especially by Cape coloreds.

The schedule, on the other hand, did protect whites in some areas in which there had been major encroachment of "colored labor," such as in the operation of winches. Wallers and another TCM Executive Committee member, A. French, suggested a compromise: the color-bar status quo should be frozen, with those already employed keeping their jobs. Thus, if a white was doing a job on one mine, that job became a white job for that mine, and vice versa. This was the origin of the Status Quo Agreement, which was initiated by the unions but formulated by mining capital.

Some of Wallers's executives were not happy about going any further than endorsing the mining regulations, but he prevailed upon them by pointing out the political dangers and mobilization potential of the color issue: ". . . It is an extraordinarily popular thing . . . it is a thing they would strike on very rapidly, the substitution of coloured for white, and it is a subject on which they would have the public behind them—here, anyway, this community, every shopkeeper in the place."[61] The political dangers of the issue also meant that the employers should not expect any help from the state. Smuts had promised that mine conditions would not be altered during the war. Moreover, he said,

> nobody will have the courage to bring forward any legislation on the subject, they are all afraid of it, have been so far, although it is felt that the position of the color bar is . . . manifestly unfair . . . the coloured person will turn it down in time. . . . *Mr. Dalrymple*: Even to the extent of managing mines: no reason why it should not be. *Wallers*: Not in our time.[62]

Finally, Wallers argued that the expansion or contraction of black employment had had little effect on working costs: ". . . The displacement that has taken place, that is taking place, of white by coloured, financially to the Industry means extraordinarily little, next to nothing; it is not quotable in your working costs, as a matter of fact."[63] Moreover, he expected black labor gradually to unionize ("combine"), and then the industry would no longer "be getting them at the very low rates of today." It was vital to agree to preserve the status quo and limit (political) "difficulties that would be a good deal more costly than the difference in rate of pay of these few men."[64]

Wallers had his way. Three days later, the TCM wrote a letter to the SAMWU, which, although it repeated the old lie that "there has been no increased employment of coloured persons on the mines at the expense of white" (and even quoted figures as proof), offered to maintain "the status quo as at present existing in each mine. . . ."

Of course, all this debate was not going on in a vacuum. Its backdrop was a strike in January 1917 on Van Ryn Deep Mine caused by the employment of nine colored waste packers. The strike did not spread because the management withdrew the waste-packers at the recommendation of the government, pending an inquiry, but it certainly impressed on the TCM the need to take public opinion into account and to offer the status quo compromise.[65] The judicial report came out at the end of 1917 and said that ". . . it is essential that some agreement should exist [that is, in addition to the statutory color bar] as to the classes of work limited to Europeans only." The report recommended state intervention to arrive at such an agreement. The government, of course, with an eye to the possible repercussions, made no such move.

In May 1917, the employers backed down again on the threat of a strike on Randfontein Estates, and on the issue of whether the agreement in their February letter referred to preserving the status quo for unskilled as well as for semi-skilled and skilled whites.[66] Though the unions did not agree officially to the status quo offer, and refused to be bound by it, they attacked the employers for infringing it. Wallers was dismayed to receive demands of a fixed black/white ratio, for example, which was one of the developments the status quo offer was designed to prevent and which capital had strenuously resisted.

The TCM continued to press the unions to ratify the agreement, but this was done only in September 1918, and then by a small margin.[67] The unions continued the attack even after this: in May 1919, the SAMWU asked for the replacement of African clerks by whites; and in November 1919, the SAMWU told the TCM (in the presence of the government's Assistant Inspector of White Labour) that it wanted to eliminate the use of coloreds for semi-skilled jobs.[68] The employers were at first accommodating, seeking a *quid pro quo*. It was more important to resume the importation of tropical black labor, said Gemmill privately, than to remove the color bar.[69]

In July 1919, the TCM said in its evidence to the LGM Commission that the phasing out of the color bar was not "within the bounds of practical politics," and confined itself to requesting the easing of some restrictions.[70] Part of the reason for the weak case was that the mining groups that comprised the TCM were divided on how to deal with the issue.[71] The LGM Commission's report was less timorous: it recommended outright the abolition of the legal color bar. The black miners' strike of February 1920—by far the largest and most effective to date—had undoubtedly influenced both the Commission's courage and its conscience.[72]

The 1920 strike was regarded as ominous throughout the industry and undoubtedly frightened those running the mines, who expected it to become a regular pattern. It did not: no similar strike occurred again before World War II. Though only a "partial strike," it "practically paralyzed" the industry from February 17 to February 24, with 71,033 men coming out on twenty-one mines. Their demands were for higher wages and lower prices for the few commodities (such as clothing) they could afford to buy. The TCM issued a press statement emphasizing the unique and peaceful nature of the strike: "This is not, as all previous native troubles have been, a riot; it is a regular strike organised on the European model, obviously by persons who are acquainted with European practices in such matters."[73]

The strike was not, however, allowed to end on the European model. Police and soldiers surrounded individual compounds, all of which were peaceful before their arrival, told the blacks quartered there that the miners in the other compounds had gone back to work, and drove back with rifle butts and fixed bayonets those who would not return voluntarily to work. Eleven persons were killed and 120 injured, all blacks, in two incidents.[74]

The TCM responded by arranging the sale of goods to black miners at reduced prices. Average wages were increased by 3 pence a shift as of January 1, to 2 shillings and 3 pence for underground work and to 2 shillings for surface workers. Blacks compared their minuscule increase with the November 1919 white increases of 8 shillings per day. Black wages had increased far slower than had white wages between 1910 and 1920, and even the whites' far larger increase had not kept pace with the cost of living. The black miners were fed and partially clothed in their compounds, but they needed money to send to dependents in the drought-stricken reserves and to buy items for themselves. Mining capital knew this and recognized it, but claimed not to be able to pay any more if the industry were to stay viable.

The demands of the black miners also led the TCM to call for, largely in private and through judicious public hints, the end of job reservation, which restricted the advance of semi-skilled blacks. The mining capitalists seemed to be planning to give the white miners a little less in future and black labor (now that it had shown that it could be militant though peaceful) a little more. The *extension* of the color bar by further Status Quo Agreements was now unequivocally rejected.

The new militance of the black miners and the call by the LGM Commission for the abolition of the color bar were not the only factors that encouraged the TCM to dig in its heels about the demands to expand the color bar. Two factors were the large white wage increase mentioned above and the large increases in white unemployment resulting partly from the return of soldiers from the war. The SAMWU continued to attack the Status Quo Agreement of September 1918, but the TCM became more emphatic in its defense and pointed out, somewhat hypocritically, that it was equally bound by the agreement to protect black jobs.[75] The TCM even began to hint that it might move on the offensive. In May 1920, it warned that, far from extending the color bar, it might even call for its contraction if other methods, such as the rearrangement of underground work, could not save the industry.[76]

This, at last, constituted the intersection and conflict of the LGM and the color-bar issue: the TCM threatened that if the costs of the LGM were not drastically cut, the status quo color bar would have to go. In return, trade unionists countered that if the color bar was to be weakened, cost-cutting suggestions would be opposed—for example, black tropical laborers would continue to be kept out of South Africa by public opinion because of the threat they constituted to unemployed whites.[77] As late as November 1920, the SAMWU was demanding a *broadening* of the Status Quo Agreement.[78]

Until late 1921, the LGM and the color-bar issues stalemated each other. Capital and organized labor sparred while the government, at this stage, merely made gestures asking for the fight to be kept clean and fastidiously avoided actual involvement itself. When the state eventually became fully involved, it did so not simply because the LGM were faced with imminent extinction. Just as important, if not more important, was the state's determination to divorce industrial action from political action and to depoliticize organized labor.

THE BLUEPRINT TO SUBJUGATE ORGANIZED LABOR

The strategic threat posed to both the state and capital by the growing politicization of organized white labor has been partially discussed. The state had to protect the industry that was both a large employer and the largest provider of direct and indirect revenue. It had also to face up to the direct physical threat to its own security that was posed by the large numbers of geographically and ideologically coherent white mineworkers who could mobilize the support of other sectors of society on certain issues.

It was strategically necessary for the employers, not only to minimize costs, but also to stabilize labor relations. Gold mines required enormous capital investment to be laid out many years in advance of any return. Therefore, stable conditions that enabled long-term planning and projections were essential. The militant white miners were thus a great threat to the stability so urgently required by both the state and capital.

Several tactical responses to the politicization of white labor were tried: the attempt to crush its resistance by naked coercion (as in 1907); the combination of formal co-optation and coercion (1909–1914); and finally, the accommodation by gradual economic concessions, including increased social-welfare benefits (1914–1920). But the accommodationist policy started coming apart in 1919: strikes proliferated and the postwar boom was rapidly overtaken by increasing unemployment and raging inflation (the cost-of-living index rose by 20 percent in 1920, the steepest increase, by far, in South Africa's history, including the contemporary era).

South Africa's problems were not unique. Throughout the capitalist world, industrial and semi-industrial states were wrestling with the problems of inflation, unemployment, and labor militance. The Department of Mines and the TCM were getting letters from state and capitalist networks as far afield as the Philippines, asking how they were dealing with labor unrest and with the urgent need to reduce inflated wages. The Australian Chamber of Mines, for example, wrote to the TCM that industrial "unrest is acute all the world over and its solution is now taxing the brains of all thinking men." London conferences on the subject were being closely followed, "and there is no doubt that the industrial world is about to be revolutionized."[79] The entire relationship of labor and capital was being reviewed, and measures that still sound radical today, such as joint control and profit sharing, were being freely discussed.[80]

The International Labour Conference held in Washington, D.C., in 1919—from which sprang the ILO—was symptomatic of world concern about labor relations and about attempts to avoid "industrial war." South Africa sent three delegates: the Secretary for Mines and Industries, Warington Smyth; an employer representative, William Gemmill; and a union representative, Archie Crawford. When Gemmill returned, he wrote two reports: "Report A" was his formal report; "Report B" was a "strictly private and confidential report" addressed to South African employers to help them "to shape their future labour policy."[81] "Report B" contains Gemmill's evaluation of three different approaches to industrial relations: the "Continental European" (governed by the danger of a "communistic revolution"); the British (achieving the same ends by peaceful methods); and the Canadian and U.S. approaches, which he thought were most relevant to South Africa.

Gemmill characterized the U.S. and Canadian industrial populations as being in many respects similar to South Africa's, where labor

> is decidedly a minority of the population. Wages, conditions of work, and standard of comfort are high. There is a large body of unskilled labour antagonistic to the skilled. There is no great cohesion in labour. It cannot sustain a really prolonged strike . . . demands . . . cannot be forced upon South African industries which are prepared to fight. . . .[82]

Gemmill called for cooperation with unions, where possible, but it is clear that the thrust of his argument called for the end of the conciliatory policy toward organized labor.

Gemmill personally addressed various organizations (for example, the South African Federated Chamber of Industries) and had fifty copies of "Report B" printed and distributed to senior government officials and all employers' organizations except agricultural associations, who did not have to deal with unionized labor. He hoped to form an employers' united front, a federation of all employers to cooperate among themselves "in dealing with labour matters" and ultimately even share the expenses of breaking strikes or "extending pecuniary assistance to members suffering from a strike."[83] Though the proposed federation does not seem to have been formed, employer response from other industries was unanimously enthusiastic and was potently mobilized by Gemmill.

A key point was the role of the state. This aspect was deliberately obscured in "Report B," which talked merely of governments that refuse to be browbeaten or that are "impartial." It cited the U.S. Government, which allowed strikes but refused to allow effective picketing. In private correspondence with Wallers, Gemmill was more forthright: he was so impressed with the methods adopted by the United States in November 1919 in smashing the coal miners' strike that he enthusiastically cabled to Wallers from the United States: "Government action coal strike here completely established labour's impotence against firm democratic capitalistic Government . . ."[84] He followed that with a letter saying that the "first-hand knowledge" he had acquired of U.S. methods was "worth a great deal," and commenting that radical trade-union resolutions in South Africa were useless, "given a firm attitude by the government."[85]

Gemmill went to work to convince the South African Government to be "firm." He sent copies of "Report B" to Sir William Hoy, the General Manager of the South African Railways, and to Warington Smyth. The latter wrote official and unofficial letters back, the unofficial letter commenting on the inadvisability of publishing "Report B," "which, by the way, I thought very interesting and very good."[86] Gemmill's "Report B" and activities generally constitute, to some degree, a blueprint for an attack on organized labor, an evaluation of its strategic strength, and the types of alliance needed to defeat it.

One of its suggestions was the joint financing of the costs of strikes by various industries. The Witwatersrand gold mines already had a strikebreaking scheme operating among themselves, and Gemmill was the principal organizer. In 1917, for example, a strike on the Meyer and Charlton Mine ran up expenses of £846, 18 shillings, and 10 pence. The mine itself paid only £7, 8 shillings and 6 pence. The rest was paid by other TCM members on a tonnage and profits basis. This meant, of course, that isolated strikes could easily be defeated, particularly as the union funds available to support strikers were always sparse.

Around the beginning of 1920, however, the employers decided to go much further. The TCM Executive Committee decided that a Reserve Fund of £50,000 should be established (it was first planned to collect £100,000), which would be collected from members on the usual basis of tonnages crushed and profits earned. Because of the financial difficulties of the LGM, however, it was decided that tonnage would only count for one-third of a mine's contribution. The actual purpose of the fund appears to have been kept from all but the inner circle of TCM members—the senior representatives of the group—and several inquiries from mines as to why they were being asked to subscribe were fobbed off with deliberate vagueness by Gemmill: ". . . The Chamber finds it necessary from time to time to provide money for various purposes on behalf of the Industry, and . . . owing to the premium now being obtained on gold, the present is considered a favourable time for the establishment of such a fund."[87]

Joint projects had previously always been financed by *ad hoc* funds established for particular purposes. Moreover, there was never any talk in the TCM of subsidizing the ordinary costs of struggling members, only their strike costs. The conclusion seems inescapable: the £50,000 Reserve Fund was, at the very least, an insurance policy imposed by mining capital on itself to face an anticipated wide-scale confrontation between labor and capital.

This insurance policy was an offensive weapon as well; the Reserve Fund was tightly controlled by the TCM, which decided the criteria that determined whether an issue concerned a matter of principle for the whole industry and thus justified the use of industry funds. The fund was also used to cement antistrike collusion among mining capitalists. Its purpose was to ensure that a prolonged strike would not result in compromise by the individual companies affected, only in the breaking of the trade unions. Ironically, the TCM Executive Committee decided later in 1920 to raise debentures to repay the contributions by its members to the Reserve Fund.[88] Basically, this means that the trade unions were broken in 1922, at least partially, by borrowed money. The TCM members were contributing only the interest payments to the Reserve Fund at that stage. Whoever had taken up the debentures was financing the employers' subjugation of their workers. Thus, the financial strength of *non*mining capital was also mobilized to crush potential strikes on the mines.

The postwar period, in general, marks a rapid growth in the influence of the TCM, which was basically an association of Witwatersrand mining finance houses and companies. The mining finance houses were also known as the mining groups, and they dominated both the companies and the TCM. The growth of influence applies particularly to negotiations with labor and the government by the TCM on behalf of employers as a whole. As the state-capital-labor relationship became more complex and volatile, the TCM, run by experts in the field such as Gemmill, became more important.

Lionel Phillips was somewhat alarmed by the growing role of the TCM, and he warned the Johannesburg partners of his firm about it from the United Kingdom. The expansion continued, however, and in September 1921, the TCM Executive Committee agreed that no decision of principle affecting labor matters would be taken by any company or group without first consulting the TCM: ". . . It was agreed that where any member of the Chamber contemplates initiating a new departure which involves important principles, the Chamber should be notified of the proposal before putting it into effect or before informing the Union."[89]

Gemmill's pivotal role in the formation of the structure of South Africa's industrial relations—for black as well as for white workers—and as the architect of the 1922 confrontation has gone virtually unnoticed. One reason has been the exaggerated importance of the role attributed to H. O. Buckle, who was appointed "President of the Transvaal Chamber of Mines and Liaison Officer between the Chamber and the Government" in 1920.[90] Buckle, the former Chief Magistrate of Johannesburg and Chairman of the Miner's Phthisis Board, seems primarily to have fulfilled the liaison role and to have had little, if anything, to do with setting TCM policy.

Buckle's qualification to be an industry spokesman was enhanced by his previous appointment, in 1919, as Chairman of the Industrial Advisory Board (IAB). The IAB was an (ultimately ineffectual) attempt to reconcile the differences of labor and capital under the umbrella of the state, the last sustained attempt at conciliation before the 1922 strike. The IAB was suggested by the SAIF to serve as "a link between organized workers and organized employers and the Government" because the Minister of Mines and the government were "too much involved in the tomfoolery of Parliament" and too little with the industrial situation.[91] The unions were quite satisfied to have Buckle as Chairman, though, by his own admission, he had no "practical experience of industrial conditions."[92] A few months later, he became TCM President at the large annual salary of £5,000, resigned as IAB Chairman, and rejoined the IAB as representative of the TCM.

The government initially had high hopes for the IAB as a channel of communication (a function that would normally be performed in industrial countries in later years by legally recognized trade unions),[93] though it would have preferred a formal government commission on industrial relations.[94] But the IAB failed, partly because it had only advisory functions, and partly because the unions were increasingly unable to speak for their members and other white mineworkers. Wildcat strikes and the breaking of union agreements by branches of unions were a recognized problem by 1917.[95] By 1920, these had become serious enough to concern the state as well.

After the LGM Commission made its report, the union representatives met the TCM Executive Committee several times to discuss possible methods of cutting costs and of keeping the LGM in operation. One proposed method was to relax the mining regulations that required personal supervision by whites of black gangs and that cut down the actual working time of black miners to about five hours daily. Employer and employee representatives met under the direct mediation of the Government Mining Engineer, Kotze, and on July 15, 1920, the union leaders publicly agreed to Kotze's draft amendments.[96] Less than a week later, the SAMWU wrote to the TCM saying that its branches had objected, and it delayed its final decision. In October, the proposed amendments were turned down.[97]

The inability of the trade unions to guarantee industry-wide agreements with employers meant continued industrial turbulence. The government responded to the turbulence by sending the Inspector of White Labour or the GME to mediate disputes or by appointing judicial inquiries. The state's desire to keep the industrial peace is shown clearly by its refusal to enforce the law and charge the strikers with criminal offenses. Magistrates who found that the strikers had broken the law were instructed "not to apply" the 1909 Industrial Disputes Prevention Act and not "to find who, if anyone, is liable for criminal prosecution."[98] (See Table 4.)

As industrial turbulence mushroomed to record levels,[99] however, it became clear to the state that *ad hoc*, patchwork solutions—arbitrating strike by strike and overseeing individual settle-

Table 4   Trade Unions and Industrial Disputes, 1910–1955

Year	Union membership ('000)		No. of persons on strike ('000)		Man-days lost ('000)	
1910	9.1		0.4		10.2	
1915	10.5		—		—	
1916		15.4		1.3		1.4
1917		39.2		3.5		18.4
1918		77.8		2.6		31.8
1919		113.8		23.8		537.1
1920	135.1		105.7		839.4	
1921		108.2		9.9		112.4
1922		81.9		29.0		1,339.5
1923		86.9		0.1		0.7
1924		87.1		1.9		10.1
1925	93.6		—		—	
1930	75.5		5.1		2.6	
1935	121.3		2.4		19.6	
1940	235.1		1.8		6.5	
1945	341.4		16.1		91.2	
1950	358.6		3.8		10.7	
1955	395.1		9.9		17.0	

Source: Union Statistics for Fifty Years 1910–1960, Pretoria, 1960, G-18.

ments—merely had the effect of entrenching industrial action as a substitute for political action. Industrial action exacerbated the threat to the stability of both industry and the state: it constituted the heart of the political strength of white labor, which did not have the numerical strength or electoral support to vote its way to political power. Therefore, the need to limit industrial action, either by force or by incorporating organized labor into the political system (which, paradoxically, would depoliticize it), became clearer as industrial action became more intense.

These, then, were the salient ingredients of the industrial crisis: the Afrikanerization of the white labor force; the large-scale white unemployment accompanying massive urbanization; and the threat to the state's stability and revenue and to the industry's LGM (corresponding to the threat to white wages and jobs). The state and capital thus shared a vital interest in the depoliticization of organized white labor, though not necessarily for the same reasons.

Both sectors needed stability above all, though there was no absolute agreement as to how this should be achieved. Unemployment and the color bar, for example, were potent political issues that no government could ignore. But the question of whether the relaxation of the color bar would extend white employment (by cutting costs and therefore expanding the volume of ore that could profitably be exploited) or reduce it (by making white jobs black) was not one that could be accurately answered.

Behind these issues was the more profound question of the proper relationship between the state, labor, and capital. Though the state and capital had long shared the desire to *depoliticize* organized labor, it took the very singular and specific events of 1920–1921 to transform the desire into a concrete plan to *subjugate* organized labor by force or by threat of force.

State intervention in capital-labor relations, long indicated as necessary for the state to assert and assure its sovereignty and impose a favorable climate for accumulation, was delayed for several years because of the war and because individual governments did not stand to gain as much from intervention as did the expanding state.

The growing economic and political problems of 1921, with costs, workers' demands, and unemployment continuing to soar as the gold price fell, swung public opinion against the miners. At last, the government felt that the electorate would accept strong state intervention against organized labor. The blueprint for subjugation had already been prepared, largely by Gemmill, but it is unlikely that it would have been fully acted upon but for the acute economic crisis in the summer of 1921.

NOTES

1. BRA3, Archives of the Central Mining and Investment Corporation, Ltd., London (henceforth CML), Phillips (London) to the head of his South African operations, Evelyn Wallers, 1915.

2. See also David Ticktin, "The War Issue and the Collapse of the South African Labour Party, 1914–1915," *The South African Historical Journal*, No. 1, November 1969.

3. *Smuts Papers*, Vol. 3, p. 169, F. E. T. Krause to Smuts, 23.3.1914.

4. Ticktin, "The War Issue"; N. G. Garson, "The Political Role of the White Working Class in South Africa, 1902–1924," unpublished ms., 1976, p. 12.

5. Johnstone, *Class, Race and Gold*, London, 1976, p. 111.

6. The term "job color bar" is becoming popular to distinguish what was traditionally known simply as the "color bar" from "wage" or "exploitation color bars." I argue elsewhere (Yudelman, "The Quest for a neo-Marxist Approach to Contemporary South Africa") that the "wage color bar" is a misnomer and that the only color bar was the job color bar. A "bar" is an enforced exclusion, not an enforced inclusion (whether at low wages or not).

7. In most, if not all, treatments of the Rand Revolt, they are mistakenly thought to be central for one or both of two reasons: first, those were the ideological terms in which the conflict was couched by its participants; second, because race seems overwhelmingly to be the central issue of South African society today, there is the Whiggish impetus to search for the "origins" of contemporary institutionalized racism.

8. John Stone, *Colonist or Uitlander: A Study of the British Immigrant in South Africa*, Oxford, 1973, p. 121.

9. *Report of the Transvaal Indigency Commission*, TG 13–1908; the Carnegie Commission reports.

10. Stone, *Colonist or Uitlander*, pp. 122–27.

11. *Report of the Low-Grade Mines Commission*, UG 34–1920, Cape Town, 1920.

12. Katz, "White Workers," pp. 145–46.

13. Ibid. and p. 151.

14. TCM S 44, 12.7.1913.

15. Ibid., 11.7.1913.

16. MM 1212/17, Vol. 372, 30.1.1917. See also Johnstone, *Class, Race and Gold*, pp. 116–18, for an account of police-mobilization contingency plans to meet the threat of large strikes.

17. Ticktin, "The War Issue"; Simons and Simons, *Class and Colour in South Africa*, pp. 180–86.

18. *Smuts Papers*, Vol. 3, F. E. T. Krause to Smuts, 23.3.1914.

19. Simons and Simons, *Class and Colour*, p. 246.

20. Garson, "The Political Role of the White Working Class."

21. For example, Hancock, *Smuts*, Vol. 2, p. 69; Johnstone, *Class, Race and Gold*, p. 235; Garson, "The Political Role," p. 11; Horwitz, *Political Economy*, p. 99; Ticktin, "The War Issue," p. 59. Hancock and Johnstone misread their source, the *Martial Law Inquiry*, paragraph 96, and Garson misread Horwitz, who quotes it correctly. Ticktin gives no source.

22. *Martial Law Inquiry*, p. 18, paragraph 96.

23. J. J. Fourie, *Afrikaners in die Goustad, 1886–1924*, Pretoria, 1978, Appendix B, says that 39.8 percent of all white mineworkers in 1922 were Afrikaners, without documenting sources. This figure should be compared to the GME's figure for South African-born whites in 1922 of 48.6 percent.

Clearly, a large majority of the South African-born whites were Afrikaners, even if Fourie's precision is somewhat spurious.

24. C. E. M. O'Dowd, "The General Election of 1924," *South African Historical Journal*, No. 2, November 1970, p. 56.

25. ARTCM, 1921, p. 151.

26. Union of South Africa, Social and Economic Planning Council Report No. 11, *Economic Aspects of the Gold Mining Industry*, UG 32–1948, Pretoria, 1948, p. 30.

27. ARTCMs.

28. Johnstone, *Class, Race and Gold*, pp. 98–99, 101.

29. Johnstone provides an excellent account of the cost crisis, pp. 93–104.

30. Johnstone emphasizes, correctly, that the LGM "problem" was more socioeconomic than a geological problem. Though this is true, it accepts the employers' position too readily and fails to take into account the use of the concept for propaganda purposes (detailed below).

31. BRA, HE 155, Phillips to Eckstein, 29.3.1909, his emphasis. See also BRA, HE 154, 13.1.1908. Bantjes mine was closed in 1919.

32. BRA, HE 155, 5.4.1909.

33. Johnstone's analysis ably summarizes the contingent circumstances but fails to show how the mine controllers were the authors of many of their own problems. Nor does he analyze the use of the LGM issue by capital for the mobilization of outside support.

34. Alan Jeeves provides useful examples in his introduction to *All that Glittered*.

35. BRA, PH1, 1911–1916, 5.4.1911.

36. ARTCM, 1917, pp. 62, 473; TCM 1911.22 Series, File L 16a.

37. TCM L 16a; ARTCM, 1917, pp. 217–22, gives texts of correspondence.

38. Smuts Papers, unpublished collection in South African State Archives, Vol. 193 (18), No. 16. Lionel Phillips to Smuts, 4.12.1917.

39. TCM L 16a.

40. Union of South Africa, *Report of the Select Committee on the Gold Mining Industry*, SC 3–1918, Cape Town, 1918, pp. v–xi.

41. TCM 1911.22 Series, File L 16b, 9.5.1919.

42. Union of South Africa, *Interim and Final Reports of the Low-Grade Mines Commission*, UG 45–1919, UG 34–1920, Cape Town, 1919 and 1920.

43. ARTCM, 1919, p. 69.

44. TCM L 16b, Buckle (Cape Town) to TCM, Johannesburg, 29.5.1920.

45. Union of South Africa, *Report of Select Committee on Trading by Mining Companies on Mines*, SC 7–1921, Cape Town, 1921, pp. 37, 309, 317; Union of South Africa, *Interim Reports of the Cost of Living Commission*, UG 13–1918, Cape Town, 1918, pp. 2–3.

46. *Interim Report*, UG 13–1918, p. 3.

47. *LGM Commission*, p. 16, paragraph 77.

48. Papers of Sir Robert Kotze, in the possession of his son-in-law F. G. Hill, in Johannesburg.

49. State Archives, Prime Minister's Papers, PM 1/1/394, No. 204/19, "Closing of Low Grade Mines."

50. Ibid.

51. See also note 55, Chapter 1.

52. Katz, "White Workers' Grievances," makes this point cogently without, however, explaining why historians have overemphasized the role of the color bar in industrial disputes.

53. House of Assembly Debates, 1914, cols. 1990–1991, cited in Lever, "Creating the Institutional Order," p. 11.

54. BRA, CML, 28.7.1916.

55. TCM File 6, 1919, "Colour Bar."

56. Ibid., 13.11.1916, 14.11.1916.

57. BRA, CML, September 1916, Phillips (London) to Wallers.

58. TCM File 13, 1920, "Cape Coloured Mineworkers," 5.5.1920; for white labor figures, see ARTCM, 1920.

59. TCM 6/1919, 21.2.1917.

60. Ibid.

61. Ibid.

62. Ibid.

63. Ibid.

64. Ibid.

65. TCM 1911.22 Series, File G8, "Government Commission and Van Ryn Deep Strike"; Johnstone, *Class, Race and Gold*, pp. 107–11.

66. TCM 6/1919, 3.5.1917, 8.5.1917.

67. Ibid. Johnstone claims this was a case of the TCM "actually initiating an extension of the job color bar" (p. 111). This is incorrect: the first approach came from the unions in 1916, and the TCM scheme was far weaker than that demanded by the unions. For the agreement, see ARTCM, 1918; Johnstone, p. 109; TCM, 54/1920.

68. TCM 52/1919; TCM 6/1919.

69. TCM L 16b, 2.6.1919, 12.6.1919.

70. TCM 6/1919, 30.7.1919.

71. TCM 43/1920, 29.3.1920.

72. *LGM Commission*, pp. 29, 33.

73. ARTCM, 1920, pp. 67, 88.

74. Simons and Simons, *Class and Colour*, p. 232.

75. TCM 75/1920, "Status Quo 1920," October 1920; ARTCM, 1920, p. 92.

76. TCM 54/1920.

77. *LGM Commission*, minority report, p. 39.

78. TCM 15/1920, 1.10.1920.

79. TCM File 61, 1919, "White Labour," 5.6.1919.

80. London *Observer*, 8.2.1919.

81. TCM File 33 (1), 1920, "International Labour Conference." See also George N. Barnes, *History of the International Labour Office*, London, 1926.

82. TCM 33 (1), 1920. A censored version of "Report B," omitting this passage and others, appeared in *The South African Quarterly*, Vol. 2, No. 3, June 1920.

83. TCM 33 (1)/1920, Gemmill to Durban Retailers Council, 12.3.1920.

84. TCM File 23, 1919 Series, W. Gemmill to Wallers, 17.11.1919.

85. Ibid., 18.11.1911.

86. TCM 33 (1)/1920, 21.4.1920.

87. TCM 1911–1922 Series, File F 4(b), 31.3.1920, 15.4.1920.

88. TCM F 4(b), 22.7.1920.

89. TCM Executive Minutes, 12.9.1921 (uncirculated).

90. See, for example, Walker and Weinbren, *2,000 Casualties*, pp. 95, 98. The TCM files show that Buckle was engaged on a four-year contract at £5,000 per annum. As Chairman of the Miners' Phthisis Board, he had earned £650 per annum.

91. Archie Crawford, "The Present Industrial Situation," SAIF pamphlet, 1919.

92. TCM 1911–22 Series, File I 18, "Industrial Advisory Board 1919–21," 26.3.1919, 12.4.1919.

93. Selznik, *TVA and the Grass Roots*, p. 14.

94. TCM I 18, Warington Smyth to Buckle, "Private and Personal," 12.4.1919.

95. Johnstone, *Class, Race and Gold*, pp. 114–15.

96. *Rand Daily Mail*, 15.7.1920; TCM 54/1920.

97. TCM 20/1954.

98. TCM 1911–22 Series, File G8, "Government Commission re Van Ryn Deep Strike."

99. See Table 4.

5

The Subjugation of Organized Labor: The Rand Revolt of 1922

My American experience has made me more convinced than
ever that employers in South Africa have the upper hand of
labour, if they care to recognise the fact, and act accordingly.
　　　　　　　　　　—Gemmill to Wallers, December 1919[1]

The Rand Revolt of 1922 has left an indelible impression on South
Africa's collective political consciousness. To this day, mass unrest
and labor action in South Africa—actual or contemplated—are
almost inevitably accompanied by media coverage explicitly suggesting an analogy with 1922. The power and endurance of the
analogy is more noteworthy than its accuracy, but it is clearly essential to bear in mind the symbolic as well as the material significance of the Rand Revolt. It was the last sustained challenge from
organized labor to the legitimacy of the South African state up until
the present. There have been bigger strikes subsequently, and public violence on a grander scale, but never in the form of a systematic, concerted rejection of the state itself.

The Rand Revolt has come to symbolize the dangers of twentieth-century violence and anarchy, as the Zulu massacres of whites
and the Battle of Blood River in Natal of 1838 symbolized similar
fears in the nineteenth century. The longevity of each as a symbol
can be attributed to the continuing nightmares of the eventual victors rather than to the real threats that confronted them. This
chapter attempts to examine some of the events and issues behind
the symbol in the hope of refining our understanding of its applica-
bility, both to the past and the present.

The long-term structural developments leading up to the 1922
upheaval have already been discussed at length: the Afrikaneriza-

tion of the white working class, the continuing cost crisis of the low-grade mines, the color bar, and the need to depoliticize organized labor—a need being felt at the time throughout the capitalist world. The more immediate cause, the deepening of the economic crisis of both the state and industry, remains to be considered. The economic crisis was genuine enough. The premium on the gold price continued to fall, and the expected drop to the official price would have made twenty-two of thirty-nine Rand gold mines unprofitable by the TCM's estimate.[2] No doubt that estimate was somewhat exaggerated, since costs would have fallen with the gold price (though more slowly), but even those who were most critical of capital's role believed that the position was then serious.

The price of gold was the key. In February 1920, it was peaking at 127 shillings and 3 pence an ounce, profits were up in spite of rising costs, and it was clear to both the government and employers that the white electorate would not have supported any attempt to cut costs at the expense of white labor. By December, the price was down to 95 shillings, and the government had begun to realize the magnitude of the state's financial problems.

The state's debt had almost doubled since 1910, while government spending had doubled since 1914.[3] Drought, locusts, and crop failures had further accelerated the flow of unemployable poor whites into the towns. The state simply could not afford to have a large part of the mining industry close down. A temporary recovery of the premium provided some respite and, once again, delayed action against the unions in the first part of 1921. But by late 1921, the gold price was falling again. The leading mining capitalists then decided to force a confrontation with the unions; the government became increasingly reconciled to a direct clash between capital and labor, and began to mobilize the coercive power of the state for probable intervention.

The intervention was to be aimed at achieving short-term economic goals for both the state and capital, but behind these goals was the more important long-term question: who should govern the mining industry? More broadly, what was the proper relationship between industrial and political action, and the proper role of the state in the industrial arena? Both the government and mining capital, each for its own reasons, wanted to subjugate the white workers; both were eventually prepared for violence if necessary. The economic crisis provided a compelling rationale for subjugation and generated the popular support to make it feasible.

For the government, however, subjugation was not an end in itself. It was clear that a more permanent solution would have to follow, in which state intervention of a less dramatic type would be institutionalized on a continuing basis. Nevertheless, though it is not obvious whether the government understood this clearly at the time, the success of formal co-optation depended on the prior sub-jugation of organized labor. Buoyant and self-confident groups, such as the mining unions were between 1919 and 1921, cannot easily be persuaded to sacrifice the substance of power for its shadow.

The immediate background to subjugation was a wide-ranging, three-pronged attack: (1) the demand for higher productivity; (2) the assault on wages; and (3) the fight for dominance in industrial relations. Whenever the price of gold dipped, the momentum of the assault increased, helped both by the fears of the state and capital of bankruptcy and unemployment[4] and by their realization that other sections of the electorate were increasingly hostile to organ-ized labor. Conversely, when the price rose, the momentum slowed.

PRODUCTIVITY AND THE FIRST STAGE OF REORGANIZATION

The general argument of the TCM was that while white wages were rising, productivity was falling. Before 1920, the shortage of black labor was blamed, but white labor was increasingly seen as the culprit. The trade unions were blamed for foisting unproductive whites on the industry, through such measures as the Status Quo Agreement of 1918, and for cutting the working hours of blacks by insisting on close white supervision.

The productivity of both blacks and whites certainly fell between 1915 and 1920, but it is not so clear whether the trade unions were fully to blame. To begin with, the idea of employing semi-skilled and unskilled white supervisors came from the employers and the government before 1910, when the employers hoped to cut costs and the government hoped to employ more Afrikaners. The 1918 Status Quo Agreement, which extended the color bar, was not thought by employers to be important to costs. (See Chapter 4.)

The employers, in fact, even encouraged the extension of the color bar to buy peace in other areas. But the tremendous increase in white wages, especially in 1920, brought a change of heart. The intermediate class of white miners was the creation of the employers, who used it as an effective method of getting around the "one man-one drill" demands of the "old school" miners. Now, many of the supervisors were also being attacked by the employers as being superfluous.

The drop in productivity, then, was, to some extent, the result of the political weakness of capital: it was unable to take its reorganization of the structure of the white labor force far enough. It now had to employ the intermediate semi-skilled class of white miners in addition to the old class of skilled labor rather than as a substitute for it. The TCM proposed another reorganization. Officially, it claimed merely to want to weed out "redundant" whites; of course, the actual aim was also to employ cheaper black labor in the same jobs. What has not been generally noted, however, because the TCM did not advertise it, was that the employers were responsible for introducing these redundant whites in the first place. The redundant whites who faced the first onslaught in 1921-1922 were precisely those men who had been deliberately brought by the employers a decade earlier to replace the skilled miners. In an about face, it was now proposed to adjust underground work to eliminate these men "and once more make the miner an 'all-round man' "[5] (that is, a miner who has artisan's skills and who is not merely a supervisor).

Equally underemphasized was the scheme of the employers to create and expand a class of nonunionized "officials," who would create a buffer between management and white miners and possibly even replace the latter as a direct link with black mineworkers. Strenuous precautions were taken to ensure that these officials would not join trade unions. As Gemmill put it:

> The Industry on this point should adopt a definite and strong attitude with a view to protecting its officials, whose interests in varying degrees, but in all cases to a greater extent than the manual workers, are similar to those of the employers. . . . The Industry should actively endeavour to get the officials on the side of the employers.[6]

The TCM took pains to widen the cleavage by such devices as giving monthly paid employees, or "officials" (many of whom were trade-union members), certain benefits that were still being negotiated by the unions. When the unions protested, the employers blandly offered to withhold the benefits from any official who wrote to them asking not to be paid the increase.[7] The unions finally lost control of the officials just before the 1922 upheavals. The only major provision of the settlement of the Crown Mines strike in November 1921 was the establishment of the principle that the unions had no right to represent officials.[8]

The Minister of Mines had intervened to push through that settlement, which also represented a defeat for the strikers in other respects. Ironically, the TCM was still involved at the time in a formal investigation aimed at publicly defining an "official."[9] The officials were extensively used in antistrike actions. They performed safety work, without which the mines would have been flooded, when miners refused, and the government allowed the breaking of regulations that this entailed. Managers were even authorized by the TCM to use officials to break rock. They were probably used in that capacity after Smuts requested the mines to restart operations in mid-February. The officials were naturally hated by the strikers, and their houses and furniture were frequently attacked and destroyed by fire.[10] Not only was the working class divided by race, organization, and ethnic factors, but it was also divided internally into union men and officials. The last division proved to be very durable: in 1976, of the 37,800 whites employed on the gold mines and collieries that were members of the South African Chamber of Mines, a full 50 percent, or 18,815, were classified as officials.[11] The ratio of one official to one union man reflects the subterfuge involved in the designation "officials."

The plan of mining capital seems, then, to have been to replace many of the unskilled and semi-skilled Afrikaner supervisors it had created earlier partly with blacks and partly by extending the class of nonunionized officials and the scope of their work. It succeeded in its first aim but never managed to get white miners to allow officials to supervise blacks directly.

The issue of supervision had a broader dimension as well. It was claimed that the "personal" supervision by whites required by government mining regulations was cutting the actual working day of the supervised Africans to five hours. The TCM hoped that the removal of the word "personal" would result in large increases in black productivity by increasing working time by up to 40 percent. In June 1921, Smuts cabled from London saying that the mining industry representatives had told him it would not be necessary to press for wage reductions if the regulations could be amended.[12] Some changes were made but they proved inconclusive, and in November, Smuts held three conferences with the unions in an effort to push through the necessary provisions.[13] Smuts had been reluctant to intervene directly but, claimed Phillips later, had agreed to act

> when I pointed out in very clear language . . . that, if we attempted to bring about these reforms without the Government at our back, there would unquestionably be a tremendous upheaval at once, whereas, if the Government would frankly face the situation, there was a possibility of averting this . . .[14]

The unions, however, correctly saw this as a partial attack on the color bar, and the limited alterations they agreed to were dismissed by the TCM as useless.[15] The following month, the TCM came up with far more comprehensive demands, *inter alia*, for underground reorganization. However, its earlier hopes of prevailing upon white labor by persuasion (with the help of government pressure) were fading. Part of the reason for worker resistance to TCM productivity suggestions was the fact that white wages were being reduced at the same time that higher productivity was being demanded.

THE ATTACK ON WHITE WAGES

The level of white wages was of vital importance to the state and mining capital, the two largest employers in South Africa. There is evidence of continuous cooperation in the setting of wages, as any concession by either employer would tend to increase pressure on the other.[16] The General Manager of South African Railways, Sir William Hoy, for example, regularly sent Wallers the wage demands made by his workers. In one "confidential" note to the Minister of Railways, he recommended resisting any reduction of the forty-eight-hour week, as the mines were doing, and passed on a copy to the TCM.[17] At times, the white miners accused the state of setting the example in reducing wages. The state also saw itself as fulfilling that role.[18]

In February 1920, the gold price was at a peak of 127 shillings and 3 pence an ounce, and workers' demands continued on both mines and railways. As Phillips pointed out, concessions by either the state or mining capital were inevitably followed by demands on the other. Because of gold's high price, "the public will certainly side with the men," and because of the imminence of general elections, the government was likely to compromise: "There is no doubt a tendency on the part of the white men to take advantage of the political situation, because they are aware that Governments are particularly supine when an election is at hand."[19]

Wallers and Hoy were, therefore, communicating "in order that we may act in the same general way." Phillips predicted, correctly, that it would be difficult to reduce wages—the minimum wage for whites had been increased by £2/8 shillings per week in November 1919—even if the gold price fell. Mine closures, however, would make everyone—workers and the general community—"much more reasonable." For the moment, it was necessary to compromise "to avoid warfare and let the future take care of itself."

The government was also clearly unhappy about wage levels, and a few months later, F. S. Malan told Buckle that he hoped unemployment (about which the government professed in public to be very concerned) might help reduce wages. Unemployment was not to be fought: ". . . If the Government took any steps now towards the prevention of unemployment, they [sic] would be met with the demand for congenial work at standard wages. He [Malan] stated that their definite policy was to let unemployment go until more moderate terms would be accepted."[20] And a week later, Malan told the SAIF that the government did not hold itself responsible to keep all its citizens in work.[21]

The large wage increases of 1919 were given on condition that wages could be cut back if the industry's situation changed or if the cost of living fell. A close watch was, therefore, kept on public opinion as well as the cost of living and the gold price. At the end of March 1921, the cost of living had fallen considerably, and the government took the lead in reducing cost-of-living allowances.[22]

Nevertheless, the TCM Executive Committee decided it was "premature to come to a decision on the general question of reduction in wages . . ."[23] After further falls in the gold price, it approached the SAIF two months later only to be rebuffed.[24] The price had risen again, and a few weeks later, Smuts told Phillips that the TCM

> would be ill-advised to force down wages at a time when the exchange value of gold is fairly high, as he thought, in the event of a strike resulting, the sympathy of the community on the Rand would very likely be with the workers and not with the gold mining companies.[25]

Clearly, this was a question of tactics only, and the Inspector of White Labour commented on the "unfortunate" fluctuations of the gold price, which sabotaged the TCM's attempts to cut wages.[26] He felt that the TCM's compromise proposal to reduce wages on a quarterly sliding scale would be accepted mainly because the unions were weak and divided.[27] The TCM, in the meantime, decided to begin a propaganda campaign justifying its cutback of wages.[28]

A few days later, on August 2, 1921, the TCM and the SAIF agreed to pin adjustments of wages to the cost of living on a quarterly basis, starting October 1 with a reduction.[29] The SAIF, however, rejected a request in September for wage reductions for the coal miners, though they earned more than the gold miners. Then the government intervened,

> pointing out that as Railway employees and others had to accept reduced salaries, in order that coal might be carried at cheaper rates, so that the Transvaal coal market might be retained, it was unreasonable for the coal miners to expect to retain a privileged position, and not to have their wages similarly reduced.[30]

The SAIF continued to refuse reductions in spite of government pressure. It offered to go to arbitration, which the TCM refused. The government warned against extreme steps because of the public interest in the coal industry and because essential utilities might be threatened by a strike "which [utilities] the Government in the interests of the community as a whole would be bound to preserve."[31]

In spite of these "mediation" efforts, the coal strike began, much to the fury of Smuts, who saw an incipient export industry destroyed. In December, a statement by Smuts (approved in advance by the TCM) charged that South African coal was no longer competitive because the British coal strike had resulted in a reduction of wages there.[32] When, in February 1922, the Witbank coal miners were told that less than half could be reemployed after the strike, Smuts was unsympathetic: "When you make a mistake like that [of going on strike] you pay for it."[33]

Thus, the stage was set for the general confrontation over the permissible forms of industrial action. Artisans were resentful because their wages were being cut, and both unskilled and semi-skilled workers were frightened that their jobs would be given to blacks. Consequently, the TCM's attempts to divide the white workers in this way failed because both artisans and nonartisans were threatened by its various proposals.

The gold price continued to fall, and the employers' panic deepened. The government and the employers were outraged at labor's intransigence and delay tactics, especially on the coal mines, in refusing to accept drastically reduced wages. Labor filibustering continued until their patience snapped. Characteristically, the deadlock was then broken by a disguised ultimatum that maneuvered the unions into the ostensible position of aggressor. In short, the unions were made an "offer" that they could not accept—and moreover, were not seriously expected to accept.

THE FIGHT FOR DOMINANCE IN INDUSTRIAL RELATIONS

In mid-1921, Phillips and Smuts met in London to discuss the problems of the industry. A concerted effort by the state and capital to modify the government mining regulations resulted, which involved attempting a covert relaxation of the color bar while carefully avoiding any frontal attack on it. Phillips was convinced, however, that this effort was merely tinkering with the essential problem: who should govern the industry? State backing was essential if organized labor was to be subjugated, and Phillips candidly admitted this to Smuts. Moreover, subjugation was necessary, not merely to lower costs, but to restore long-term employer (or state) sovereignty over the industry.

Aiming above all to swing the state fully behind the employers, Phillips contrived to accompany Smuts and the former Unionist party leader, Sir Thomas Smartt, on the long voyage back to South Africa; he even delayed his departure when Smuts did. A breakdown of the ship en route extended the time available to him and enabled him to drive home at length the point that "those responsible for the operations on the mines must, by hook or by crook, get discipline restored and be able to dismiss anybody who will not give a fair day's work for the good pay he receives."[34]

After their return to South Africa, Smuts and Phillips conferred with Wallers, and they decided to attempt further alterations in the mining regulations. Smuts met the unions but proceeded with caution. He had been made vividly aware, in both 1907 and 1913–1914, that the interests of the government and employers during strikes were not identical, even though there was considerable overlap. He was equally aware that white labor was a volatile political force.

One of Smuts's major concerns, expressed earlier to Phillips, was whether the Rand "community" would support labor or capital. Capital, too, was aware of the importance of the floating allegiance of groups like shopkeepers and white-collar workers, and the TCM Executive Committee decided on July 29, 1921, to initiate a propaganda campaign to publicize its point of view, concentrating on press advertisements. The fact that it was necessary to advertise shows graphically the limitations of direct industry influence on the editorial content of the South African press, even though a large part of the press was owned by mining capital. By March 1922, the TCM's Propaganda Subcommittee had run up expenses of at least £10,000. Large *ad hoc* payments of 400 guineas and 250 guineas were made the same month to two prominent journalists, Owen Letcher and H. A. Chilvers, "for their services in regard to propaganda."[35]

While the TCM campaigned for public and government support, it began to take an increasingly tough line with the white workers. On September 12, 1921, it sent a circular to mine managers, reiterating that the standing costs of any mine hit by a strike on what was considered by the TCM to be a general issue of labor-capital relations would be met by the employers as a whole. The principle of "open shop"—supporting the right of workers not to join unions—was reaffirmed shortly afterward.[36]

Finally, a meeting of the TCM Executive Committee on October 24 made the momentous decision to force a confrontation with the trade unions. Wallers pointed out that there was strife between unions and that the SAIF was weakening. He asked whether "the industry wished to reaffirm its policy of collective bargaining and assisting unions, or whether it wanted to assist in the disintegration of the Federation."[37]

Professor J. G. Lawn, Joint Managing Director of Johannesburg Consolidated Investments, the second largest mining group (Wallers's was the largest), said that only drastic action could save the industry. Such action, if rejected by the unions, would result in a strike. "The position was, What was the Chamber to do after passing through the strike? Were they only to insist on the reduction of wages and let all agreements stand? He thought the time was ripe when they should resume the management of their own mines." Wallers, the erstwhile accommodationist, went further, making it clear that an attack on the color bar as a whole was contemplated, which would involve the amendment of the Status Quo Agreement and of the statutory (or legal) color bar itself and the dismissal of large numbers of whites, some of whom would be replaced by blacks.

The only dissenting voice was that of Buckle, the outsider who had been brought in as the TCM's first paid president. Although his was the lone voice on the TCM calling for moderation in its policy toward the unions, he was shortly thereafter to be used as its hatchet man; thus he attracted a great deal of white worker odium that should more properly have been directed elsewhere. Buckle suggested that he understood the TCM policy to favor the recognition of "properly constituted unions." He was pointedly ignored.

Sir Ernest Oppenheimer, already one of the most influential men in the TCM, suggested the appointment of a committee of gold producers to "go into the question," and it was agreed to do so, with each group appointing one member. This was an extremely important move because it streamlined the decision-making process by completely bypassing the cumbersome TCM Executive Committee and it centralized control of the industry in the hands of the six or seven mining groups. The committee was the precursor and model for the Gold Producers' Committee (GPC), officially formed after the 1922 revolt. From its formation to the present, the GPC has always been the industry's true Executive Committee and an instrument for imposing the will of the large groups on the industry as a whole.

The following month, Wallers expanded his proposal to attack the color bar. He suggested to the Executive Committee that it might be necessary to fix a black/white ratio for the total work force for a period of, say, three years and allow the industry to use its labor in whatever way it saw fit without trade-union restrictions. The government would probably support this plan. After discussion, a suggested ratio of 11:1 was settled on. The TCM had always vehemently opposed fixed black/white labor ratios, and Wallers's mention of government approval probably indicated a tentative agreement or trade-off with the government. The employers possibly guaranteed to preserve some white jobs (though far fewer, as the ratio was 8.2:1 at the time) in exchange for the state's help in subordinating the unions and, implicitly, the state's renouncement of color-bar mining regulations.[38]

However, when Wallers asked Smuts publicly whether the state would intervene in broader issues than regulations—such as trade-union restrictions and the reorganization of the underground labor force—Smuts evasively suggested that labor and capital discuss these among themselves, though the Minister of Mines would help if called upon.[39] He had already received a memorandum from Kotze showing that the need to reduce white wages was far more important to cutting costs than amending the regulations.[40] Phillips commented at the time that Smuts was hanging back out of "moral cowardice." Phillips himself was very optimistic about the strength of the employers' position, about public support for it and the weak, divided state of the trade unions: ". . . The outlook for getting back to control, discipline and efficiency is better than it has been for years."[41]

He was energetically engaged in giving press interviews "to educate the public" (because "its memory is painfully short") and to "warn the workmen." He had no doubts then, as early as November, about what was in store: ". . . the serious battle with the men's leaders on the Status Quo agreement, modification of contract systems, etc."

Phillips's letter shows clearly that the decision had been taken by mining capital not to compromise or negotiate with the workers. The question was no longer whether to attempt radical changes, but how these would be achieved. The key, as always, was the government's decision on what role the state should play: "If only Smuts and his Government will be strong I think we may get radical reforms without all the disorganisation and loss which a general strike would involve, but we are quite determined to see the necessary changes effected." Smuts, he said, feared the unpredictability of a strike. Phillips, smelling blood and realizing that he might make the kill without dirtying his own hands, was more intrepid: "Smuts accused me of *wanting* a strike. This is of course furthest from my desire, but there are worse things than a strike (deplorable as it might be) viz:—to sit supinely by and watch ruin overtake half the Industry with all its disastrous effects."[42]

In spite of his caution, Smuts and his Cabinet had by now decided that organized labor should not be allowed to dictate industrial policy to either the state or capital. Amid reports that a strike was imminent on the Witbank coal fields (which fed, *inter alia*, the Rand power stations), F. S. Malan called a meeting on December 9 of representatives from the government, the police, the South African Railways, and the mining employers. He asked for and received agreement that a press statement be issued that wage reductions were essential and a strike unjustified. Referring to strikes, he pledged firm but neutral state action: "It has never been the Government's policy to stop strikes, only to maintain law and order and the protection of property."[43]

He seems to have chosen as his model Gemmill's description of the U.S. Government: "A strong capitalistic but nominally democratic government."[44] To enforce this "day to day and hour to hour," he appointed a small committee. The police representative suggested that the army be invited to send a representative, but Malan turned it down because "using the military causes more bitterness." On December 19, a meeting of the committee resolved to keep the mines working, under police protection if necessary.[45] On December 30, the Inspector of White Labor recommended a mobile military force, to be held out of sight, for use anywhere on the Reef at six hours' notice.[46]

On the employers' side, feverish preparations continued for the confrontation with labor. The Federated Chamber of Industries, representing manufacturing employers, passed a resolution on December 5 supporting the Crown Mines in resisting a strike. The next day, the TCM gold producers' committee met and decided to ask for the unions' agreement to alter the system of underground contracts, modifying the Status Quo Agreement and rearranging underground work.

Wallers and Buckle clashed at length over whether the TCM should keep the demands vague "so as not to alarm the general public" or attempt to spell out their implications for the unions. Wallers, advocating vagueness, prevailed. He also repeated his suggestion of a black/white ratio of 11:1. The TCM technical advisor replied that the ratio would mean the replacement of 5,500 white men, which was neither feasible nor politically practicable.[47]

The letter eventually sent to the SAIF on December 8 made no reference to ratios. (It was not until January 28, 1922, that a ratio was first publicly suggested by the industry: 10.5:1.) The TCM promised the dismissal of not more than 2,000 semi-skilled and unskilled whites, or 10 percent of the total whites employed. On December 15, forty-one representatives of the TCM, the SAIF, and the S.A. Mine Workers' Union (SAMWU) met. Buckle made a long speech asking the unions definitely "to give up that [Status Quo] agreement" and to consider the TCM's other two proposals. In other words, the statutory color bar was not at first attacked, though it was already under private discussion within the TCM. Only jobs covered by custom and the Status Quo Agreement were threatened by the first public TCM demands.

The Status Quo proposal was rejected out of hand by E. S. Hendriksz of the SAMWU. He represented largely the unskilled miners, who were most threatened by such an action. Hendriksz asked for details of the other two proposals, but Buckle, following Wallers's orders, claimed that it was impossible to provide details of the proposed measures. This deliberate vagueness was tellingly attacked, and on December 23, the TCM sent the SAIF some details, though the scope of its demands remained obscure.[48] On December 28, the TCM gave notice of its intended withdrawal from the Status Quo Agreement on February 1, 1922, without prejudice to negotiations then going on.

Also on December 28, the government attempted to get the SAIF and the colliery companies to accept compulsory arbitration. The companies refused, which meant that even if the conciliation machinery of the Industrial Disputes Prevention Act had been invoked, no settlement would have been binding on either party.[49] On January 2, 1922, the collieries went on strike; on January 10, after several mediation attempts by Smuts, an SAIF strike ballot voted 10–1 in favor of a strike. Only two months earlier, the majority for the Crown Mines strike had been a mere 2–1, with the artisan trade unions opposing the SAMWU and actually rejecting a strike.[50] The magnitude of the 10–1 majority indicates how the sweeping demands on all sections of the white labor force had reunited the divided unions. Phillips had written on November 23 that "all the other unions are against the [Miners' Union]" and Miller, the government Inspector of White Labor, wrote on December 30 that the SAIF was breaking up and its affiliated unions were not paying fees. But Phillips had also warned that "class cohesion is so strong that we have to walk very warily to prevent a situation that might consolidate them all against us."[51]

Partly because of increasing panic at the continued fall of the gold price (it fell 9 shillings an ounce in four weeks of November–December and another 5 shillings, down to 98 shillings, by mid-January), and partly because of the active desire for a confrontation, neither the TCM nor the state trod at all warily, and the tactics of the TCM, in particular, united the warring trade unions against them. Though wage reductions were already under way by mid-1921 and strike stoppages were far smaller than in 1919 or 1920, the employers wanted larger cost cuts and complete control of labor and industry as a whole. They were not, moreover, concerned with being particularly tactful in making these demands.

THE STRIKE AND REVOLT OF 1922[52]

By the beginning of 1922, then, the state was seen by the workers as firmly allied to the employers; in most senses, this was true. The unions, seeking alternatives, proceeded to make contact with two of the opposition political parties. The South African Police, which had thoroughly infiltrated the unions, said in a confidential report that contact had been made between Tielman Roos, the Transvaal leader of the National party, and Hendriksz, the SAMWU secretary, at the end of 1921. Roos allegedly told Hendriksz to hold off the strike until Parliament was in session.[53]

On January 9, Smuts sent a long telegram from Pretoria to Henry Burton, his Minister of Finance, in Cape Town, saying that he was "certain that there are political motives to upset the Government behind the movement." He predicted violence and the stopping of essential services, and he argued that the meeting of Parliament on January 20 should be delayed as its "attitude may also be singularly unhelpful and embarrassing at [this] most difficult stage of the trouble." Burton replied, "Strongly agree," and the session of Parliament was duly delayed to February 17.[54]

Smuts's best biographer to date has alleged that the delay proved that Smuts wanted to stop a confrontation. He cites the many meetings Smuts had with both labor and capital and his calls for a peaceful solution. At the same time, the Labour and National parties are castigated for seeking political profit from the confrontation.[55] What this fails to take into account was the fact that Smuts *had* to take the stance of peacemaker, and that Smuts was himself seeking political profit (or trying to minimize political loss) by delaying the opening of Parliament and by emphasizing the general dangers of an upheaval. Smuts had finally decided that organized labor had to be crushed, but he did not want the odium of being seen (as in 1914) as the aggressor in its defeat.

Thus, Smuts talked a great deal about conciliation, but he exerted little serious pressure on the TCM to make any compromises. He directed his genuine efforts to preparing for the violent confrontation that he felt was almost inevitable. On January 27, for example, he publicly called for a settlement but prejudiced any such possibility by saying the issue was the LGM, not the color bar.[56]

On January 28, the TCM came out with a new offer, ostensibly a response to Smuts's call, which offered far tougher terms than before, including its first public mention of a (10.5:1) black/white ratio. The ratio, if fully carried out, would have eliminated more than twice as many white workers as the maximum of 2,000 suggested the previous month. Moreover, the ratio was only guaranteed for two years and threatened even the statutory color bar by implication, since a TCM condition was that it would be given a free hand within the confines of the ratio. The TCM also demanded the abolition of paid holidays on May Day and Dingaan's Day, thus offending, at one stroke, both Anglophone and Afrikaner workers.[57]

The TCM's offer was clearly calculated to inflame the workers. Two days later, Smuts wrote resignedly to the Governor-General that he expected the strikers to interfere in the next week with pumping equipment on the mines and that the police would resist.[58] All this is not to say that Smuts (or the TCM) necessarily wanted a strike; they both wanted the power of the unions crushed and far fewer white miners employed, at far lower wages. Since it was (quite reasonably) felt that these goals probably could not be achieved without a fight, both military and political measures were taken to prepare for that fight.

Politically, the TCM courted public support with propaganda that heavily emphasized the danger to the community as a whole if the industry collapsed; the government courted public support by emphasizing the threat to the state posed by a selfish sectional interest (the white mineworkers) within it. In this action it was supported by such powerful interests as the Federated Chamber of Industries and the Transvaal Agricultural Union, which wrote indignantly to Smuts saying that no single section should have the power to paralyze the country, and which demanded a permanent solution to the industrial problem.[59] The opposition Labour and National party leaders denied that there was any real threat to the state, and Tielman Roos even called publicly for Afrikaners to refuse to fight if called up for army duty to suppress the strike.[60] But neither party (particularly not the National party) was prepared to support extralegal actions by the strikers.

Smuts sought, first, to take up the neutral stance of an umpire: "If a strike were to take place the Government would draw a ring around both parties, do its best to maintain law and order, and let the two parties fight it out."[61] Merely maintaining law and order in this situation was to take sides, but the intervention of the opposition parties complicated matters. As Smuts himself put it, in a private letter dated February 3: "The intervention of Roos and others has utterly spoiled this business. The strikers now simply look to the collapse of the Government in Parliament for their salvation. Poor deluded people."[62] He was right. No viable South African government at the time would have forced all the workers' demands—or even most of them—on the mining capitalists.

On February 12, Smuts called on the mines to reopen and pledged police protection for strikebreakers. Serious clashes between the South African Police and the strikers' military arm, the paramilitary groups they called their "commandos," date from that speech. The use of the word "commando"—the name given to units of the Boer republican armies—was itself a challenge to the legitimacy of the state and to its monopoly over the legal use of force. In addition to the tougher tactics of the government, it was now clear to the strikers that the Labour and National parties would only provide political and charitable support and would do nothing unconstitutional to help organized labor.[63]

The government, for its part, continued to refuse to intervene beyond recommending capitulation by the strikers to TCM demands, pending further investigation. On March 1, the Secretary for Mines wrote to Smuts asking him to stress publicly that the TCM was not being pressed by the government to make compromises and to call on the strikers again to return to work.[64] The government clearly refrained from direct physical intervention for political reasons: it wanted to assume the role of neutral guardian of public order rather than that of strike-repressor. So, although the TCM itself had urgently asked as early as February 21 for martial law to be declared, the government did not do so.

In early March, the SAIF made overtures of peace to the TCM, but they were rejected in a letter of such towering contempt (signed by Gemmill) as to constitute a direct provocation.[65] Incidents of violence increased, a general strike was declared (it failed because other unions did not join in), and strikers attacked blacks. Confidential government reports indicate that the attacks were deliberate attempts by strikers to provoke retaliation and thus recruit public support by introducing a racial dimension.[66] This speculation certainly makes more sense than the trade-union theories that the blacks were attacked by employers' representatives: both the state and capital had every reason to avoid any racial flare-up.

Still, Smuts hesitated. As he explained afterward, he was

prepared to take the risk of losing control of the Rand for "a couple of days," and the risk of "a great deal of outrage and destruction":

> If there are revolutionary forces brewing in this country; if we are continuously walking on the edge of a volcano, let the country see it, let us even at the . . . very serious risk of a couple of days of revolution, delay the declaration of martial law and let the situation develop.[67]

That is exactly what did happen, though the major revolutionary outbursts and armed resistance, on March 10, were coincident with the declaration of martial law and were not its cause. Smuts wanted to make the point that groups of organized white workers had revolutionary intentions and could justifiably be put down by state coercion. As far back as mid-January, it was known that certain Afrikaner miners, in particular, favored armed insurrection;[68] whether they could have mobilized the mass support they achieved without the systematic policy of alienation followed by the state and the TCM is open to doubt.

Smuts rushed up from Cape Town to deal with the situation personally, arriving on March 11. He had called up 70,000 men to suppress the 1914 general strike; now he called up less than 20,000, supported by aircraft, artillery, and tanks. Although the strike of 22,000 miners had failed, an estimated 10,000 rebels took over most of the Reef on "Black Friday," March 10. Their triumph was very short-lived, however, and the state forces—of whom a large proportion were Afrikaner burgher commandos[69]—totally defeated the revolt in three days, by March 13. The following day, Smuts cabled his Cabinet colleagues in Cape Town, asking their approval of summary trials and executions of leaders. They dissuaded him with some difficulty.[70] Smuts, like Joseph de Maistre, believed that behind every civilization stands a hangman. As he explained ten days later to a friend: ". . . Life with all its beautiful flowerings rests at last on a granite foundation. Unless Society is to go to pieces there must be a solid guarantee of force in the background."[71]

THE MYTH OF THE "RED REVOLT"

Both during and after the strike, the role of communist revolutionaries was emphasized and exaggerated. Throughout February, it is true, control of organized labor had been slipping from the SAIF Augmented Executive Committee in Johannesburg to an informally constituted Council of Action. The council was militant, some of its members were communists, most were English-speaking, and all of them supported revolutionary action.[72] Police reports, however, show clearly that the real revolutionary threat came largely from Afrikaner urban commandos, or miners' militia.[73] Even the boastful account of one of the council members, W. H. Andrews, tending to inflate his own role, admits that the council of commando leaders (known as the "generals") turned him out of his own office when they wanted to discuss their plans for revolution.[74] The communists, though providing vocal and effective leaders, had little overall impact, particularly outside of Johannesburg.

The miners' commandos had started military drilling in late January, at first encouraged by the authorities, who feared a possible rising of black miners as a result of the general unrest. Outside of Johannesburg, where English-speaking unionists kept control of the Fordsburg commando, the vast majority of the commando members were Afrikaners.[75] Their leaders were also largely Afrikaners: the Supreme Commander was known as "General" Piet Erasmus, and other "generals" were W. A. D. Coetzee and I. J. Viljoen. In the Afrikaner urban commandos, one finds the uneasy mixture of republicanism and working-class revolutionary thought that resulted in the notorious slogan, "Workers of the world unite and fight for a white South Africa." In 1918, it was said at a trade-union conference that the whole Dutch (Afrikaner) population would oppose by force any attempt to remove the color bar. In December 1921, there was already talk among Afrikaner miners of the necessity for political action and of the resurrection of the old republican *Vierkleur* flag.[76] In Benoni, a predominantly English-speaking town extremely loyal to the Empire, a rash of *Vierkleurs* appeared, even on the Trades Hall, the workers' headquarters. English-speaking workers claimed to have been intimidated into joining the commandos, at times by physical assault.[77]

The urban commandos hoped to get armed help from the rural burgher commandos, but it did not happen.[78] There was some "passive" help, however, with reports of the burgher commandos turning back when they realized they would be fighting not merely foreign communists and English city slickers, but fellow Afrikaners as well. Many of the burgher commandos illegally refused their mobilization orders, and the government was privately requested that the law punishing offenders be applied leniently or that burghers be allowed to pay their fines in instalments.[79]

Smuts, who was fighting a losing battle with the National party for the rural Afrikaner vote, did not pursue the burgher commandos who had refused to fight. On the contrary, he chose to glorify the role of the burgher commandos who had helped put down the revolt:

> . . . In the hour of danger . . . when they realised that it was more than an industrial dispute, and that the very foundations of public life were in danger . . . they did not ask for reason, they did not urge politics, but a vast bulk of them took to the field, got their horses and rode to the rescue.[80]

It is true that the burgher commandos comprised a large proportion of the state's forces—one estimate suggests 6,400 of 20,000, but the proportion could have been as high as 8,000 of 13,000[81]—and that these mounted men were a very effective fighting force. Smuts, for all his lavish praise, was uneasy about using the commandos and quickly relieved them, and the army as a whole, of any further role once the principal conflict was over.[82]

As for placing responsibility for the revolt, there seems to have been almost a conspiracy of silence about the major role of the urban Afrikaner. Both the state and mining capital played it down for their own reasons. Smuts perpetuated the idea that the 1922 revolt was a foreign-led aberration rather than the product of genuine indigenous tensions. Russian immigrants to South Africa, the argument goes, were responsible for a Bolshevik-type Rand Revolt. Essentially, this meant Russian Jews, since a vast majority of Russian immigrants were Jews. In other contexts, Smuts was a firm supporter of Jewish and Zionist aspirations, but he refused the private entreaties of the Jewish Board of Deputies to scotch allegations that Russian Jews were responsible for the revolt, even though they clearly were not and he knew they were not.[83] Historians, particularly Afrikaner historians, have also subsequently downplayed the major Afrikaner responsibility for the revolt.[84]

The significance of the role of the Afrikaner—rural and

urban—in the events of 1922, and the reaction to it of the state and mining capital, is complex, and it is beyond the scope of this study to do it full justice. What is clear, however, is that the two major potentially radical forces confronting the state and capital were once again—as in 1914—not able to operate in alliance. Once again, rural commandos helped put down an urban uprising. In 1922, the urban Afrikaner miners attempted to recruit the support of their fellow Afrikaners in the countryside. They failed, partly because of a combination of poor communication and the concerted propaganda campaign that the state and mining capital had waged since 1914 to recruit the support of the "general public"; and partly because a significant section of the burgher element, as we have already seen in Chapter 4, was as concerned with holding the center as was mining capital.

The need for the center to hold against possible radical threats is also shown by the gentle treatment of parliamentarians such as Tielman Roos, the Transvaal leader of the National party, and Bob Waterston, a Labour party member of Parliament who had been among those union leaders deported by Smuts in 1914. Waterston publicly called for the proclamation of a republic and presided over a meeting in Benoni at which cases of rifles were distributed. Roos advised rural Afrikaners not to act without deep thought if they were called up for military duty. Yet no action was taken against either man. This strategy of conciliation did not prevent the government from losing the next election to a coalition government of the National and Labour parties. But it was a success for both the state and capital, as it rapidly became more evident that the National and Labour parties had been consolidated into the center rather than alienated by the events of 1922. The center did not confront as great a physical threat in 1922 as it did in 1913–1914, but the Rand Revolt showed it that a radical alliance of nationalist republicans and working-class revolutionaries was still possible.

On March 17, the SAIF called off the strike and the workers streamed back to work. Eventually, eighteen men were sentenced to death for murder by a special court. After appeals, four were hanged: all were trade unionists, English-speaking, and went to the gallows singing "The Red Flag." The miners had been physically crushed, and the permissible limits of direct industrial action had been more closely circumscribed. But both the state and mining capital still needed to develop a stable, institutionalized relationship with organized white labor.

Though labor had been roundly defeated, it was clear that it would be necessary to defuse permanently its explosive potential or at least to diffuse it by establishing a new institutional framework for the formal co-optation of organized labor into the state apparatus. Such a framework would be intended, ideally, both to reinforce the legitimacy of the state and to establish the administrative framework for the orderly governing of the industry.

The subjugation of labor had provided a favorable climate for the government to co-opt organized labor formally into the state structure. It made the unions amenable to accepting the trappings of power and the responsibility for it as a substitute for power itself. In close cooperation with mining capital, the state now proceeded to lay out the concrete terms of co-optation. Organized labor was about to be depoliticized by the very action of making it officially part of the political process. The fact that it had been physically broken made it possible for the state and mining capital to impose their own terms in exchange for granting official recognition to the trade unions.

NOTES

1. TCM 33(1)/1920, 22.12.1919.

2. ARTCM, 1921, p. 132.

3. De Kiewiet, *A History of South Africa*, p. 169.

4. Closure of several mines would cause unemployment and starvation, according to the 1920 *Report of the Low-Grade Mines Commission*: "Starving men are not given to be reasonable and a tendency to disturbances would almost inevitably assert itself," p. 15.

5. TCM 54/1920, 26.4.1920.

6. TCM 61/1919, "Private and confidential" note by Gemmill, 25.9.1919.

7. TCM 5/1920, 28.1.1920, 29.1.1920.

8. MM 847/21, Vol. 565.

9. ARTCM, 1921, p. 41.

10. TCM E 15d, 10.1.1922, 13.2.1922; Hessian, "An Investigation into the Causes of the Labour Agitation on the Witwatersrand, January to March 1922," pp. 31, 134.

11. Chamber of Mines of South Africa, *Statement of Evidence to the Commission of Inquiry into Labour Legislation* (Wiehahn Commission), 1977, Table O.

12. MM 3261/20, Vol. 544, 18.6.1921.

13. MM 1311/22, Vol. 617.

14. BRA, CML, Phillips to F. R. Phillips, 2.3.1922.

15. TCM M 41d, 14.11.1921; TCM E 15d, 18.11.1921.

16. For example, BRA, CML, 19.12.1917, Phillips to Wallers, instructing him to discuss with the government and protest against the increased wages given to *railwaymen*, though "in view of the higher cost of living and the direct concessions which the Industry has been obliged to make its own workmen, it may well have been impossible for Burton to resist the demands of the railway men."

17. TCM 5/1920, 12.1.1920; TCM 61/1919, 26.9.1919.

18. MM 2416/21, Vol. 581, Inspector of White Labour, Johannesburg, to Chief Inspector of White Labour, Pretoria, 11.7.1921; Hessian, "An Investigation," p. 31.

19. BRA, CML, 9.2.1920.

20. TCM L 16b, 27.5.1920.

21. MM 3024/20, Vol. 540, 5.6.1920.

22. MM 2416/21, Vol. 581.

23. TCM E 15d, 30.3.1921, 1.6.1921.

24. MM 2416/21, Vol. 581.

25. BRA, CML, Phillips (London) to Skinner, 22.6.1921.

26. MM 2416/21, Vol. 581.

27. Ibid., 11.7.1921.

28. TCM E 15d, 29.7.1921.

29. ARTCM, 1921, p. 42.

30. MM 1311/22, Vol. 617, Secretary for Mines to SAIF, 10.12.1921.

31. Ibid.

32. PM 1/1/422 File 3/22, 24.12.1921.

33. Hansard, 24.2.1922, quoted in Hessian, "An Investigation," p. 129. Also Hessian, p. 32, Hansard, 21.2.1922.

34. BRA, CML, 28.7.1921, Phillips to J. L. Leish; BRA, 2.3.1922, Phillips to F. R. Phillips.

35. TCM E 15d, 29.7.1921, 23.3.1922, 17.3.1922 (Executive Committee minutes).

36. Ibid., 9.12.1921, 18.10.1921.

37. TCM 41/1921.

38. TCM E 15d, 10.11.1921.

39. Ibid., 18.11.1921, describing conference of 15.11.1921.

40. MM 3153/21, Vol. 600, 3.11.1921.

41. BRA, CML, Phillips to Sothern Holland, 23.11.1921.

42. Ibid.

43. PM 1/1/422, No. 3/22, 9.12.1921.

44. TCM 23/1919, Gemmill to Wallers, 18.11.1919: ". . . The ease with which the extreme revolutionary sections of the [U.S.] labor party were

dealt with by a strong capitalist but nominally democratic government is an excellent object lesson."

45. TCM E 15d, 19.12.1921.

46. Ibid., 30.12.1921.

47. TCM 41/1921, 6.12.1921.

48. ARTCM, 1921, pp. 145–48.

49. Hessian, "An Investigation," and Hancock, *Smuts*, Vol. 2, both argue that the failure of the unions to attempt to use the machinery of the act shows that the unions were also eager for a confrontation; but it was fairly clear in the context of the time that the procedures would merely have made for a delay, not a settlement.

50. PM 1/1/422, File 3/22, 30.12.1921.

51. BRA, CML, 23.11.1921; PM 1/1/422, File 3/22, Vol. 1.

52. The best factual account is in Hessian's unpublished master's thesis. Extensive documentation is available in ARTCM, 1921, pp. 129 ff. See note 24 in Chapter 1 for citation of other accounts.

53. PM 1/1/424, 3/22, Vol. 15.

54. PM 1/1/422, 3/22, Vol. 2, 9.1.1922.

55. Hancock, *The Fields of Force*, pp. 67 ff. Hancock's two-volume biography constitutes a good but by no means definitive treatment of the enigmatic Smuts.

56. Elsewhere, he made it clear that the issue was labor's stubborn refusal to accept economic realities current throughout the world: "The men have chosen to be unbending just at a time when all over the world labour has either to bend or break before the wild economic storm which is raging," *Smuts Papers*, Vol. 5, p. 113, Smuts to M. C. Gillett, 23.2.1922.

57. ARTCM, 1921, p. 158.

58. PM 1/1/422, 3/22, Vol. 3, 30.1.1922.

59. PM 1/1/422, 3/22, Vol. 2, 21.1.1922.

60. Hancock, *The Fields of Force*, p. 71.

61. Ibid., p. 67; newspaper reports on 10.1.1922.

62. PM 1/1/422, 3/22, Vol. 3, 3.2.1922.

63. Hancock, *The Fields of Force*, pp. 71–72.

64. MM 2101/20, Vol. 521.

65. ARTCM, 1921, pp. 162–63 for full text.

66. MM 1311/22, Vol. 617; PM 1/1/424, 3/33, Vol. 15.

67. *Smuts Papers*, Vol. 5, pp. 128–29.

68. PM 1/1/442, 3/22, Vol. 15.

69. Hessian, "An Investigation," p. 155. These were traditional *rural* Afrikaner fighting units, now reduced to a shell of their former selves and beholden to the state.

70. PM 1/1/423, 3/22, Vol. 7, 14.3.1922, 15.3.1922.

71. *Smuts Papers*, Vol. 5, p. 115, 24.3.1922.

72. R. K. Cope, *Comrade Bill: The Life and Times of W. H. Andrews*, Cape Town, n.d., p. 244.

73. PM 1/1/424, 3/22, Vol. 15.

74. Cope, *Comrade Bill*, p. 272.

75. Hancock, *The Fields of Force*, p. 85; Humphriss and Thomas, *Benoni, Son of My Sorrow*, p. 170; Cope, *Comrade Bill*, p. 257; J. J. Fourie, *Afrikaners in die Goudstad, 1886–1924*, Pretoria, 1978, pp. 91–92.

76. Humphriss and Thomas, *Benoni*, p. 169, 192.

77. Ibid., pp. 203, 206–208, 257.

78. J. J. Fourie, *Afrikaners in die Goudstad*, p. 91.

79. PM 1/1/424, 3/22, Vol. 2, 27.3.1922.

80. *Smuts Papers*, Vol. 5, pp. 129–30.

81. Hessian, "An Investigation," p. 155; communication to author from the Office of Comptroller (Directorate, Documentation Service), S.A. Defence Force, Ref. No. KOMPT/DOK D/19/3/5/2, 20 May 1976, which details a "Mobilization Plan B," calling for 8,000 commandos from Krugersdorp, Potchefstroom, Heidelberg, Standerton, Pretoria, Bethal, Ermelo, and Middelburg to be called up to comprise the great majority of a total force of 12,976. Unfortunately, no details are known of "Plan A," and these figures merely give an indication of the importance of the rural Afrikaner commandos rather than a detailed breakdown of their actual participation.

82. Ibid. Follow-up letter, dated 3 September 1976. By March 16, the various detachments of the S.A. Police—probably under 3,000 men in total—who had been under military command during the revolt were once again in charge of public order. The army took over patrolling duties and was ordered merely to render assistance to the police "when called upon."

83. PM 1/1/424, 3/22, Vol. 9, Vol. 11, 16.3.1922, 20.3.1922. Simons and Simons, *Class and Colour*, p. 296, point out that in spite of the contemporary accounts blaming the revolt on a Bolshevik conspiracy, not one communist stood trial for treason.

84. D. W. Kruger, *The Age of the Generals*, Johannesburg, 1961, p. 123, blames the revolt on the Council of Action and does not even mention the existence of the miners' commandos; J. J. Fourie, *Afrikaners in die Goudstad*, pp. 91–92, documents the rise of the commandos, only to blame the communist leaders of the Council of Action for "misleading" the Afrikaner miners, some of whom received long-term sentences. Besides the blatant distortion of the locus of responsibility involved here, it should be pointed out that the imprisoned strikers were speedily released under the Strike Condonation Act of 1922.

6

The Co-optation of Organized Labor, 1922–1924

I thank you for your voices, thank you;
Your most sweet voices.

—Coriolanus, II.iii.

The breaking of the 1922 strike and the revolt resulted, as had happened in 1907 and 1914, in the immediate slashing of white wages; they fell by 17.7 percent in real terms (see Table 1) and considerably more in cash terms. White earnings as a percentage of total gold mining revenue fell from 24.8 percent in 1921 to 18 percent in 1922, according to the figures published by the Government Mining Engineer. In 1907 and 1914, mining capital and the state had allowed their satisfaction with the cost reductions on the mines to blunt their desire to follow up their advantage in a truly concerted way. The aftermath of the events of 1922, however, showed that they had learned a lesson from the previous strikes.

There had been an intensive propaganda campaign since 1921 to justify various measures taken by South Africa's two major employers—mining capital and the state—against organized white labor and to mobilize public support for those measures. After the 1922 revolt, the campaign did not fade away but, if anything, broadened and intensified. The employers were no longer seeking merely cost-cutting measures; they were seeking a far more comprehensive reorganization of the industrial structure itself. The method and scope of the cost-cutting measures has had enduring significance, and they will be dealt with first, before considering how South Africa's industrial structure was transformed.

THE SPOILS OF VICTORY

The changes brought about by the various employers were, of course, uneven. Within the gold mining industry itself, there were considerable differences. Some mines merely paid lower wages, employed fewer miners, and reduced contractors' incentives. Others, like the large conglomerate Crown Mines, set out immediately to reorganize their entire method of operation.[1] In general, those mines with short anticipated lives made fewer operational alterations.

In spite of the variety and unevenness of the immediate post-1922 changes, three major areas can be distinguished: (1) changes in the ratio of black to white miners; (2) reorganization and mechanization of the underground labor force; and (3) the attack on contract labor.

The first change—the so-called attack on the color bar—had the most publicized result. The proportion of blacks to whites in the mine labor force increased from 8.2:1 to 11.4:1—the highest figure ever recorded for the gold mines. In 1923, it dropped to 10.0:1; but it did not return to the 1917–1921 levels until 1937. The color bar's scope was thus reduced, but it was far from abolished. Nor had the mining employers ever seriously thought that the abolition of the color bar was politically feasible.[2] (See Table 5.)

Table 5   Employment on the Gold Mines, Selected Years, 1918–1937

Year	Blacks	Whites	Ratio (B:W)
1918	179,628	22,764	7.9
1920	176,057	22,198	7.9
1921	172,694	21,036	8.2
1922	161,351	14,207	11.4
1923	177,855	17,727	10.0
1924	178,395	18,457	9.7
1926	181,577	19,713	9.2
1929	193,221	21,949	8.8
1934	249,200	28,334	8.8
1937	303,087	38,327	7.9

Source: ARTCM, 1980.

The second area of change was the seldom-mentioned but relatively more severe singling out for attack of highly paid white *underground* labor (the statutory color bar generally applied only to underground labor). The proportion of blacks to whites underground increased from 13.6:1 to 18.8:1 in 1922. The reason for this tendency, which surprised and perturbed the Inspector of Mines,[3] was an abortive attempt to make the miner once more an "all-round man," dispensing with "redundant," semi-skilled (generally Afrikaner) supervisors. This also explains why the percentage of South African-born miners *fell* in 1922, the only year between 1907 and the present that that had happened.[4] The attempt was short-lived, however: the predominance of the all-round man was not to return.

The economically rational reorganization, begun in 1907, which cut the numbers of skilled, all-around miners, was now brought to fruition. Although semi-skilled supervisors were at first dispensed with in large numbers as "unproductive and redundant," the tendency did not last. Eventually, the foreign-trained artisan miners began to be squeezed out again, and new, locally born men were engaged to do semi-skilled supervisory work. This time, however, they were required to do a great deal more supervision.

The increased supervision done by each white miner allowed the employers to make proportionately more use of black miners. A parallel reorganization of the black labor force and mechanization of many of their jobs thus took place. Together, these developments resulted in dramatic increases in both black and white worker efficiency: productivity increased by 15–20 percent for blacks in the year after the strike and almost doubled for whites in the same time. (See Figure 1.)

A third area of change, also inadequately analyzed to date, was the attack on contract labor. Contractors were a privileged and generally highly paid group of white miners whose earnings fluctuated with the results achieved by the "gangs" of black laborers they supervised. The contractors suffered slightly more than did the average white miner in the aftermath of 1922: pay per shift dropped from 49 shillings and 10 pence to 30 shillings and 4 pence, compared to 33 shillings and 5 pence and 21 shillings for noncontract miners. Their wages also recovered more slowly subsequently.

Behind these alterations, other related changes were occurring.

Figure 1   The Growth of Productivity

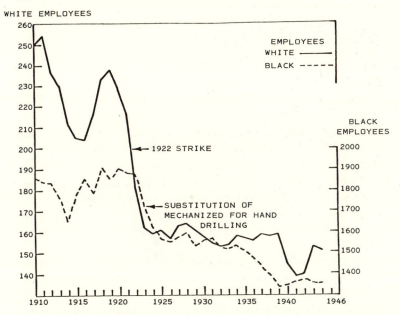

WHITE EMPLOYEES

EMPLOYEES
WHITE ———
BLACK - - - -

BLACK EMPLOYEES

← 1922 STRIKE

← SUBSTITUTION OF MECHANIZED FOR HAND DRILLING

Source: ARGMEs, collated in *Economic Aspects of the Gold Mining Industry,* Report No. 11 of the Social and Economic Planning Council, UG32-1948 Pretoria, 1948, p. 30.

*Miners at work per 1,000 tons (about 1,100 metric tons) hoisted per day on large producing mines, 1910–1944.

Though they are not as easy to quantify, they go to the heart of what the struggle of 1922 was about. Mining employers had said often enough in private[5] that their aim was not merely to reduce wages, but to regain control of the industry and reduce costs by increasing productivity. This they proceeded to do. Mine managers were once again made virtual dictators and were encouraged to take whatever steps were necessary to cut costs. By the beginning of 1923, average working costs had dropped from 25 shillings and 10 pence in 1921 to about 20 shillings per ton. (See Table 6.)

The renewed dominance of the mine managements following the strike is not always fully reflected in the figures. There was, for example, a widespread victimization of the strikers, many of whom

Table 6   Working Costs on the Gold Mines, Selected Years, 1911–1939
(Per ton Milled, in Shillings and Pence)

1911 — 18/1	1919 — 23/0	1923 — 20/1
1916 — 18/2	1920 — 25/8	1926 — 19/1
1917 — 19/3	1921 — 25/10	1929 — 19/10
1918 — 21/7	1922 — 23/7	1935 — 18/11
		1939 — 19/5

Source: Ralph Horwitz, *The Political Economy of South Africa,* London, 1967,
    p. 237.

could never regain their jobs. A large number of the miners
employed in 1924 were new to the gold mines and were employed
even though experienced men—exstrikers—were applying for the
same jobs. Thus, a higher percentage of the prestrike workers were
purged by the reorganization than appears in the raw employment
figures.

This understatement was later noted by the Secretary for Labour
for the new Department of Labour that was created by the Pact
government. The Secretary, however, made no further suggestion
that the government should take action on behalf of the workers.[6]
The hiring of "new" men was no doubt an attempt to depoliticize as
well as to discipline the organized labor force, to staff the mines
with men ignorant of trade-union practices and ideology, and at
lower wages. The overall effect was to reestablish the long-term
trend of the accelerating Afrikanerization of the organized labor
force (see Table 2).

Besides the drastic reorganization of the labor force, important
technical advances brought a greater degree of mechanization.
Pneumatic equipment and other mining tools (which had made
great advances in Europe during the war) were introduced on a
large scale to South Africa for the first time. The light jackhammer
drill, in particular, was important: it replaced the heavy recip-
rocating type of machine drill and almost eliminated hand stoping
(that is, chiselling holes at the face to take charges of dynamite).[7]
The combined effect of the reorganization and the technological
revolution led to an unbroken decade of increases in labor productivity and restored the prosperity, or at least the viability, of the
industry.

It also resulted in great bitterness, however, among the white workers. The employers were notably unconcerned, but the government, which still needed the miners' votes, made some half-hearted attempts to persuade the TCM to be gracious victors. Smuts, for example, received a letter from a friend pointing out that the TCM "should not be allowed to forget that the country saved the mines because it realised that it was a National asset,"[8] and asking that the employers make sacrifices to help unemployed Afrikaners. Smuts wrote unofficially to Wallers a few days later, asking for the employers to be humane but refraining from alleging that the industry owed its survival to the state.[9] He was not hopeful that the TCM could be convinced, however,[10] and he proved to be correct.

THE LEGITIMATION CAMPAIGN

Mining capital was more concerned with reducing working costs than with placating the defeated strikers. But it was developing a far greater awareness of the need to mobilize the support of various outside groups and interests. In June 1922, the Gold Producers' Committee was formed, partly out of the desire "for an entirely new start," and partly because it was felt that the 1922 strike should have been handled more tightly and diplomatically.[11] Buckle, still nominally the TCM President, was made a scapegoat and was excluded from the GPC; Gemmill, far more culpable than Buckle, nevertheless survived as GPC Secretary and was the author of its first constitution.

Gemmill had orchestrated the antistrike propaganda, and he wrote a confidential note to the GPC a few months later, reminding it how successful the propaganda had been. He suggested, not for the first time, that a regular propaganda service be run by the TCM, modeled on the "new profession" in the United States, where there were "several firms engaged in nothing else but propaganda for groups of industries."[12] Gemmill was particularly keen to start an industrial "News Service," which would not only distribute "news" that was "favourable to the employer," but also "information from all over the world in favour of the employing class." The South African Industrial News Service, edited by Owen Letcher, a well-known journalist, was formed a month later. By October

1924, it had succeeded in getting South African newspapers to publish 8,032 of its releases.[13]

Gemmill was a born manipulator of public opinion, adept at tricks such as arranging questions to be asked in Parliament that only the employers could answer. The TCM's answers would then be presented to the public through the mouths of government spokesmen. He next spearheaded a move by the TCM to consolidate the cost-cutting gains of 1922 by directly influencing Parliament and public opinion.

Mining capital had always vacillated about its political role. Directly after Union in 1910, the most important mining employers (including Phillips) had entered Parliament and had openly represented the employers. Gemmill, briefing the new "outsider" TCM President, H. O. Buckle, in 1920, explained: "Subsequently, however, the policy was definitely adopted that the Industry should take no part in politics, it being thought that its importance to the country ensured that it would be well looked after by the Government and fairly treated in the House." But, the letter continued lugubriously, "This policy has proved a mistaken one; and now [in 1920], not only is the Industry the subject of inroads from all sides, but it is still looked at with suspicion and there is no one either inside or outside of the House to take up cudgels on its behalf."[14]

This view of mining capital—that it was politically isolated and without influential spokesmen—is a far cry from the generally accepted view that, for example, sees the Unionist party (or even the S.A. party) as its mouthpiece. However, it was a view shared by Smuts, who told Buckle that "nothing in the interests of the mines ever got any support from the Rand members, which made it very difficult for the government to do anything,"[15] and by Patrick Duncan, one of the most influential of the Unionists and, after the party's absorption in 1921, a leading S.A. party member. The general political unpopularity of mining capital was frequently deceptive: members would bitterly attack it in Parliament to court popularity with their constituents, but their actions would not match their words, as the various LGM Committee reports testify.

Nevertheless, the employers decided, after the 1922 strike, to seek the direct support of various third parties. Gemmill suggested that "expenditure on this work would be recouped many times over by its results. Public opinion in South Africa is instinctively hostile to the mining industry, but a well-conducted propaganda system on the lines indicated above would alter this atmosphere."[16] Part of the effect of that campaign was to exert a degree of pressure on Parliament by addressing public opinion directly.

The period after the strike was clearly going to be a very sensitive one since Parliament and the government had to attempt to put together a viable labor-relations system that would not again threaten the stability of the state. The first step in that direction was the appointment of the Brace Commission, or Mining Industry Board, in April 1922.[17] Gemmill later pointedly justified his arguments to the GPC for a massive propaganda assault by citing the successful taming of the Brace Commission:

> As is well known, the Board at the beginning was hostile to the industry. By steadily placing before it the true facts of the position (biased no doubt in favour of the industry) and controverting everything said against the industry, the attitude of the Board was entirely changed, and at the end was generally favourable.[18]

Gemmill was being too modest. The industrial conciliation machinery set out in the Brace Commission was, in fact, as the government Inspector of White Labour pointed out in a private memorandum,

> Without doubt the Chamber's scheme; the workers' representatives had very little to do with the draft. The trade unions were in a hopeless position to do other than to agree to the scheme. They were hopelessly outnumbered and in their disorganized state had to accept any scheme.[19]

Later, in a letter to Sir Ernest Oppenheimer, Gemmill admitted as much, saying that the Brace Commission's conciliation scheme was "really drawn up by the Industry."[20]

After the completion of the report, William Brace wrote to Smuts that the conciliation machinery was designed to be applied to all important industries, though only the employers and employees of the mining industry had agreed to follow its provisions.[21] Less than three months later, a draft of a new bill, for all industries and incorporating the Brace machinery, was in the hands of the Minister of Mines, F. S. Malan. Gemmill, who had proved to the GPC how effective his propaganda machine could be, was now given a free hand to ensure that the final legislation did not differ too significantly from the scheme that the employers themselves had covertly drawn up, the so-called Brace Plan.

THE ORCHESTRATION OF THE 1924 INDUSTRIAL CONCILIATION (I.C.) ACT

The use of force alone is but *temporary*. It may subdue for a moment; but it does not remove the necessity of subduing again: and a nation is not governed, which is perpetually to be conquered.
                    —Edmund Burke, on American taxation, 1774

The employers' reorganization of the industry was paralleled by the state's reorganization of industrial relations. The Brace Commission was appointed on April 15, 1922, less than a month after the use of force had ended both the revolt and the strike. It reported on September 29, with a relatively new but very significant warning, that "the interests of the State should be regarded by every section of industrial life, however important and powerful that section might be."[22]

A month later, the Under Secretary for Mines wrote to F. S. Malan, the Minister of Mines, about the urgent need for legislation to give concrete expression to the report's recommendations.[23] Within three days, the Minister authorized the drafting of a new bill based on the aborted 1913–1914 legislation (see Chapter 3). Kotze, the Government Mining Engineer, who was one of the four members of the Brace Commission, was instructed on November 3 to prepare the new bill, and by November 25, he had completed a first draft. The draft was approved by the Inspector of White Labour, R. H. Miller.

Within a week, Kotze was forwarding his third draft. An analysis shows that fifteen of eighteen clauses in this draft were taken over, sometimes in condensed form, from the aborted 1914 bill, which also failed to be passed in 1919.[24] The three new clauses proposed that trade unions be registered and become corporate bodies capable of suing and being sued; that machinery for state-backed conciliation boards be established; and that strikes or lockouts were illegal unless conciliation machinery (to settle disputes) had already been tried. Previously, under the Transvaal Industrial Disputes Prevention Act, state mediation had to be specifically requested. Now it becomes compulsory to try state intervention before strikes or lockouts. Kotze also asked that the Minister consider another alternative, which would rely on public opinion rather than on the threat of legal action to force disputants to use the machinery first.[25] That option was not taken up.

On December 11, after the intercession of the Associated Scientific and Technical Societies of South Africa and of the Prime Minister's office, Kotze added a clause that would make compulsory arbitration (otherwise eschewed in the bill) obligatory in the case of "essential services" such as power stations and water suppliers. The same day, Miller met trade-union officials and claimed to have transformed their initial "point-blank opposition," particularly to the compulsory use of conciliation machinery, to unanimous agreement "individually." This reservation probably meant that they were unsure whether their members would also agree.[26]

Finally, on December 29, Smuts made several amendments to the new bill, the most important being that the conciliation machinery should only deal with large issues, not "matters of minor importance," and that strike ballots be left under the control of the unions because "government control of ballots will meet with a good deal of opposition."[27] On January 9, 1923, the first version of the Industrial Conciliation (I.C.) Bill was published.[28]

Though the unions had been consulted in the prepublication stage, they do not seem to have inspired, or even asked for, any amendments. Smuts's amendments in favor of organized labor originated with his anticipation of parliamentary opposition, and they were effected in spite of the fact that the trade unions had agreed to less favorable terms.[29]

The TCM did not take the initiative in asking for the formal co-optation of organized labor, but it accepted the fact that the use of force alone to settle industrial disputes could not solve the problem of governing the industry. Having accepted the state's insistence that industrial relations be institutionalized, the employers played a vital part both in 1914 and in 1922 in drafting and amending specific provisions of the institutional framework. Not surprisingly, then, they were content with the first published Bill.

The Bill, of course, applied to all organized industries, and some of its most important aspects originated outside the gold mining industry. For example, it made provision for permanent employer-employee councils, if both employers' organizations and trade unions wanted them. The agreements of such a council were made legally binding and could be imposed on a whole industry if the Minister decided that the negotiators' organizations were representative.

The South African model for these industrial councils was probably the National Industrial Council of the Printing and Newspaper Industry of South Africa, a voluntary body representing employers and employees that had successfully prevented any major labor disputes in the printing industry from its inauguration in November 1919. The Secretary for Mines and Industries wrote to the council in 1920 saying "that this Department highly appreciated the great advantage, not only to the trade but to the Country, of such an organisation as your Council. . . ."[30]

In fact, the advantage of industrial councils within the printing trade (and others, too) was limited to the large established employers and trade unions. They could get together and agree to barter industrial peace for higher wages because it was possible to pass on the increased wage bill to the consumer by raising prices. The only threat to this joint monopoly was the smaller firms who conducted their business "on unfair lines" by paying less and selling cheaper. If, however, minimum-wage rates for everyone in the printing industry were to be set by government proclamation (by establishing an industrial council under the I.C. Bill), the smaller firms and labor groups would suffer. The printers' voluntary National Industrial Council made this very clear in writing to the government after the publication of the I.C. Bill saying, in effect, "We will provide industrial peace if you provide us the means of forcing higher wages on the whole industry."[31]

The joint monopoly implications of the state's sanctioning large employers and trade unions to represent complete industries have been ably dealt with elsewhere.[32] It has also been pointed out that the joint monopoly system of collective bargaining tended to create cleavages within both organized labor and capital. Within labor, it opened up differences between industrial and craft unions because the craft unions could more effectively protect the benefits gained through the bargaining system by maintaining a closed shop.

Within capital, it opened up differences between primary and secondary industries. The primary industries, including the mining industry, objected to the joint monopoly system because higher wages could not, in their case, be passed on to the consumer in the form of higher prices: world markets determined these prices. The parliamentary Select Committee on the I.C. Bill, which sat from February 12 to May 18, 1923, provides some examples of these sorts of cleavages.[33]

They never became a serious problem, however, largely because joint monopolies (in the form of state-chartered industrial councils) were not imposed on either large employers or trade unions in any industry, but were voluntary: the state left it to the large (or "representative") employer and employee organizations to decide if they wanted joint monopolies.

The nature of the gold mining industry determined that there were to be no "small firms" and that the bulk of the white labor force was in industrial unions, as opposed to craft unions, or not unionized at all. Thus, no industrial council has even been formed in the mining industry, in spite of considerable pressure from various governments to do so. The I.C. Bill also made provision for *ad hoc* conciliation boards to be constituted, especially in the event of industrial disputes. This was the procedure actually adopted in the mining industry. All large organized industries, then, would be legally mandated to try state conciliation procedures before lockouts or strikes, but they were to have the choice of procedures.

In broad outline, all the large employers supported the I.C. Bill because it promised a greater degree of labor stability through statutory underpinning of industrial agreements; many of the established trade unions also supported it because they sought higher wages through joint monopolies rather than through strikes. Even the National and Labour parties "were hard put to it to offer vigorous opposition . . ." to the I.C. Bill.[34]

Only the once-powerful South African Mine Workers' Union

(SAMWU), which represented the semi-skilled and unskilled whites who stood to lose the most from a joint monopoly structure, was in the position to offer significant opposition to the I.C. Bill. But it had been so crushed and demoralized by the events of 1922 that its opposition to the proposed new structure was negligible. Crawford, General Secretary of the South African Industrial Federation (SAIF) and spokesman for the SAMWU, lamented the loss of the strike power and publicly criticized the joint monopoly implications of the I.C. Bill.[35] But in private, he had been prepared to accept the first I.C. Bill (the one least favorable to labor) and even sneered at other trade unions that sought a Select Committee to amend it.[36]

It should be noted, however, that the unions were well aware of what they were losing in signing away their effective (though not *de jure*) right to strike. To be truly effective, strikers had to be able to control the timing of their strike. To agree to institutionalized delay was to destroy the power of the lightning strike. Various trade unions, estimated by the Department of Mines and Industries to represent 25,000 workers, met on February 5 and May 2, 1922, and prepared two comprehensive memoranda that made this very clear:

> We recognise . . . that by so agreeing that there shall not be a strike until the Conciliation Machinery has been used and for a fortnight afterwards we are depriving ourselves of our most effective weapon, viz. that of the immediate strike and giving the Employers concerned a period of at least six weeks in which to make arrangements to employ men in our place if we strike.[37]

They pointed out that the delay could be stretched out almost "indefinitely" by various stratagems. This, of course, was precisely the hope of the employers.[38] In spite of their articulate skepticism, however, the trade unions supported the principle of state-sanctioned conciliation: ". . . We are agreed that the system of Conciliation before Strike shall have a full and fair trial, and if it proves a failure it will not be from lack of effort on our part."[39] The Inspector of White Labor noted with some surprise the subdued and conciliatory attitude of the union representatives; so did the

Secretary for Mines and Industries. The unions made many suggestions for amendments of specific details, but few, if any, challenged
the basic principles of the Bill.

The reasons for the failure of the unions to oppose the I.C. Bill
are complex. The breaking of the strike and the attempted revolution by the commandos resulted in large numbers of resignations
from the unions. They had, in any case, been weaker and far more
divided before the strike than their militance suggested to the
public. Smuts, Wallers, Gemmill, and Phillips, among others, had
been well aware of this weakness and were more concerned about
public opinion than about the resistance of the unions.

After the strike, the unions, particularly the more brittle industrial unions, were virtually smashed, bankrupted, and even less
able to speak with authority for their rank-and-file membership.
The SAIF had split, and two federated unions now purported to
speak for the white worker in general. The rivalry between the two
was petty, but it was strong enough at times to override the
strenuous pursuit of the workers' best interests. Crawford, the
erstwhile radical, was a notable example of the selling out of his
members' interests and of his indulgence in personal whims and
rivalries.

The final, and possibly most important, reason for the unions'
acceptance of the I.C. Bill was that it left a great deal of power in
the hands of the Cabinet minister administering it. Even before the
election of the Pact, organized labor realized its basic inability to
dominate the employers, and it hoped that the state's power might
redress the balance. In its weakened position after the strike, it was
more prepared than ever before to put its fate in the hands of the
state.

The principle of establishing a new framework of industrial relations was, therefore, supported by both capital and organized
labor; many of the details, some of them important, were not. The
first I.C. Bill satisfied mining capital, which was itself largely instrumental in drawing up the Bill's major provisions. After the
Select Committee, however, a greatly expanded bill was published
at the end of May 1923 that included several new provisions less
favorable to the employers.[40]

One provision, in particular, allowing individual workers with
personal grievances to invoke the conciliation machinery, incensed

the TCM. The employers claimed that the previous conciliation machinery had been unworkable precisely because it was most frequently used for petty disputes between individual workers and management, thus undermining management's authority.

H. O. Buckle, the TCM President, cabled from Cape Town that F. S. Malan, the Minister of Mines, was to blame for the new, unfavorable I.C. Bill and that Malan had proposed all but one of the amendments. This was unusual, as Malan would normally be expected to defend his own bill: "Minister himself moved all amendments changing comparatively harmless Bill into measure most hostile to Employers. Obviously put up job. Have pointed this out to David Harris [a mining magnate M.P.] who will speak on it. Do everything to arouse other employers."[41]

Gemmill proceeded to do exactly that: he orchestrated a campaign during June 1923 that mobilized virtually every large employer organization in South Africa except the agricultural associations: the Bill did not apply to farming labor. He was particularly furious that the TCM had not been given the chance to give evidence to the Select Committee. Malan had told Buckle that no evidence would be taken, but extensive trade-union testimony was in fact taken, and advance copies of the report were held back from the TCM. Gemmill responded by flooding Malan and other members of the government with complaints, memoranda, and suggested amendments.

Virtually every time he sent a cable or letter, he sent copies to the many employer associations with whom he had established contact after returning from the International Labour Conference. And he appended requests that they protest as well. Most of them then sent identical letters or cables, with copies to the TCM. They included at least forty organizations drawn from, *inter alia*, the banks, the Associated Chambers of Commerce, and the Federated Chamber of Industries.

By July 12, Gemmill was boasting that the Bill would be scrapped because of employer protest, and on October 5, the Secretary for Mines and Industries wrote a letter to the TCM, the contents of which Gemmill found "highly satisfactory both in substance and in tone" and which confirmed that Malan had agreed to the suggested amendments of the amendments. Gemmill later sent copies of that letter to all the employer organizations, adding somewhat gloatingly: "You will observe that the Minister is adopting a reasonable attitude in regard to the Bill."[42]

A month later, however, the *Rand Daily Mail* reported that the unions objected to some of the TCM-inspired amendments.[43] Shortly thereafter, Warington Smyth wrote to the TCM, once again reverting to several of the Select Committee's clauses. Gemmill, in turn, went back on the attack, arguing that the lack of industrial discipline before the strike was disastrous. The latest I.C. Bill would reestablish the opportunity for interference by allowing individual employees to bypass managers and utilize the machinery for minor personal issues. This would be tragic after all the post-1922 reorganization: "At great cost, the Industry has eliminated these conditions."[44] The letter writing campaign was cranked up once more, and within a week, six large employer organizations had protested to the Minister and forwarded copies to the TCM.

The government backed down again with alacrity. The TCM was sent a copy of the proposed new bill, with the crucial amendments it had insisted on restoring reinserted in Warington Smyth's handwriting. Sections 4 and 10 were changed yet again so that only a "representative" number of employees could apply for a conciliation board (the Minister being the final judge) and conciliation boards could not deal with the conditions of service of individual employees.[45]

A clause forcing employers to allow workers to join unions if they wished, Section 22, was deleted at the TCM's request. The TCM regarded the deletion as vital because of the position of officials "who," Gemmill said, "in no circumstances should be allowed in the workers' unions."[46] The 1921 Crown Mines strike had been fought largely on that issue. Even before the 1922 strike, the employers, or some of them, began to force workers out of the unions by signing on men as "officials," who were compelled to agree not to join a union. This probably accounts, in part at least, for the large decline in trade-union memberships: from 135,000 in 1920 to 108,000 in 1921 to 82,000 in 1922 for all South African unions.[47]

The Inspector of White Labour was aware of the practice. He noted that at ERPM, one of the largest gold mines, men were being employed "as officials who can never be officials in the accepted meaning of the term and . . . compel(led) or induce(d) . . . to leave the trade union . . ." ERPM was also introducing a scheme to pay engine drivers monthly: ". . . One of the conditions of acceptance is that they are not members of a Trade Union . . ." And some companies were even making daily paid employees agree not to join the unions. The Inspector recommended that the TCM be threatened with the reintroduction of clause 22,[48] but it was not done (neither, apparently, did the Pact government do so subsequently). Nevertheless, the employers were approached informally, and they agreed to stamp out such practices if they existed. But the ranks of the "officials" continued to grow. Today, they comprise about 50 percent of white mineworkers and can, with the help of (nonunionized) black miners, easily keep the mines going, even in the event of a total strike of union members.

This was to be Malan's final vacillation, having changed his mind on crucial details four times since the publication of the first Bill in January 1923. On January 5, 1924, the third version of the Bill was published, containing all the major amendments the TCM had asked for. Much of Gemmill's time in the next three months was devoted to mobilizing employer support, putting intense pressure on Malan not to succumb to pressure to restore the "objectionable clauses." There was nothing subtle about the campaign. The employer organizations generally simply transferred Gemmill's suggested protest to their own letterhead paper and sent it otherwise unaltered to the Minister. Nevertheless, it had the desired effect. Malan stood firm at last, and the I.C. Act became law on March 31, 1924.

Gemmill's campaign built on the propaganda ideas and organization he had been forming since his first exposure to U.S. techniques in 1919, but its intensity was unprecedented for South Africa. He unsuccessfully tried a similar campaign in 1925 against the Wage Bill. It is doubtful whether such all-out campaigns were ever tried subsequently by capital, partly because there were few issues on which all employer opinion, including nonmining employers, was so united; partly because U.S. direct lobbying techniques do not necessarily work as well in the Westminster parliamentary system; partly because Cabinet ministers as pliable as F. S. Malan are few and far between.[49] It is clear that the GPC allowed Gemmill enormous scope to act on his own, even though one purpose of its formation had been to regain control over industrial policy for the mining groups at the expense of the TCM bureaucracy. Illustrating Gemmill's relative autonomy was his technique of replying immediately to letters from Malan or his department and then circulating *ex post facto* copies of his own letters to the GPC.

He was not allowed to make decisions of principle, but he did introduce new tactical approaches to the vital relationship of the state and capital. His abrasive, almost contemptuous tone was noted by Warington Smyth:

> The Department has noticed . . . during the last twelve months a marked change in the tone of communications from the Chamber of Mines which is in consonance with the general attitude which seems to have been adopted. . . . I will ask Mr. Malan to discuss the matter with the Prime Minister.[50]

Smyth was mainly concerned that this change of tone was indicative of the tough treatment being handed out to white miners in the wake of their crushing defeat in 1922—which treatment, he felt, was greatly resented and could eventually lead to further industrial turmoil.[51]

The TCM's success in imposing some of its own tactical objectives on the final I.C. Act, moreover, should not be overemphasized. The *principle* of the legislation—to force labor and capital to negotiate under the state umbrella—was firmly established by the I.C. Act, but this principle was accepted rather than initiated by the TCM. Wallers, speaking as TCM President, was even somewhat churlish about the I.C. Act:

> I do not believe that conciliation by Act of Parliament can ever hope to achieve anything approaching that which can be achieved voluntarily by free direct discussion between employer and employee . . . what is known as the Brace plan provided for this in a liberal and reasonable manner. . . .[52]

The TCM's reservations, of course, show more about the brevity of its memory than about the real effect on the industry of the new legislation. Mining capital had never been slow to seek shelter under the state umbrella during the economic storms before the crushing of organized labor in 1922. But it was slow, now that the danger was temporarily past, to realize that a new industrial order had necessarily to emerge.

THE NEW INDUSTRIAL ORDER

The I.C. Act of 1924 created an industrial order of state-chartered joint monopolies and of nominally self-governing industries narrowly circumscribed by the vital interests of the state. The idea of a fully autonomous gold mining industry had always been largely an illusion. Now the merest remnant of the illusion remained, and there can be little doubt that the state was saving mining capital from itself by insisting that even that remnant be stripped away.[53]

In this respect, organized labor grasped the situation more quickly in 1922. It lamented but accepted its loss of the strike weapon as a necessary compromise: "I have received her dowry," someone in a similar situation had once said, "and in return have parted with my authority."[54] Labor had been forced to part with its authority on trust, in the hope of a future dowry from a sympathetic state. Capital had immediately received enough of its dowry to give it the short-lived and ludicrous hope that the dowry might be used in a highly unorthodox way: to finance a divorce from the state.

The idea was sensibly dropped, however, and capital's dowry came to fulfill the traditional role of dowries: it cemented what was to be a long, generally very happy, and, to date, unbroken marriage with the state. This limited sense was the only one in which it could be said that the mining capitalists lost a war; they had to accept a "dependent" position in a marriage. As in the case of most individual marriages, however, the dependence of partners is mutual, though each brings something different to the marriage.

To analyze marriage as merely a relationship of dominator and dominated, moreover, is as much a travesty in the case of the state and mining industry as it is in the case of individual human beings. The type of individual marriage most analogous to that between the South African state and the gold mining industry is that found in many traditional African societies: the state is the hunter and protector of the overall order; its wives control the household. The subtleties of the power relationships within such symbiotic relationships are immense, which is why zero-sum conceptualizations are so sterile.[55]

Notwithstanding the TCM's propagandistic mutterings that the industry did not need a protector, the employers were extremely satisfied with the final form of the I.C. Act. Even capital's loss of "autonomy" was nominal compared to labor's loss: the loss of capital's right to lock workers out before going through negotiating procedures was unimportant compared to the workers' loss of the right to the lightning strike. Moreover, no one was compelled to form an industrial council, the permanent negotiating body that gave the state its maximum leverage over industries. The employers, consequently, had no intention of forming one.

The I.C. Act, then, achieved the comprehensive institutionalization of the principle that justified state intervention to enforce industrial peace, a principle sought by governments with varying degrees of urgency since before the 1910 unification of the four provinces of South Africa. It did not, however, have equal impact on capital and labor, though it nominally applied to both. The effect of the new industrial order was formally to co-opt organized labor into the leadership structure in order to avert threats to the stability of that structure (see also Chapter 3). The manner of the co-optation was such that organized labor "shared . . . responsibility for power rather than power itself." Labor had lost the power to use the strike as a real political and economic weapon; it had been depoliticized by its very incorporation into the political and administrative structure of the state.

The employers, on the other hand, were also, to some extent, formally co-opted. But they did not draw their major power from the right to lock workers out *en masse*. They were more interested in being free to alter the conditions of service of individual employees without notice and without resorting to formal procedures, and that right had been written into the I.C. Act with the help of Gemmill's concerted lobbying campaign. Thus, the formal co-optation of capital was nominal, and we must continue to look elsewhere (though not necessarily in the same places as before) to unravel the nature of the state-capital relationship.

It should be pointed out, however, that the I.C. Act left the Minister who administered it—after 1924 this was the Minister of Labor, Creswell—with enormous discretionary powers. The

Minister could decide how many workers were "sufficiently representative" and whether their complaints should be submitted to conciliation procedures or merely dealt with by the employer or mine manager. He could also decide whether disputes were "issues of principle" or individual disputes between employer and employee.

Although he could not legally impose a settlement on either party if they had not previously agreed to be bound to one, he had the considerable power of publicizing conciliation board decisions and invoking "public opinion." Both sides realized that the I.C. Act was one more example of the state's accretion of administrative power, or "government by regulations."[56] Finally, they were also aware of the increasingly sophisticated technique of governing by the *threat* of regulations, which has been referred to earlier as government by the sword of Damocles principle.

The Minister's interpretation of the I.C. Act was recognized by both labor and capital to be more important than the interpretation of the judiciary.[57] But in terms of the electorate in general, the law gave the incumbent Minister ample opportunity to appear to be even-handed while, in fact, he could and did favor one of the disputants.[58] This, of course, is another major illustration of the efficacy of formal co-optation:[59] it creates apparent distance between the state and the warring parties by setting up regular procedural machinery while, in fact, giving the state increased control over the shape and outcome of the conflict.

Formal co-optation also creates the opportunity for the state to *refrain* from making decisions while the machinery is grinding through the motions of resolving a dispute. Thus, although the actual provisions of the I.C. Act were tilted in favor of the employer, a determined Minister of Labour had a great deal of power to create enormous problems for capital on the issue of white labor, if he wished to do so. This could be achieved either by action or inaction, by making decisions or nondecisions.

What remains to be considered is the state-industry relationship after 1924 and the measures taken by the Pact government to give more comprehensive and systematic form to the new industrial order whose foundations had been so securely laid by the South African party government.[60] Most important, however, it is necessary to analyze the impact of the new government-industry relationship on labor and capital and on the ongoing development of an interventionist state.

NOTES

1. MM 658/22, Vol. 609, Johannesburg Inspector of Mines, March monthly report.

2. Johnstone, *Class, Race and Gold*, p. 149, convincingly argues the same point but fails to note its significance: that the mining capitalists achieved what they were aiming for in 1922, and that the election of 1924, and the subsequent reentrenchment of the statutory color bar, did not reverse this.

3. MM 658/22, Vol. 609.

4. C. E. M. O'Dowd, "The General Election of 1924," p. 56, argues in defiance of the statistics that British workers left the Rand immediately after the strike and were replaced by Afrikaners.

5. A government commission also said it in public. *The Report of the Mining Industry Board* (also known as the Brace Commission, or Solomon Commission), UG 39-1922, Cape Town, 1922, p. 7.

6. MM 1699/24, Vol. 723, Secretary for Labour to Under Secretary for Mines and Industries, 8.8.1924.

7. *Report of the Low-Grade Ore Commission*, UG 16-1932, Pretoria, 1932, p. 31; Johnstone, *Class, Race and Gold*, pp. 136–45, provides an extended account of the introduction of this and other technological innovations.

8. PM 1/1/424, 3/22, Vol. 6, 23.3.1922.

9. MM 2375/22, Vol. 628, Smuts to Wallers, 28.3.1922.

10. PM 1/1/424, 3/22, Vol. 13, 11.4.1922.

11. TCM 22/1922; verbal communication by C. B. Anderson, son of P. M. Anderson, a leading mining figure and member of the first GPC. Father and son were each President of the TCM several times.

12. TCM 22/1922, 31.10.1922.

13. TCM 97(1)/1924, 4.12.1924.

14. TCM E 15d, "private and confidential" briefing note to the new TCM President, Buckle, 3.6.1920.

15. TCM L 16b, 29.5.1920.

16. TCM 22/1922.

17. See note 5 above.

18. TCM 22/1922.

19. PM 1/2/57, File 15/11, 12.1.1924.

20. TCM 21(1)/1923, 30.5.1923.

21. PM 1/2/95, 34/2, 20.9.1922.

22. Brace Commission, p. 43.

23. MM 2931/22, Vol. 637, 30.10.1922.

24. MM 1699/18, connected to Vol. 637; MM 2931/22, 2.4.1918, 11.6.1918.

25. MM 2931/22, 4.12.1922.

26. Ibid., 11.12.1922.

27. MM 2931/22, 30.12.1922.

28. *Government Gazette Extraordinary*, Vol. 38, 1923. For a concise summary of its major provisions, see Lever, "Creating the Institutional Order," p. 14.

29. MM 2931/22, Vol. 637, 30.12.1922.

30. MM 3055/20, 14.9.1920.

31. MM 2931/22, 11.4.1923.

32. Particularly by W. K. Hancock, *Survey of British Commonwealth Affairs*, Vol. 2, *Problems of Economic Policy, 1918–1939*, Part 2, London, 1940, pp. 55–57.

33. SC 5-1923.

34. Lever, "Creating the Institutional Order," p. 15.

35. Ibid., p. 16

36. MM 2931/22, Vol. 637, 12.2.1923. The membership of the SAIF had fallen from a peak of 60,000 to about 2,000, according to Simons and Simons, *Class and Colour*, p. 321.

37. MM 2931/22, 5.2.1923. The new trade-union federation was called the Associated Trade Unions of South Africa. It was a bitter rival of the SAIF but, like it, acquiesced in the general principles of the I.C. Bill.

38. P. M. Anderson, at the time on the GPC, later told his son that this was the whole point of the I.C. Act, "to delay and delay and delay." Verbal communication to author, August 1976.

39. MM 2931/22, Vol. 637, 5.2.1922.

40. SC 5-1923.

41. TCM 21(1)/1923, 1.6.1923; see also ARTCM, 1923, pp. 183–84, where Buckle points out that it is virtually unprecedented for a Minister to initiate moves to radically amend his own bill in Select Committee.

42. TCM 21(1)/1923, 24.10.1923.

43. *Rand Daily Mail*, 24.11.1923.

44. TCM 21(1)/1923, 6.13.1923.

45. TCM 21(2)/1923, 14.12.1923.

46. Ibid., 16.12.1923.

47. See Table 1. Simons and Simons, *Class and Colour*, p. 321, imply that the Rand Revolt caused the decline, though members started drifting away (willingly or otherwise) in 1920–1921.

48. PM 1/2/57 File 15/11, 12.1.1924.

49. For an alternative view, arguing the evenhandedness of Malan's

guiding influence, see Lever, "Creating the Institutional Order," p. 22. See also Peter Kallaway, "F. S. Malan, the Cape Liberal Tradition, and South African Politics."

50. PM 1/2/57, File 15/11.

51. A. P. Cartwright, *Golden Age: The Story of the Industrialization of South Africa and the Part Played in It by the Corner House Group of Companies, 1910–1967*, Cape Town, 1968, p. 120, argues that employer-employee relationships were *improved* after the 1922 revolt. Cartwright, a prolific and much-underrated chronicler of the mining companies, is almost certainly wrong, though the quiescence of the workers may have been mistaken by the mining companies for acquiescence or even active support.

52. ARTCM, 1924, p. 55.

53. The need for groups of capitalists to accept a relative degree of state autonomy in their own best interests is well covered by Marx's "Eighteenth Brumaire of Louis Bonaparte," *Surveys from Exile*, Harmondsworth, 1977, and is developed further by Nicos Poulantzas, *Political Power and Social Classes*, London, 1973, passim.

54. Titus Maccius Plautus, *Asinaria*.

55. George Eliot, *Middlemarch*, London, 1961; Yudelman, "Capital, Capitalists and Power in South Africa: Some Zero-sum Fallacies."

56. ARTCM, 1924, p. 57, complained that this type of government usurped the powers of Parliament. This was not something that had unduly bothered the TCM before, as it was notoriously unpopular in Parliament. It was still nervous at this stage, however, that the new Pact Minister of Mines might not be as "rational" in his dealings with the industry as the S.A. party Minister of Mines had been. This fear turned out to be needless.

57. For the labor recognition of this, see Lever, "Creating the Institutional Order," p. 20.

58. It even allowed Ministers the luxury of *believing* that they were acting in an evenhanded way while their decisions were consistently skewed by their perceptions of the overall "public good" or needs of the state.

59. Though not one developed by Philip Selznik, from whom the concept "formal co-optation" used here is drawn: Selznik, *TVA and the Grass Roots* and passim.

60. For details of other S.A. party legislation concerning apprentices and factory and wage regulation, see F. S. Malan autobiography, Chapter 20 and Hancock, *Survey*.

Government Proposes, State Disposes, 1924–1933

> Hegel remarks somewhere that all the great events and charac-
> ters of world history occur, so to speak, twice. He forgot to
> add: the first time as tragedy, the second as farce.
> —Karl Marx[1]

THE EIGHTEENTH BRUMAIRE OF THE PACT GOVERNMENT

In 1913–1914, it has been argued earlier, there were two genuinely radical movements afoot in South Africa, which, if they had
managed to collaborate, would have shaken the fledgling South
African state to its foundations. Even as late as 1922, an alliance of
rural burgher commandos and radical unionized workers would
have had considerable impact. But, as we have seen, nationalist
revolutionaries and class revolutionaries were so far apart that it
seems almost pure counterfactual speculation to suggest that they
would have been extremely powerful together. After all, it might be
countered that one could also argue that if organized white labor
and migrant black labor had combined, they would have formed
an extremely powerful revolutionary force.

The difference between the two forms of "might-have-been"
counterfactual speculation is that some would argue that the two
radical streams—nationalist and class—did eventually combine, in
the Pact between the National and Labour parties. Having lost the
battles of 1913–1914 and 1922, they won the war in 1924 (see
Chapter 1). This view sees the Pact, and its victory in the 1924
general election, as the culmination of an era and a triumph for the
forces of nationalism and trade unionism.[2] This is an extremely im-

portant judgment about contemporary South African history, with implications that necessarily color one's entire interpretation of the subsequent period. In addition, it is a strikingly pervasive view, held by social scientists, historians, and political commentators whose views encompass the entire ideological spectrum from the far left to the far right. Almost unanimously, they see 1924 as a radical break, a turning point in contemporary South African political development.

The 1913–1914 and 1922 "battles" have been dealt with in this study, but they have been interpreted differently: as milestones to the eventual *loss* of the "war." By the end of the Rand Revolt, it has been argued, any possibility of a "white workers' state" or even an Afrikaner republican state was dead forever. The center had held. It is conceded that in 1913–1914, the combined forces of worker radicalism and republican nationalism could have challenged both the state and big business. Counterfactually, if there had been a Pact in 1913–1914 between rural and urban rebels, they might conceivably have succeeded in destroying the symbiotic relationship of the state and capital and helped shape an entirely different state. But no such Pact occurred in 1914, and the threat to the center—the "burgher elements and capitalist classes," to use the terminology of the time—was defeated.

If this argument is to be sustained—particularly since the weight of the literature is so directly opposed to it—one needs to show in some detail that the Pact was not what it was (and is) thought to be; that its actual impact—as opposed to its rhetoric—was not to create a significant break with the past and a reformulation of the structures of power. It is suggested in this study (in Chapter 1 and elsewhere) that the above argument is not difficult to demonstrate, and that one might, in fact, go even further and categorize the Pact as not merely conservative, but as counterrevolutionary. Not only did it continue to operate as its predecessor had done in all significant respects, but it created the impression of significant change, which legitimized the state and actually strengthened the symbiotic relationship of the state and capital.

Expressed another way, while the events of 1913–1914 may be seen by some as tragedy, the election of 1924 should be seen by all as farce. Archie Crawford, the deported radical of 1914, becomes Archie Crawford, the collaborationist clown of 1924. Like Louis

Napoleon, however, the Pact government was a crucially important farce. The Pact government claimed to represent primarily the
white worker, the small businessman, the Afrikaner nationalist,
and the petit bourgeois. It is not the intention of this study to question the sincerity of that claim. The fact that the proposals of a
government may be overridden by the imperatives of a state is not
necessarily evidence of hypocrisy. What is important is that (1) the
Pact almost certainly did not achieve significantly more for those
groups than other governments had done or would have done; and
(2) the Pact isolated populist opposition and estranged it from the
majority of the electorate by the simple technique of vociferously
legislating supposedly pro-white populist policies.

In this way, the Pact immeasurably strengthened the symbiotic
relationship of the state and capital. Its policies, which were in-
herited from the S.A. party and enthusiastically expanded by post-
Pact Keynesian governments, have made it difficult for populists to
mobilize general support for their attacks on the state and capital,
even when personified by the vitriolic caricature of "Hoggen-
heimer" (which came to convey in one fell swoop anticapitalism,
antisemitism, and an acute antipathy to the mining magnate Ernest
Oppenheimer). Only in the 1980s is the duumvirate of the state and
capital once again being remotely challenged, this time by the cry
of *"geldmag"* (money power) from the sinking white worker and,
far more important, by the incipient rise of organized black labor.
All the feverish mental activity now being expended by high-
powered committees of the state and capital pondering "constitutional reform" is, in a very real sense, a quest for a new Pact
government.

THE REVOLT AND THE 1924 ELECTION

The TCM, for all its real reservations about the S.A. party
government, definitely regarded it as the best of the available alternatives. It even broke with usual policy (possibly flushed by the
success of its propaganda machine since 1921) and publicly
said—in a statement it claimed contained "nothing political"—that
the S.A. party policy on various issues was least damaging.[3]

The GPC was asked to raise money to support the S.A. party as
soon as Smuts dissolved Parliament, and it was to be laundered
through a slush fund. Phillips wrote to Wallers in Johannesburg

asking for information on "what the gold producers have done and how the fund is being administered. I take it for granted it was raised . . ."[4] Some money was raised,[5] but the S.A. party, the supposed mouthpiece of the mining magnates, continued to suffer from poor financial backing.[6] There were distinct limits, moreover, to the quality as well as the quantity of help mining capital was prepared to offer: when the S.A. party's General Secretary approached Gemmill to ask if white mineworkers might be given higher wages before the general election, he was flatly turned down.[7]

In spite of the TCM's support, or even, to a limited extent, because of it, the S.A. party was defeated in the 1924 general election by the Pact, which comprised an electoral combination of the National and the Labour parties. It is not within the scope of this study to establish the degree to which the Rand Revolt was responsible for the defeat of Smuts's S.A. party, since it is primarily the effect on the state rather than on individual governments we are concerned with. But the confident assertion by some historians that it was the major cause[8] is, at the very least, debatable.

There are several reasons for questioning the line of direct causality drawn between the revolt and the 1924 election. The electoral combination was no doubt of some importance and had been hastened by the events of 1922, but feelers between the leaders of the Pact parties, Hertzog and Creswell, pre-dated the strike by several months.[9] Moreover, the actual importance of the Pact has probably been overstated, as the really important swings were to the National party in the country districts;[10] and the Labour party, even with the help of the National party, polled a smaller proportion of the vote in 1924 than in 1920.[11] Finally, the direct culmination of 1922, the 1924 I.C. Act, did not appear to have been an important issue in the election.[12]

One should not, however, confuse either the employers' preference for the S.A. party or the results of the 1922 upheaval with the *impact* of the new government. Specifically, this study is less concerned with the reasons for the election of the Pact government than with the effect of that new government on the relationship of the state, labor, and capital. The Pact introduced legislation and policies in its first three years that were to have important effects on both industrial and race relations for the next fifty years.

It is necessary to ask, first, whether the legislation and policy package was a significant departure from the new industrial order inaugurated by the S.A. party or whether it was built logically on its foundations; second, whether the package as implemented constituted a real attack on mining capitalists by the state on behalf of other interests; and third, the extent to which white labor generally (including nonmining labor) and/or manufacturing capitalists (the "national bourgeoisie") benefited from the new regime.

It has been pointed out that the conventional answers to all these questions—whether supplied by liberal, nationalist, or neo-Marxist historians—suggest that a radical break, or turning point, occurred with the election of the Pact. Thus, if a case can be made to indicate a substantial continuity of state policy in these areas after 1924, a good deal of modern South African history might need to be revised.

THE PACT GOVERNMENT AND THE MINING CAPITALISTS

The employers greeted the victory of the Pact with some trepidation. Creswell, a former mine manager and the head of the Labour party, was not made Minister of Mines, much to the relief of the employers. He was, however, put at the head of a new department as the Minister of Labour (a department that the S.A. party government had been thinking of creating since 1910); C. W. Beyers, inexperienced in mining matters, was made Minister of Mines.

From London, Phillips counselled his son Frank to make personal contact with the new ministers. In 1906, when government-employer relations were bad, he wrote, "I made it my duty to cultivate the new masters and in the end greatly modified the relations. You and Wallers will have to try to get upon good personal terms with Hertzog, Beyers & Co. . . ."[13] It was essential, he added, to get to the relevant minister before important issues were publicly debated, partly because the government often harmed the industry without intending to do so.

Phillips was advising the continuation of a tried and tested principle. Given the general unpopularity of the industry, it was considered vital to get prepublication drafts of proposed legislation or policy announcements and incorporate capital's proposed changes in them at that stage. Thus, the first public announcement would already be relatively acceptable to the employers but would appear to come from the government alone. The State and TCM Archives are replete with industry precautions ensuring that vital "first bite" at government legislative and policy drafts.

Nevertheless, Phillips's analogy was faulty. In 1907 (his memory was also faulty), he and others had begun to build up a *modus vivendi* with government and the state that went far beyond his doctrine of friendly intercourse. As the bureaucracies of both the state and industry developed and institutionalized the relationship, it became increasingly less important for leaders of government and industry to be on "good personal terms" or on any terms at all. Nevertheless, Phillips was expressing a lingering and pervasive fear among mining capitalists that the change of government might endanger what was previously a categorical imperative for the state: the commitment to the centrality of a profitable gold mining industry, able to supply revenue and, directly or indirectly, employment opportunities.

The new Pact government also had fears about the state-capital relationship. With the exception of General J. M. B. Hertzog, the new Prime Minister, none had previously held a Cabinet post. Creswell, though he had had very extensive experience in the gold mining industry, retained a dangerously simplistic and paranoid view of the state-capital relationship. He posited a dichotomy of the government's political power and the mining capitalists' economic power, and he passionately urged the necessity for the government to act "to get South Africa out of the thrall of this [industry] monopoly." In short, he showed no understanding of the symbiotic nature of the state-industry relationship.[14]

Creswell did not get his way. He failed, as we shall see, to force the white labor policy—which would have phased out all black miners over a period of time—on the employers, and could not even get the mining capitalists to shoulder the burden of substantially relieving white unemployment. The one policy he followed that most affected and annoyed the mining capitalists—the restriction on recruitment of black migrant labor from Mozambique— was merely a continuation of a policy initiated by the S.A. party government to ensure fuller employment of South African black nationals. Even that policy was seriously questioned by the Pact government, and Creswell found it necessary to write at length to Hertzog to justify its continuation, saying lamely that the restriction had been an integral part of the S.A. party government's policy.[15]

Some of Creswell's paranoia rubbed off on other members of the

new government, particularly while the Cabinet was still inexperienced and did not fully understand the overlapping nature of
state-capital interests. The Minister of Mines, Beyers, sent Kotze's
replacement as Government Mining Engineer, Dr. Hans Pirow, on
a blind search through state statistics to check that the government
was getting its full share of profits from leased mines.[16] Pirow,
a very able GME but still young and inexperienced, labored dili-
gently before reporting that he could find no irregularities. He
plaintively suggested that "my task would naturally be made easier
if you could obtain an inkling as to the direction in which it is considered that investigation is necessary."[17]

Not surprisingly, then, there were some changes in the
government-employer relationship under the Pact, and the relationship became more formal. The TCM found it more difficult, at
least to begin with, to get prepublication drafts of proposed
government legislation, particularly on politically volatile issues
such as organized labor. The lack of detailed private consultation
between the state and capital before issues became public naturally
resulted in government-employer relations becoming strained. The
lack of collusion was especially marked in the early years of the
Pact government, before it began to realize that taking its differences with the TCM into the public arena could create difficulties and inflexibilities for the government as well. On more
than one occasion, Creswell and Beyers exchanged insults with
mining capital on public platforms and in the press, and the TCM
formally accused Beyers of curtness and hostility toward the
employers.[18]

This friction could damage the government as well as mining
capital. Creswell's loudly proclaimed but unenforceable white
labor policy, for example, turned into a political embarrassment
for the government.[19] Beyers also found that "going public" could
be a double-edged sword, when he tried and twice failed to impose
government representatives on the boards of directors of gold mining companies.[20] Although both GMEs, Kotze and his successor,
Pirow, poured scorn on the proposal, Beyers only withdrew it
when it became clear that the measure would be totally im-
practicable. His enforced retreat was naturally also politically
embarrassing.

The TCM, for its part, attempted to gain more parliamentary

support through such measures as inviting all the members of both houses to visit the Rand goldfields at the TCM's expense. About ninety members, many of whom had never before even visited the Rand, accepted in 1925.[21]

The question that arises from the change of political climate following the takeover of the Pact is whether it marked any fundamental change in the state-capital relationship (as opposed to the narrow government-employer relationship). It is also necessary to assess whether it had any significant impact on the relationship of capital and organized labor.

THE PACT'S PROGRAM AND ITS IMPACT

The program embarked upon by the Pact government, encompassing the Wage Act of 1925, the Mines and Works Amendment Act of 1926, and the "civilized labor policy," is generally taken by historians to be the manifest evidence of how the mining industry lost the war in 1924. No doubt, Creswell and Beyers were sincerely concerned with the problem of protecting white miners from the competition of poorly paid black labor and with the problem of finding jobs for poor whites and unemployed whites generally. But previous S.A. party governments, as we have seen, had been concerned with exactly the same problems.

It has been argued that in "passing the Industrial Conciliation Act, the S.A. Party government had in a very real sense preempted the actions of the NP-SALP governing coalition. The Pact government thus came into power with part of its industrial programme in existence."[22] The reverse would be more accurate: the Pact proceeded, once it came to power, to appropriate the S.A. party program. The Mines and Works Amendment Act, for example, largely restored those portions of the 1911 Mines and Works Act that had been found by the courts to be *ultra vires* in 1923, and the Wage Act was preceded in 1917 by the S.A. party's exhaustive Select Committee on the Regulation of Wages (Specified Trades) Bill, and its Wage Board Bill of 1921, which was never passed.[23] The cornerstone of the new industrial order, the I.C. Act, was (as has been shown in detail) an S.A. party measure that was drafted by the government and by mining employers with no significant input from either the National or Labour parties. Its basic principles were not changed by the Pact and, indeed, still apply today.

Naturally, it could be argued that the S.A. party government did not deal with these problems as urgently as did the Pact, and that both the Mines and Works Amendment and the Wage acts went further than did their precursors. There is something to that view, and it is also true that Smuts's party strenuously opposed the program in Parliament. Nevertheless, there is no doubt that the Wage Act, in particular, builds on the I.C. Act and closes certain loopholes that any government preoccupied with the political threat of white labor—as both the S.A. party and the Pact were—would have had to close. It should also be recognized that the "adversary procedure" encouraged by the structure of Parliament, with its government and official opposition, also tended to exaggerate relatively slight differences between the parties.

Smuts and the mining capitalists were more concerned about how the new Wage Act and Mines and Works Act might be administered against the mining industry than about the principles introduced by these laws. The Pact program established precisely what the S.A. party had been aiming at in a more random way: state control of the powerful "organized" industries while maintaining a substantial illusion of industrial autonomy; and state control of the "unorganized" industries. There was no conflict in principle between the industrial programs of the S.A. party and the Pact. Though it cannot be denied that the Pact gave its program somewhat higher priority, even that emphasis was greatly exaggerated by the nature of the adversarial party political system, by Pact propaganda, and by its more systematic and ideological exposition of the new industrial order.

Both the S.A. party and Pact governments greatly expanded the range of administrative powers delegated to the government: government by regulation, as has been noted in Chapter 3, has been a notable characteristic of the executive's undercutting of the legislature and the judiciary from Union and even before. This policy opened the way for vastly increased state intervention in all sectors of industrial life without being subject to regular public and parliamentary review and criticism.

It is not proposed to reiterate here all the details of the Pact industrial legislation or of its civilized labor policy,[24] but it would be instructive to examine how the I.C. Act, in particular, and the S.A. party's industrial program, in general, relate to the Pact program. This examination once more addresses the question of whether the Pact program was a departure or a turning point; or whether it was merely the logical development of the S.A. party's program.

The I.C. Act had three main loopholes:

1. It allowed employers generally to substitute lower-paid blacks for whites once the act's machinery (which did not apply to blacks) had set white wages at levels considered by the employer to be high enough to take the social and economic risks of substitution. The act thus had the unwanted effect of pricing whites out of the employment market by forcing employers to pay them more. The loophole was closed by an amendment in 1930 that enabled industrial councils to regulate black wages and hours of work, should they feel that the ends of the I.C. Act were being defeated by the substitution of (otherwise unregulated) black labor.[25] The issue illustrates the complexity of state intervention into the labor market, and the double-edged nature of such intervention.

2. The I.C. Act could only be applied to "organized industries" that could muster representative bodies of both employers and employees. This loophole was closed by the Wage Act, which was specifically designed to deal with unorganized, "sweated" industries, on the lines of British and Australian legislation on the same issue. The Wage Act was the logical corollary of the I.C. Act, which was confined to dealing with organized, "self-governing" industries. There was no possibility of the unorganized industries even appearing to be self-governing, so the Wage Act operated on an openly compulsory basis.

3. The I.C. Act could not force an important organized industry, such as the mining industry, to accept the recommendations of the I.C. Act conciliation machinery unless both parties agreed in advance to be bound by state arbitration. Thus, it was clear that the I.C. Act left unresolved to what extent either the state or capital controlled the new industrial order.

The major potential weapon in the hands of the government—should a clash occur between the state and capital—was the Wage Act, which empowered the Minister of Labour to investigate any industry if he deemed it not to be cooperating under the I.C.

Act. Such an investigation under the Wage Act could, for example, empower him to set the same minimum wages for whites and blacks. This would effectively eliminate the economic incentive to employ black miners by setting their wages as high as those of whites.

Creswell, in fact, threatened to do precisely that when the GPC refused to be bound by the Pact government's de Villiers report recommendations under the I.C. Act concerning minimum rates of pay and cost-of-living allowances.[26] At first, he responded by introducing a bill, the Mineworker (Minimum Rates of Pay) Bill, attempting to force his will directly on the industry. The TCM President, P. M. Anderson, responded by threatening to ignore the I.C. Act if "special legislation" like Creswell's bill—which abrogated the "mutual consent" principles of the I.C. Act—were passed.[27]

The bill was dropped, but Creswell did not relax the pressure. In September 1925, he publicly threatened to use the Wage Act, if necessary, to force the de Villiers report on the industry. The government was to rule South Africa, he said, not the TCM.[28] The GPC bowed symbolically a few days later, awarding a very limited, "temporary arbitrary increase," pending (it said), the findings of the Economic and Wage Commission then sitting. The Commission's report heavily favored the mining employers, but the matter was not allowed to rest there, and the TCM finally accepted a (binding) arbitration board on October 26, 1926. The SAMWU had previously been prepared to be bound by the de Villiers Conciliation Board's decision, but the TCM had refused. In 1927, the board issued its award, which increased the industry's wage bill by less than 1 percent (an increase of £75,000 annually, of a total £8 million).[29] Creswell finally dropped the issue, and the employers were not again compelled to accept arbitration.

The government-TCM clash over the de Villiers report was illuminating for several reasons. First, it shows that the Wage Act, although a powerful weapon, was also a blunt, almost apocalyptic, one. If Creswell had imposed a Wage Board on mining capital to force it to raise white wages, he would have had to face all sorts of other possibilities, such as economic slump in the industry, leading to drastically reduced white employment and government revenue.

For that reason, the Pact finally settled on the Mines and Works Amendment Act to protect white mineworkers from displacement—much to the private relief of the employers. The act gave the Minister the power to reserve jobs for whites more openly and directly. As in the case of the 1911 Mines and Works Act, it could potentially be used as an offensive weapon to cut drastically the number of jobs available to blacks, but it, too, was not used to any large extent to do this.[30] Thus, the Pact did nothing to reverse the failure by white mineworkers to expand the semi-skilled categories of jobs available to whites.

The struggle, which was masked by the white workers' attempt to abolish the Status Quo Agreement and move into jobs occupied by blacks at *higher wages*, was, in a very real sense, the precursor of the Pact's civilized labor policy. Basically, that policy involved paying "civilized labor" (white labor) a "civilized rate" (higher wages) for doing the same jobs being done by blacks. The irony of all this—especially for commentators who doggedly cling to the idea that the 1924 election marked a defeat for mining capital at the expense of *industrial* capital,[31] or secondary industry—was that the Pact's civilized labor policy was imposed upon virtually everyone *except* the primary industries, mining and agriculture.

In a sense, then, the manufacturing industries paid for the tariff protection they were being given by the Pact (which was not, in any case, as we shall see, dramatically higher than the "revenue-gathering" tariffs previously imposed by the S.A. party). The "protected" industries were compelled by various Pact measures to employ more whites in semi-skilled and unskilled jobs at far higher wages.

In contrast, the mining industry, on which there had been intense pressure before 1922 to employ more whites in an expanding array of jobs, was now virtually free from the burden of attempting to alleviate South Africa's white unemployment problem. The mining unions' attempt to impose an informal civilized labor policy on the mining industry between 1916 and 1921 was totally dropped after 1922. When the Pact formally implemented the civilized labor policy in 1924, it imposed the economic burden of employing whites on its own bureaucracy and on secondary industry, which, because of its dependence on the government's protection program, had little choice in the matter.

The effects of the Pact program with reference to its effect on white labor in the mining industry can be summarized as follows:

1. Creswell, who had sincerely tried to get his Cabinet to accept the necessity of a white labor policy for the industry (gradually replacing all black
labor by white), did not even succeed in having a half-baked white labor
policy imposed on the employers. Instead, the expense of the civilized
labor policy was borne by precisely those groups and interests the Pact
was supposed to represent—the state bureaucracy and manufacturing
industry (or the "national bourgeoisie"). In this way, secondary industry
paid for the tariff protection it was getting from the Pact government.
The major price the mining industry paid for the civilized labor policy
and tariff protection under the Pact government was the price paid by
the population at large—a relatively higher cost of living.

In actual fact, however, the cost of living was falling in absolute
terms, and mining costs were being kept at the low post-1922 levels (see
Tables 6 and 7). Much has been made of the increased burden through
tariffs suffered by the gold mines. The argument that the Pact increased
direct or indirect taxes on the gold mining industry to finance its civilized
labor policy is sometimes used in attempting to salvage the idea that the
election of the Pact marked a defeat or a setback for mining capital.[32]

That claim is something of a last-ditch stand for advocates of the
turning-point theory, and it is as incorrect as are the cruder versions
dealt with earlier. The direct cost of tariffs to the industry was, of
course, negligible. The Commissioner of Customs estimated these to be
1.37 pence per ton milled in 1929. If one compares that figure to the
reduction of costs between 1920 and 1929 of 70 pence per ton milled, the
unimportance of the protective tariffs becomes manifest (and this does
not even take into account the fact that the S.A. party's "revenue tariffs"
of 1920 would also have imposed direct tariff costs on the industry). The
tariff costs were so low that the Gold Producers' Committee of the TCM
openly admitted they were "not heavy" and declined to press for their
removal.[33] Direct taxation rates of the industry did not increase after
1924 either.

This does not mean that the TCM had no complaints, of course: the
industry was headed for yet another crisis for a complex set of reasons
(such as a progressive decline in ore values), none of which had anything
to do with the Pact's policy. The TCM, however, was seeking various
types of help from the state, ranging from direct subsidies to permission
to recruit black labor from areas closed to the employers (for the comprehensive shopping list, see the 1932 *Report of the Low-Grade Ore
Commission*).

One of the TCM's justifications for asking for state help was the claim
that the Pact's protective tariffs increased the general cost of living 6 percent and gold mining costs by a shilling a ton. The Commissioner of
Customs quite properly contested that figure.[34] But even if it were ac-

curate, it is not impressive when placed next to the 6-shillings-a-ton reduction in costs since the early 1920s, a reduction achieved largely through state intervention in the organized labor arena.

In addition, the cost of living, or, more accurately, the level of prices, fell by 30 percent between 1920 and 1930. Though the pact probably had little to do with this decline—it was part of a worldwide trend—it is pointed out to indicate how little real grievance the mining industry had with the Pact. The figures in Table 7 indicate how the state's revenue receipts from the gold mines actually fell under the Pact—in spite of the fact that gold output and revenue *rose* (though only slightly) over the period.

2. A second aspect of the impact of Hertzog's Pact government on the gold mining industry is that neither the wages nor the conditions of white mineworkers were markedly improved, in spite of the public pressure and the threats exerted by Creswell. The threats and the employers' "capitulation" were, in retrospect, more symbolic than actual. Creswell may conceivably have meant what he said, but he never mustered the support (inside or outside the Pact) for a major attack on the TCM. While it made good political sense to mouth meaningless rhetoric defying (on behalf of the government and the electorate as a whole) mining capital's supposed attempts to govern the country, it did not concretely aid organized white labor.

This was one of the few periods, in fact, when the white miners actually lost ground to the black miners, both in numbers and in terms of

Table 7   The Gold Mines' "Burden," 1920–1939

Year	Costs (shillings and pence per ton)	Witwatersrand retail price index	State revenue receipts from gold mines (£'000)
1920	25/8	144.0	1,359
1921	25/10	130.8	2,002
1922	23/7	109.6	1,579
1924	19/8	107.2	1,827
1926	19/1	104.9	1,611
1930	19/8	101.6	1,623
1933	19/5	91.3	12,548
1939	19/5	99.5	13,119

Source: Ralph Horwitz, *The Political Economy of South Africa*, London, 1967, p. 237; Leo Katzen, *Gold and the South African Economy*, Cape Town, 1964, pp. 56–57; *Union Statistics for Fifty Years*, 1910–1960, Pretoria, 1960, H-23.

real wages. In other words, it was during the tenure of the Pact, which strongly proclaimed its intention to defend white labor against black competition, that white miners fared worst. This does not mean, of course, that the Pact was secretly conspiring to achieve the opposite of its proclaimed policy. Rather, there were various reasons for the increased use of black labor as its training improved, paralleled by the use of more unskilled and semi-skilled white labor (which was either new to mining or which had been thoroughly subdued by the breaking of the 1922 strike and the passing of the Industrial Conciliation Act of 1924).

Overall, both black and white miners show a decline of real earnings, stretching two decades and more from Union. The major reasons for the decline in black wages were probably a greater supply resulting from more efficient monopsonistic recruiting techniques of migrant blacks, and migrant blacks' increasing dependence on mine jobs. For whites, the decline can be attributed to the substitution of semi-skilled for artisan miners in more mechanized situations and, most important for the purposes of this study, the growing intervention of the state in capital-organized labor relations and its *de facto* destruction of the strike option in ongoing industrial relations.

The statistics strikingly illustrate the decline in monetary rewards for white miners, a decline that was not reversed by the Pact government, nor even arrested by it. These statistics are shown in Table 8.

Table 8   Black/White Earnings on the Gold Mines, 1911–1975

Year	Index of real earnings, 1936 = 100		Earnings-gap ratio W:B
	Blacks	Whites	
1911	100	102	11.7:1
1916	90	94	12.0:1
1921	69	90	15.0:1
1926	88	85	11.2:1
1931	92	90	11.3:1
1936	100	100	11.5:1
1941	89	94	12.1:1
1969	99	172	20.1:1
1975	—	—	8.4:1
1980	—	—	5.5:1

Source: Francis Wilson, *Labour in the South African Gold Mines, 1911–1969*, Cambridge, England, 1972, p. 46. 1975 figure derived from 1975 ARTCM and reflects (a) the shortage and militance of black labor in the early 1970s; and (b) the ability of the mines to pay more following the freeing of the gold price.

3. White employment opportunities were not markedly increased as a result of the Pact's takeover (see Tables 1 and 5). In fact, whites lost ground to blacks in the mines during the tenure of the Pact government, both in terms of wages and in employment levels. It could be argued that the Pact's program prevented the TCM from even more drastically reducing white wages and jobs: in spite of the TCM's protestations that it had no such intention, there is some evidence the reductions might otherwise have occurred without the countervailing presence of the Pact's proclaimed policy to protect the jobs of the white miners. This was, at most, a holding operation at the precise time when the Pact was taking offensive measures in other areas to force the increased employment of poor whites (of whom there were an estimated 300,000 by 1929).

While employment opportunities were being forced open by the Pact for whites in secondary industry and in the state bureacracy, very little was being achieved for the white miner in spite of the tremendous amount of effort that went into restoring the legality of the color bar. (See Table 9.)

Table 9   Employment Opportunities on the Gold Mines, 1904–1941

Year	White gold miners Witwatersrand (A)	Transvaal white male population (B)	A as % of B
1904	13,027	178,478	7.3
1911	24,746	236,917	10.4
1918	22,764	260,840	8.7
1921	21,036	285,185	7.4
1926	19,713	313,773	6.3
1931	22,654	357,504	6.3
1936	35,393	424,470	8.3
1941	41,424	487,727	8.5

Source: Union Statistics for Fifty Years, 1910–1960, Pretoria, 1960; ARTCMs.

THE PACT'S ADMINISTRATIVE IMPACT

The previous section has largely considered the impact of the Pact government's formal program on the mining industry. It is necessary also to consider whether the Pact, by informally using the administrative and regulatory power available to it, significantly altered the balance between capital and labor in the mining industry. Phillips was less worried in 1924 about the Pact's formal legislative program than about its potential to exercise administrative leverage:

> I have no doubt the new Government will be fairly chary in regard to alterations of the law which would have to stand the fire of criticism in Parliament, where the effects would be exposed and warnings of the consequences uttered in no uncertain voice, but the danger lies in insidious acts of administration or the multiplying of vexatious regulations.[35]

In fact, there is little sign that any concerted harassment campaign was mounted against the employers, particularly in the area of white labor, other than the unsuccessful effort to foist the relatively innocuous de Villiers report on them.

The government did hold down the importation of migratory black labor from Mozambique, a policy justified largely by the need to change to a white labor policy in the industry. But the S.A. party government had initiated that policy (justified by the need to give the jobs held by foreigners to South African blacks, particularly in times of crop failures). The Pact government did not apply the policy in markedly more draconian fashion, and in 1928, the gap between the theory of its policy and its practice was openly derided in Parliament by Sir Drummond Chaplin, formerly a senior figure in the mining industry:

> The Minister of Defence [Creswell] has talked for twenty years or more as to the necessity for doing away with what he calls servile labour, and for stopping the importation of natives from Portuguese East Africa. The Minister, however, is sitting in a Cabinet, which is sending one of its members to Lisbon to make sure that this labour is maintained.[36]

It was somewhat unfair of Chaplin to single out Creswell, whose belief in a white labor policy for the industry had never wavered. Creswell wrote several long, detailed, and impassioned private memoranda to his fellow Cabinet members on the subject, but he appears to have elicited little response. As late as October 1927, having lost his portfolio of Minister of Labor in 1925, Creswell circulated an analysis that argued that the mining industry needed to be restructured to use "civilized" (white) labor.[37] Either the rest of the Cabinet had not taken Pact electoral propaganda as seriously as had Creswell, or they learned quicker than he the impracticality of such a policy, given their revenue and employment imperatives. He received little apparent support.

Creswell also criticized "our own officials" for ignoring Cabinet directives. In 1926, while he was Acting Minister of Mines, Creswell had dismissed the brilliant Government Mining Engineer, Sir Robert Kotze, over a minor dispute. Kotze had always been a strong opponent of the white labor policy and had conducted a running battle with Creswell after the Pact's election (supported by Warington Smyth, the Secretary for Mines)[38] in which he argued that whites should rather be absorbed in secondary industry. He wrote a memorandum, advocating state encouragement of manufacturing industry.[39]

Kotze was replaced by a young engineer, Dr. Hans Pirow, who had little experience in the government mining bureaucracy or in mining engineering[40] and was, therefore, a "political" appointee (bureaucratic promotions were generally made on seniority). Nevertheless, he turned out to be a very able successor to Kotze. Kotze subsequently became a S.A. party Member of Parliament and was appointed to the boards of several mining companies, but he was something of an exceptional case: there was generally relatively little interchange of elites between the state and mining capital.

In 1928, the Secretary for Mines, Warington Smyth, retired and was replaced by L. P. van Zyl Ham. Thus, the two key civil servants in the Mines Department were Pact appointees, and Creswell himself established the Department of Labour in 1924. At the lower levels, the Mines Department shows a predominance of former Transvaal civil servants well into the 1930s, whereas the Labour Department was at first dominated by former Cape civil servants.[41] But these people were largely clerks, and anyone below the rank of Under Secretary was not even in the position to stall the implementation of Cabinet directives.

Thus, it is unlikely that the heads of the bureaucracy could, to a significant extent, be blamed for the failure to implement the Pact's proclaimed policy. It is more probable that a majority of the rest of the Cabinet—becoming increasingly sensitive to the overlapping interests of the state and mining capital—was Creswell's major stumbling block. Creswell regained the Minister of Labour portfolio in 1929, when Tom Boydell was nominated to the Senate,[42] but he appears to have had a more peaceful relationship with mining capital until the demise of the Pact government ended his tenure in 1933.[43]

For the rest, the Pact government does not appear to have multiplied "vexatious regulations" or "insidious acts of administration." Other than Creswell, there was no one in the Pact implacably opposed to the mining capitalists, and the state-capital relationship attained a large and fairly stable degree of "benign neglect." The Pact did not stifle the progress of the industry for the benefit of the white mineworker; on the contrary, the white mineworkers received few benefits from the Pact. Moreover, when the Depression and the continuing lowering of grade on the central Witwatersrand gold fields in 1930 began to threaten the low-grade mines (as the inflation of 1920 had once threatened them), the Pact appointed a Low-Grade Ore Commission, which advocated measures against white labor as severe as those suggested by the S.A. party-dominated 1919–1920 LGM Commission. The 1930 recommendations included the widespread substitution of blacks for whites underground (on health grounds!), a reduction of 10 percent in white wages (a minority opinion), and the reintroduction of black migratory labor from tropical areas (banned by the government in 1913 because of shockingly high mortality rates).[44] The government was saved from having to implement any of these recommendations by the massive change of fortune in the industry following the devaluation in 1932 and the large U.S. dollar increase in the gold price.

After 1922, the South African state, whether the government was S.A. party or the Pact, seems to have given up any serious idea of placing large numbers of unemployed Afrikaners in the mining industry. It settled for (1) protecting those whites who were already there, and (2) ensuring a stable labor-capital relationship through the greater state intervention in the new industrial order, the final aim being industrial "peace" and secure state revenues.

The state, in other words, ceased looking to the gold mines as the key to fulfilling both its legitimation and accumulation imperatives; the pacification and co-optation of organized white labor made the legitimation imperative less pressing. The gold mines were to continue as the major source and generator of state revenue, but the government now designated secondary industry and the state bureaucracy to bear the responsibility of expanding employment opportunities for the white electorate.

Thus, the results of 1922 were far from being a defeat for the gold mining capitalists. They did suffer a limited loss of autonomy in the sphere of collective bargaining, but it was a victory for the interventionist state that mining capital was happy to concede in exchange for the industrial peace it brought. And there can be no doubt that the increased role of the state did bring a virtual end to militant white worker resistance. As Table 4 shows, from 1919 to the Rand strike, 2.8 million man-days were lost to all South African industries as a result of industrial disputes, the bulk being on the gold mines. By contrast, in the nine years of Pact government, from 1924–1932, only 114,000 man-days were lost.

In all the vital areas, moreover, such as costs, internal reorganization of the industry, and overall control over white employment policies, 1922 resulted in a considerable victory for mining capital, which the Pact government made no serious effort to reverse. The Wage Act was not applied to the mining industry and, contrary to the employers' fears, the Mines and Works Amendment Act of 1926 was not invoked to force them into employing larger numbers of whites; at most, it was used to hold the *post-1922* status quo and protect organized labor from further attacks.

As for the suggestion that 1922 was merely a temporary defeat for organized labor pending its shared victory with the Pact in 1924, this was plainly not the case for the white miners, who, in almost every conceivable way, suffered as a result of the 1922 revolt and continued to do so throughout the two terms of the Pact government.

VARIATIONS ON THE THEME OF "TURNING POINTS"

The Pact government, it has been suggested earlier, marked neither a defeat for mining capital nor a victory for white miners. The question remains whether it might not have marked a victory or defeat for capital or organized white labor outside the mining industry.

A comprehensive answer to that question is outside the scope of this study, but the issue needs to be addressed for two main reasons. It has been suggested that (1) though the Pact may have allowed the position of the white miners to deteriorate, it never-theless represented white labor in general; and (2) the Pact was the instrument of a new group of capitalists (the manufacturers) or even a new form of capital ("national" as opposed to "Imperialist" or "metropolitan" capital).

The reasons these alternative explanations[45] need to be dealt with here is that they offer a variant of the old turning-point explanation that does little to revise or refine its manifest weaknesses. The alter-native explanations still see 1924 as a break with the past and periodize the development of the South African state accordingly. Instead of the Pact representing white miners against mining capitalists, the alternative version suggests that it represents white labor in general against white capital, or that it represents the manufacturers and farmers (or "national bourgeoisie") against min-ing capital, with white labor a very subordinate ally to "national" capital.

Such explanations, while one can at a stretch make them tenuously plausible, ignore the growing and qualitatively changing role of the state, which began well before 1924. They also continue implicitly to confuse "state" and "government." They overem-phasize what was (genuinely) unique to South Africa—the color- and skill-divided working class, and the political strength of Afrikaner nationalism—while underemphasizing world trends in state economic intervention and their causes. In seeing the state merely as an instrument or representative in the hands of one or other group or class, these explanations misconceptualize the political process as fundamentally as do the turning-point theories previously discussed (which refer only to the *mining* industry).

As with the latter, a misperception of the problem leads to answers that are empirically misleading or false. Once again, one needs to look at the actual impact of government decisions and nondecisions after 1924 to arrive at a possible alternative explana-tion. This alternative will emphasize the changing nature of the economy and the state's role in it, and will concern itself less with the factional disputes, whether of political parties or "fractions" of capital.

The Pact and White Labor

The argument that the Pact represented organized white labor in general has already been largely refuted in the course of dealing with the relationship of the Pact to mining labor. The figures quoted above (text and Table 4), which indicate the level of organized labor's militance by number of strikers and man-days lost, were for *all* industries, not just for the mining industry. The figures show clearly the destruction of the membership of various unions representing various industries. They also show steep declines in minimum-wage rates after 1920, and no significant improvement under the Pact (see Table 10). And these include wages in the engineering, metal working, printing, building, and transport industries.

Collectively, the figures show conclusively how the crushing of the 1922 strike and the subsequent co-optation of organized labor by the Industrial Conciliation Act marked the end of effective white labor militance until the present day. Even the apparent resurgence of militance indicated by the 1946–1947 strike figures does not con-

Table 10   Index of Minimum-Wage Rates, Various Sectors, 1920–1933 (1938 = 100)

	1920	1922	1925	1930	1933
Gold mining	130.7	92.6	94.4	100.0	99.7
Engineering, metal working	126.8	94.7	95.6	99.6	97.7
Printing	131.8	113.9	107.2	107.2	97.2
General manufacturing	115.2	96.1	93.8	93.2	92.1
Building	113.8	93.3	93.3	96.4	86.2
Transport	133.6	103.4	106.4	108.2	90.5
All groups	121.8	98.2	98.7	99.3	93.6

Source: Union Statistics for Fifty Years, 1910–1960, Pretoria, 1960, G-31. The index is largely based on minimum-wage rates and prescribed cost-of-living allowances for adult white male workers.

tradict this judgment, since those figures are explained by a black migrant workers' strike and by an internecine fight within the white miners' union.

The level of white miners' wages on the Rand was a leading determinant of the wage levels of organized labor throughout South Africa. As was shown in Chapter 5, the government actively and directly colluded with mining capital over wage levels in the periods before 1924. The state itself was a major employer, anxious to keep wages down.

It is unlikely that this cooperation continued at the same explicit level after Creswell became Minister of Labour, but the state's need to minimize costs and maximize revenue did not change after 1924. Indeed, because of the Pact's ambitious and therefore expensive program of industrial expansion and diversification, the need became more acute. Not surpisingly, then, the wages of white miners and other sectors of white labor between 1920 and 1933 moved similarly: they dropped sharply in response to the physical defeat of 1922 and general deflation and then lingered at this much-reduced level throughout the tenure of the Pact government. A striking illustration of this is the failure of the Pact to increase substantially even the scale of *minimum*-wage rates, though it was an explicitly proclaimed policy objective that was far easier to achieve than general wage increases, and far cheaper.

All this indicates that organized white labor, in general, suffered much the same fate as did the white miners: in spite of its propaganda, the Pact did not really represent the interests of white labor. While production, profits, and dividends rose steadily in most sectors of the economy, the rewards of organized labor generally stagnated at the low post-1922 levels.

There is, however, a vital second aspect to the Pact's relationship with white labor: employment. The Pact government promised to give every white man in South Africa a "civilized standard" of living. Given the scale of unemployment and poor white problems, that promise was a tremendous undertaking. In 1921, South Africa's entire economically active white population was about 540,000.[46] In 1929, the Carnegie Commission estimated the number of poor whites at 300,000. This meant that the Pact was promising to create a very large number of new jobs relative to those already in existence, in addition to significantly increasing the wage rates of many of those already working in the "unorganized" industries.

This goal was, to a large degree, incompatible with the goal of protecting and improving the living standards of organized white labor.[47] In fact, it marks the basic division between the two parties in the Pact. Hertzog's National party was based in the rural areas, but it was growing in strength in the industrial areas as the Afrikaners trekked into the town; therefore, the party's priority was employment. Creswell's Labour party was urban-based and heavily dependent on the support of organized white labor, and it represented those who already had jobs and skills.

Unless employers in general could be persuaded to accept large reductions in profits and other sacrifices (which the Pact did not even seriously ask them to do), the goals of organized and unorganized labor were in conflict. To employ more whites at higher wages than the blacks they were competing with (the "civilized labor policy") and at the same time increase the rewards of those whites already employed would doubly increase the level of costs.

As we have seen, the Labour party's priority goal, to protect and improve organized labor's position, was largely frustrated. It was very much the junior party in the Pact, with 18 parliamentary seats compared to the National party's 63 seats. The question of how successful the National party's civilized labor policy[48] was in achieving its objects is still an open one, which cannot be fully answered here.[49] But it is clear that the Pact made a far greater effort to apply that policy than it did actively to aid organized labor.

That effort was wholly consistent with the previous policy of the S.A. party. For many years, the S.A. party had conducted its own policy of sheltered employment for white labor on state projects such as irrigation works and railway lines. Many of these projects were initiated as much to provide employment opportunities for whites as for any other reason and bear a striking resemblance to President Roosevelt's New Deal projects of the 1930s. The Pact's civilized labor policy was largely an expanded and formalized version of the previous S.A. party policy, an appropriation similar to the Pact's appropriation of the S.A. party's new industrial order for the co-optation of organized labor.

This is not to deny that the Pact treated the problem of the employment of unskilled and semi-skilled whites with somewhat more urgency than did the S.A. party. On the railways, for example, it increased white employment from 39,024 in 1924 to

58,306 in 1930 while reducing black employment from 47,157 to 42,245.[50] The Pact also made concerted efforts to cajole or coerce private manufacturers to employ more whites by using tariff-protection incentives and requirements to encourage lower black/white labor ratios. In the area of ratios, it was less successful: the proportion of white workers only increased from 36 percent in 1924–1925 to 39 percent in 1929–1930, though the general develop-ment of secondary industry created many more jobs in absolute terms (up from 114,876 to 141,616) and therefore represented a fairly substantial increase in white jobs.[51]

Overall, however, one must still question how high the civilized labor policy was on the Pact's agenda. For example, through its power to set minimum wages, the Wage Board was potentially an extremely powerful lever for forcing employers to use white labor. But it was used both sparingly and wastefully.[52]

Moreover, the increased employment of whites was paralleled by a decrease in white wages in real terms, suggesting that the more skilled white workers, in particular, paid part of the price for the employment of their less skilled white colleagues. On the railways, for example, total salaries and wages fell from £16.5m in 1924 to £16m in 1930. Adjusting for the fall in prices,[53] total wages actually *rose* in real terms from £16.5m to £21m. A breakdown of black and white wages is not available, but in real terms, the per capita salary for *all* workers rose from £183 per annum to £208 in 1930. There were, however, 58,000 whites employed in 1930 as against 43,000 whites in 1921, an increase of 35 percent. The greatly increased relative and absolute size of the white labor force is not paralleled by an equal increase in the total work force's real wages. Therefore, unless one posits a large decrease in black wages (which does not seem to have happened), the real wages of white railway men declined during the middle and late 1920s. Part of this decline was no doubt due to the higher proportion of unskilled and poorly paid whites employed in 1930, and part was due to the reluctance and inability of the Pact government to pay more than its predecessor had.

The Pact's policy toward white labor, then, was basically similar to that of previous S.A. party governments: an increase in the employment of unskilled and semi-skilled whites, particularly Afrikaners (see Chapters 2 and 4), achieved by pressuring and en-couraging private industry and by the expansion of white employment in the state bureaucracy; and the limitation of both the militance and the rewards of organized, unionized white labor by formal co-optation into the state administrative and political system (see Chapters 3, 5, and 6). Government policy under both the S.A. party and the Pact was, to a large extent, circumscribed by the imperatives of legitimation and accumulation that operated on the South African state. And both governments required the increasing intervention of the state to pacify and politically neutralize organized white labor, and to provide employment opportunities for the newly urbanized sections of the white electorate.

The Pact and the "National Capitalists"

The imperatives of the South African state were also vital in determining the Pact's policy toward local manufacturing industry. The state's encouragement of local industry and its expansion after 1924 has recently suggested to several historians a variant of the turning-point theory, which argues that a new capitalist class, the manufacturers, or an alliance of agricultural and manufacturing capital (cheered on by white labor from the sidelines), seized control of the state through the Pact government in 1924.[54]

This is not a new theory; others have been deceived in the past by the vociferous arguments of free traders and protectionists.[55] What is new is the neo-Marxist effort to refurbish the turning-point theory with a new "hegemonic fraction" and a new state, which, it is alleged, primarily represented "national capital." This post-1924 state is contrasted with the old state, which is said to have represented primarily Imperialist, or mining, capital.

Innumerable problems arise from that theory. The role of agricultural capital, for example, is fundamental but is hardly touched on, except to mention one or two instances where it benefited from additional protection granted by the Pact. In fact, agriculture had always been heavily protected by all South African governments, including Smuts's S.A. party.[56] Why agricultural capital should suddenly have made the transformation from subordinate to dominant fraction of capital in 1924 is a mystery that those who espouse the theory wisely decline to untangle. Curiously, the Pact government's two Cabinets were the only two in South African history that did not contain any farmers.[57]

An even more fundamental problem is encountered in the idea

that manufacturing capital in some ways became hegemonic by its joint seizure of power with agricultural capital. This is an argument that is "proved" by alleging a radical tilt of policy by the Pact toward local manufacturing industries. Thus, national capital, previously almost ignored by the S.A. party (the representative of international capital), now utilized the state (through the Pact government) to impose a protectionist policy on an unwilling mining capital.[58]

But to what extent did the Pact directly favor national capital in its actions? It is very much a moot point to what extent the Pact tariff-protection measures increased state aid to manufacturing industry: customs-duty revenue did not rise appreciably between 1924 and 1930.[59] Nor did the Pact receive a higher proportion of its total revenue directly from the mines (see Table 11). In any case, the state had for many years been encouraging the development of local manufacturing.[60] The mining capitalists themselves had actively discussed and provided for the financial encouragement of local industries as early as 1916 "inasmuch as the existence of important industries in the country apart from mining and farming would tend to broaden the basis of taxation, and distribute the attention which is now focused on the Mining Industry over a number of industries."[61] The mining capitalists were not hostile to the development of local industries *per se*, though they did resist any policy that would increase the cost of living generally and thus inflate their operating costs. On November 27, 1916, the mining houses and banks voted £100,000 to start the proposed Industrial Finance Company, which was intended to help finance promising local ventures.[62]

The take-off of local manufacturing can be dated from World War I, when it became profitable to fill the gaps in the market created by the clampdown on imports from Europe. This import-substitution industrialization did not speed up markedly during the Pact's tenure, especially taking into account that the economy prospered between 1924 and 1929.[63] As with gold mining and other sectors of the economy, the real increase in the number of factories, employment, and the gross domestic product contribution by manufacturing came after the Pact government. This was in the boom years after 1933, when the large increase in the gold price had a prodigious multiplier, or ripple, effect throughout the economy.[64]

Table 11   State Revenue from the Gold Mines, 1911–1960

Year	Total ordinary revenue (A) (£ million)	Total revenue from gold mining (B) (£ million)	B as % of A
1911	14.2	1.0	7.0
1915	13.2	1.3	9.5
1920	25.7	1.4	5.2
1921	24.6	2.0	8.0
1922	22.7	1.6	7.0
1923	24.3	2.0	8.4
1924	25.3	1.8	7.2
1925	27.0	1.5	5.4
1926	28.6	1.6	5.6
1927	30.1	1.6	5.3
1928	30.5	1.6	5.5
1929	30.5	1.6	5.2
1930	28.6	1.6	5.8
1935	39.7	10.6	33.6
1940	66.6	22.3	33.6
1945	136.1	16.6	11.5
1950	169.2	20.3	12.0
1955	284.5	15.1	5.3
1960	365.4	28.9	7.4

Sources: Official Yearbooks; Reports of the Auditor General, cited in Leo Katzen, *Gold and the South African Economy*, Cape Town, 1964, pp. 56–57.

Thus, it is at least debatable whether the Pact government actually encouraged local industrialization by its much-vaunted and politically successful protection policy. Moreover, even if manufacturing industry had grown, this would not in itself have shown that the growth was the result of a conscious Pact program, nor that the South African state had been seized and utilized by a new hegemonic group. In this case, there are some doubts to begin with that manufacturing industry grew faster under the Pact than it would have under any other government, given the prevailing rate of economic growth and the improving general economic climate.[65]

The argument that the Pact government and the South African state after 1924 favored national capital at the expense of the other sectors of capital, then, is not convincing. The further argument, that national capital took over the state and imposed its interests directly on and through it, is even more implausible. Almost the opposite was in fact the case. Manufacturing capital in South Africa was then—and in fact still remains today—the creature of mining capital and, more particularly, the state. In the 1920s, manufacturing capitalists did not even enjoy a limited autonomy. Their very existence was dependent on the state, which could make or break them by simple tariff changes. The South African manufacturing capitalists share much in common with the "national bourgeoisies" of states such as Mexico and Brazil: they are all created by the state and remain its supplicant for as long as they cannot compete freely in international markets.

Even today, though manufacturing has far surpassed mining as a source of revenue and employment in South Africa, it remains in need of substantial protection and exerts minimal political influence. The Secretary for Commerce and Industries is in the habit of summoning leading manufacturing capitalists and lecturing on rather than discussing desirable industry policies.[66] Manufacturing capital in South Africa has been encouraged by (one can almost argue it has been *created* by) both the state and mining capital because both of them realized that (1) gold is a wasting resource and, like all mining products, is not inexhaustible; and (2) that employment opportunities offered by primary industries are limited.[67] Both the state and mining capital have diversified directly into manufacturing capital, and they actually control the major manufacturing industries. Thus, to talk of manufacturing capital taking over or acting contrary to or dominating against the interests of either the state or mining capital is literally nonsensical. If the interests of manufacturing capital are favored at any stage, it is because that policy is in the interests of the state and mining capital.

Whatever the South African state was then, (or is today), it was not the instrument of manufacturing capital.[68] Nor can one preserve the idea of the takeover of the state by national capital through the invocation of a powerful ally in the form of agricultural capital. Though the two sectors shared some limited objectives with regard to protective policies, their differences (especially the fundamental difference: between primary and secondary industries) were far more important than were their agreements.[69] The omnibus description encompassing them both, "national capital," creates more confusion than insight.

It is not meant to suggest that the Pact was merely hypocritically pretending to represent a group or groups that it was only marginally concerned about, though elected governments must do this to some extent as a matter of course, and the Pact was no exception. Rather, the point is that any government, given the structure of the state and society, would have operated roughly within the same broad constraints at the time. Individual governments and new policies obviously do make some difference, but it is easy to forget the imperatives and structures that limit them all.

No nonrevolutionary, white-elected government in the Pact's situation would have been able to create a viable white workers' state, ignore the cost imperatives of the gold mines, or fail to intervene to stabilize labor relations on the gold mines and keep down mining costs. The Pact continued to face the legitimation and accumulation problems of previous governments, and it continued to respond to them in notably similar ways.

The mere fact that the Pact had to act in a way so basically contrary to its electoral promises is a striking illustration of the strength of the structural factors shaping the development of the increasingly interventionist South African state. Though the South African case, like all cases, was unique, similar processes were occurring throughout the industrial world.

NOTES

1. Karl Marx, "The Eighteenth Brumaire of Louis Bonaparte," in *Surveys from Exile*, Harmondsworth, 1977, p. 147.

2. A variant of this argument, dealt with in Chapter 1 and below, sees the triumph as mainly that of national capital, or manufacturing capital. It shares in common with the others the central belief that 1924 marked a turning point and a significant change in direction.

3. *Party Programmes and the Mines: A Business Statement*, 15-page pamphlet pub. by TCM on June 2, 1924.

4. BRA, CML, March 1924, Phillips (Arundel Castle) to Wallers.

5. At least £7,000, according to Paul Rich, a researcher who has worked in the TCM Archives. I was unable to check the reference.

6. Richard Bouch, "The South African Party in Opposition, 1924–1929," University of Witwatersrand, honors diss., 1972, p. 28.

7. TCM 97(1)/1924, 1.2.1924.

8. C. E. M. O'Dowd, "The General Election of 1924," *South African Historical Journal*, No. 2, November 1970, p. 55; D. W. Kruger, *The Age of the Generals*, Johannesburg, 1961, p. 125.

9. Margaret Creswell, *An Epoch of the Political History of South Africa in the Life of F. H. P. Creswell*, Johannesburg, 1956, pp. 78–82.

10. A. W. Stadler, "The South African Party," University of Witwatersrand, mimeographed, n.d., pp. 19–20.

11. N. G. Garson, "The Political Role," p. 13: 13.96 percent in 1920, 13.04 percent in 1924.

12. Jeffrey Lever, "Creating the Institutional Order," p. 22.

13. BRA, 3 PH1, 1921–1924, 31.7.1924.

14. PM 1/2/56, File 15/1, Vol. 2, November 1924, Creswell memorandum to Hertzog, for later discussion by the Cabinet.

> We may have the political power, but the Mining Controllers have the economic power . . . If we tell them they ought to help relieve the unemployment position they smile and do nothing. If we suggest to them that their methods of administering white labour are calculated to stir up strife, we are met with polite evasions natural to those who think they are in an impregnable position. They enjoy in consequence an immense political power from whose thrall the electorate for the first time for 25 years has for the time being escaped.

15. MM 2489/25, Part 2, Vol. 802, 23.9.1927.

16. Leased mines were those that had been ceded certain mineral rights owned by the state in exchange for a share of profits, which were calculated on a formula mutually agreed by the company exploiting the rights and the state. There was generally a public tender to determine who should win the rights.

17. MM 2489/25, Part 2, Vol. 802, 3.3.1927. Though this extract sounds somewhat sarcastic in isolation, Pirow's letter was actually extremely humble.

18. MM 1709/25, Vol. 784.

19. See note 36 in the text for Drummond Chaplin's scathing comments on the gap between Creswellian rhetoric and government policy.

20. MM 450/25, Vol. 762.

21. ARTCM, 1925, p. 162; ARTCM, 1926, p. 59.

22. Lever, "Creating the Institutional Order," p. 22.

23. SC 4.1917; UG 49A-1921; MM 2931/22, Vol. 635.

24. They have been exhaustively dealt with elsewhere. The best treat-

ment is probably to be found in Hancock's elegant *Survey*, pp. 46–63, which draws heavily on *Report of the Industrial Legislation Commission*, UG 37-1935, Pretoria, 1935.

25. See *Report on the Industrial Conciliation (Amendment) Bill*, SC 9-1930, Cape Town, 1930.

26. ARTCM, 1924, pp. 56, 81–100.

27. ARTCM, 1925, p. 146; TCM 167/1925, 23.4.1925.

28. Johannesburg *Star*, 25.9.1925.

29. *Report of the Low-Grade Ore Commission*, UG 16-1932, Pretoria, 1932, p. 21.

30. See Table 5, Chapter 6.

31. Jon Lewis, "The New Unionism: Industrialisation and Industrial Unionism in South Africa, 1925–1930," *South African Labour Bulletin*, Vol. 3, No. 5, March–April 1977, pp. 37–38; see also David Kaplan, "The State and Economic Development"; Mike Morris, "The Development of Capitalism in South Africa."

32. Lewis, "The New Unionism," p. 38.

33. *Low-Grade Ore Commission*, p. 61.

34. Ibid., p. 62.

35. BRA, CML, Phillips (London) to Wallers, 26.6.1924.

36. House of Assembly Debates, 1928, Col. 2781, cited by Lever, p. 29.

37. MM 2489/25, Part 2. This was the argument of *The Report of the Mining Regulation Commission*, UG 36-1924, Cape Town, 1925, and appears to have been taken up again by contemporary writers on the industry, for example, Charles Perrings's review article, "The Production Process, Industrial Labour Strategies and Worker Responses in the Southern African Gold Mining Industry," *Journal of African History*, Vol. 18, No. 1, 1977, pp. 129–35. It does not appear to apply particularly well to the gold mining industry, given the technology of the time and the extreme difficulty of mechanization. Even today, strenuous efforts to restructure the gold mining industry to use less black labor are having scant success. See *South African Financial Mail* cover story by David Yudelman, "Mines: Race Against Time," February 28, 1975.

38. MM 1745/25, Vol. 786.

39. MM 2610/74, Vol. 742, 6.8.1924. In the same memorandum, Kotze recommends the reestablishment of the legislative, or statutory, color bar in the "national interest" even though he warned that mining and other industries would be detrimentally affected. Gemmill was also saying in private at that time that white miners would be best protected by the statutory color bar, which was then *ultra vires* (though the employers had not taken much advantage of the court decision to cut down on whites formerly protected). Both Gemmill and Kotze seemed to be saying that the statutory color bar, while unwelcome, was infinitely preferable to the pro-

tection of white workers by the state's laying down minimum wages for particular jobs. Creswell threatened to use the Wage Act for this purpose, supported by the *Mining Regulations Commission*, UG 36-1925, Cape Town, 1925, but he never did so.

40. When he was sent abroad to study on a government scholarship from 1924 to 1925, he was still a lowly Assistant Inspector of Mines, earning £675 per annum. His new job as GME paid £2,000: MM 1412/24, Vol. 719.

41. For details, see Union of South Africa *Public Service List*, annual.

42. See *Parliamentary Register, 1910-1961*, Cape Town, 1970; Horwitz, *Political Economy*, p. 218, says, incorrectly, that Creswell was Minister of Labor from 1924-1933.

43. *Report of the Low-Grade Ore Commission* (appointed August 15, 1930), UG 16-1932, Pretoria, 1932.

44. Ibid., pp. 14, 13, 111.

45. See Chapter 1.

46. *Union Statistics*, G-2.

47. W. K. Hancock, *Survey of British Commonwealth Affairs*, Vol. 2, Part 2, pp. 46-47.

48. The Prime Minister's office described the policy in a circular issued on 31.10.1924, which defined civilized labor as "labour rendered by persons whose standard of living conforms to the standard generally recognized as tolerable from the European standpoint," quoted in Hancock, *Survey*, p. 48.

49. Sheila van der Horst, "The Effects of Industrialisation on Race Relations in South Africa," in Guy Hunter, ed., *Industrialisation and Race Relations: a Symposium*, London, 1965, argues that the post-1932 boom and World War II solved the poor white and white unemployment problems rather than the civilized labor policy. *Union Statistics*, especially section G1-G32, seems to confirm this.

50. *Union Statistics*, G-15.

51. Ibid., G-10. See also C. G. W. Schumann, "Report of the Customs Tariff Commission, 1934-1935," *South African Journal of Economics*, Vol. 4, 1936, p. 176; and David Kaplan, "The Politics of Industrial Protection in South Africa, 1910-1939," *Journal of Southern African Studies*, Vol. 3, No. 1, October 1976, pp. 86-90. Schumann questions the employment-creating function of the protection tariff. Kaplan summarily dismisses it. On the other hand, Kaplan and three coauthors argue the opposite case in Robert Davies, David Kaplan, Mike Morris, and Dan O'Meara, "Class Struggle and the Periodisation of the State in South Africa," *Review of African Political Economy*, No. 7, September-December 1976, pp. 11-12. Of his two diametrically opposite versions, Kaplan's "Industrial Protection" appears to be the more correct.

52. Hancock, *Survey*, p. 52.

53. *Union Statistics*, G-15, H-23.

54. Davies, et al., "Class Struggle," p. 6: National capital "seized hegemony from mining capital, the principal fraction of international or Imperialist capital, which exercised hegemony before that date." Kaplan, "Industrial Protection," p. 91: "The industrial and agricultural fractions . . . found an identity of interest in the encouragement of local industry and . . . acting in concert, prevailed upon the state to effect a positive protection policy. That these fractions were able to prevail upon the State in opposition to the policies advocated by mining and import-oriented commerce, provides a major index of where legitimacy lay in this period."

55. Horwitz, *Political Economy*, p. 245, published in 1967, poured scorn on the exaggerated role attributed to the protectionist policy and manufacturing industry in general.

56. As Kaplan himself shows in "State and Economic Development," p. 8.

57. Newell M. Stultz, "Who Goes to Parliament?" Occasional paper No. 19, Institute of Social and Economic Research, Rhodes University, 1975. This is not mentioned in the belief that, in itself, it contradicts the notion of the new hegemonic role of agriculture; but agriculture was clearly as powerful, if not more powerful, before 1924 as it was after 1924.

58. Kaplan, "State and Economic Development" and "Industrial Protection"; Davies, et al., pp. 9, 30. The dangers of marrying the distinct processes of the rise of protectionism and the South African transformation to locally oriented capitalism are pointed out by Belinda Bozzoli, "The Origins, Development and Ideology of Local Manufacturing in South Africa," *Journal of Southern African Studies*, Vol. 1, No. 2, April 1975, p. 214. Bozzoli's careful study avoids the worst of the turning-point pitfalls.

59. D. J. J. Botha, "On Tariff Policy: The Formative Years," *South African Journal of Economics*, Vol. 41, No. 4, 1973, p. 343.

60. H. Warington Smyth, "Fostering of Productive Industries."

61. TCM E5, Wallers addressing TCM subcommittee on local industries, 17.7.1916.

62. Ibid.

63. Botha, "On Tariff Policy," provides a sensitive and cautious treatment of the equivocal impact of the new government's protection program. Kaplan, "Industrial Protection," p. 72, accuses Botha and others of giving "purely descriptive" accounts "narrated in journalistic fashion"; but his own account, where it does not naïvely accept mining industry propaganda, treats the statistics and events in characteristically procrustean fashion. See also Introduction.

64. J. J. Stadler, "The Gross Domestic Product of South Africa,

1911–1959," *South African Journal of Economics*, Vol. 31, 1963, pp. 185–208; *Union Statistics*, L-3.

65. Smuts, admittedly an interested party, argued in considerable detail that the Pact had not nearly fulfilled its election promises, *Smuts Papers*, Vol. 5, pp. 396–98, 30.4.1929. He was not able to convince the electorate of this: the pact won by a large margin in 1929, in spite of the loss of 10 seats by the Labour party.

66. Personal communication from George Palmer, foreign editor of the U.S. magazine, *Business Week*, September 1977. Palmer was formerly a senior economist with the South African Federated Chamber of Industries, and sat in on such meetings.

67. William Weiler, "The State and the Economic Life of South Africa: A Study of Government Measures Taken with Reference to Home Economy and External Trade," University of the Witwatersrand, political philosophy honors thesis, 1937, pp. 14, 38. See also note 60 above.

68. Horwitz, *Political Economy*, p. 244: "Industrialists exercised virtually no political influence in the early Union Parliaments." He might have added that they still exercise little or no influence, unless they represent mining capital as well.

69. Bozzoli, "Local Manufacturing," p. 203.

The State Comes of Age, 1933–1939

A quarrel between philosophers should be taken as seriously
as a philosophical argument between two bricklayers.
— Friedrich Nietzsche, *My Sister and I*

The focus of this study has been on the developing relationship of
the state and capital, particularly as that relationship was shaped
by the incorporation of organized labor. The subjugation and co-
optation of organized labor was largely completed with the passing
of the Industrial Conciliation Act of 1924. But Chapter 7 went into
the events of 1924–1933 in some detail with the object of demon-
strating that the Pact government of that period did nothing significant to reverse the situation of organized labor. Even more important, it did nothing to alter the basic relationship of the state and
mining capital.

The 1924–1933 period, then, was more remarkable for its continuity than for the basic changes it is usually said to mark.
Organized labor did not experience a new lease on life, the state did
not fall into new hands, and a new fraction of capital did not come
to be hegemonic over all the others. All this needs to be said, not
merely to confound conventional explanations, but also to enable
one to understand more fully the developing relationship of the
state and capital. There was a deeper logic to that development than
can be teased out by referring to the vicissitudes of party politics or
the wars of words between protectionists and free traders.

The deeper logic is as evident in the period 1933–1939 as in the
previous period. In 1924–1933, superficial developments implied a
turning point: an apparent political resurgence of organized labor,
the emergence of manufacturing and national capital, and a cor-

responding weakening of mining capital. In 1933–1939, by contrast, superficial developments implied a political renaissance of mining capital. The Minister of Mines between 1933–1936 was Patrick Duncan, a former member of the Unionist party which was so often stigmatized as the creature of mining capital; and no Laborite or Afrikaner nationalist was to regain control of the portfolio until 1948. The economic policies of the old South African party dominated the new United party government. Yet the superficial developments of this period were as misleading as were those of the previous period.

The deeper logic, the ever-increasing state intervention in an economy dominated by large-scale aggregations of capital, again predominated. Accelerating interventionism has possibly been overstated in analyzing, for example, Roosevelt's New Deal. If anything, it has been understated in the case of the South African state as governed by Hertzog's new United party. Perhaps this is partly because state policies providing subsidized sheltered employment for the (white) unemployed on public works were common in South Africa many years before the Great Depression and the New Deal. The perennial problems of legitimation and accumulation in South Africa took on new forms during the post-1933 period. The state and capital came up with new responses, which were influenced by developments abroad and which themselves influenced these developments.[1]

In this period, organized labor continues to recede as a major issue between and within the state and capital. One must, therefore, increasingly move into other areas to keep up with the developing relationship of the state and capital. Organized labor does not, from the point of view of this study, warrant as detailed a treatment as was necessary for the pre-1933 period. Only in the 1970s, in fact, does the issue of organized labor—this time, black—begin to regain its former centrality.

The truly vital development for both the state and capital in South Africa after the Pact government occurred in an entirely different area—the (internationally determined) price of gold. All over the world, capitalist states (and others) were vastly increasing their intervention into societies and economies; in South Africa, the decisive event in this long-standing process was the dramatic increase in the price of gold in 1933–1934. If one were to insist on the necessity of tracing turning points—which this study does not do—then 1933–1934 would be a far more convincing date as a turning point for the emergence of modern South Africa than the 1924 or 1948 general elections.

THE GOLD PRICE

Although the period from 1924–1928 had been a period of recovery for the gold mining industry, it was still thought of as a dying industry, as it had been most of its life (and was to be later, for example, in the late 1960s). The onset of the Depression had far less effect on the industry than on other sectors of the economy, as world demand for gold at a fixed price was theoretically infinite. But the continuing decline in ore values (the lower proportion of gold per ton of ore milled) inspired debates on how the state might help in reducing costs. To prolong the life of the industry, it was necessary to increase greatly the proportion of ore that could be profitably mined.

The Low-Grade Ore Commission reported on the problem in 1932, and the prognosis was understandably gloomy for the white mineworkers, for in a dying industry that was once again attacking costs, white labor was one obvious target. In 1920–1921, when its wages had constituted 25 percent of total gold mining revenue, it was admittedly a more urgent target. By 1929, while its wages now constituted only 19 percent of revenue, white labor was hemmed in by the new industrial order and the state conciliation procedures and was still one of the cost factors most vulnerable to employer action. The Low-Grade Ore Commission made precisely that point in February 1932, but by the end of the year, the position had entirely changed.

At the end of 1932, South Africa decided to leave the gold standard and allow its currency to depreciate—in effect, lifting the price of gold. The following year, the liquid capital exported from South Africa in 1931–1932 because of the Pact's refusal to leave the gold standard poured back. At the same time, the United States devalued the dollar, and the *world* price of gold rose, in addition to the increase through devaluation in terms of South African currency.

Within a year, the price per ounce rocketed 45 percent, from £4 12 shillings and three pence to £6 9 shillings and three pence. The next year it went to over £7 and continued to climb for the rest of the decade. For an industry as cost-sensitive as the gold mining industry, this was a dramatic development. Not only did it mean sharply increased revenue from realized gold (see Table 12), it also meant that enormous blocks of previously unpayable ore now became payable. Moreover, this ore could be easily extracted from existing mines, and therefore, no large capital expenditure was required to extract it.[2] Finally, the meteoric price rise stimulated the opening of an entire gold field, known as the West Wits line.

It is instructive to analyze how this bonanza was divided. To start with, the mining companies made both working and share profits, as one private company history put it, "beyond the dreams of avarice."[3] The state, though now governed by the new United party (which included all those groups and people conventionally thought to be the "instruments" of the mining industry), imposed "surplus profit" taxes at a level previously unheard of in South Africa. It increased its total receipts from gold mining from £4.3m in 1932 to £14.5m in 1933. Revenue from gold mining as a percentage of total revenue rose from 8 percent to 33 percent in the same time (see also Table 11, Chapter 7).

Taxation increased almost overnight to levels that the Pact, sometimes thought to be the instrument of interests opposing mining capital, could never have dreamed of applying during its tenure. This is not to suggest the Pact would not have taxed the in-

Table 12   Capital's Revenue from Gold, Selected Years, 1905–1940

Year	(£ million)
1905	20.9
1910	33.9
1915	38.6
1920	45.6
1925	40.8
1930	45.0
1931	46.2
1932	49.2
1933	68.7
1934	72.3
1935	76.5
1940	118.0

Source: ARTCMs.

dustry more severely if it had thought it was possible, or that the new United party government was not in fact more sympathetic toward the industry. Rather, it suggests that there were certain intractables in the South African politico-economic situation that limited the power of any government, in dealing with the industry, to fairly circumscribed parameters.

As Gemmill had put it, South Africa's government was capitalistic and "nominally democratic." He might have added that the state was the white man's preserve, which, by and large, only recognized the black man's presence as a labor unit. Besides these relative "constants," one must examine the nature of the South African economy. South Africa was a late-developing capitalist state, with only one reliable source of foreign exchange with which to mount a program of import-substitute industrialization (local manufacture of items previously imported). That source of foreign exchange, moreover, was a wasting asset heavily dependent on continuing flows of foreign investment. Its producers, moreover, were unable to control its price.

Nevertheless, while it cannot be denied that different governments may have represented (or collaborated with) mining capital in differing degrees, there were large areas of the state-capital relationship outside the control of *either* party. While an "enemy" of capital, such as Creswell, could make things awkward, or a "friend," such as Smuts, could smooth out situations, one cannot draw conclusions about the nature of the state-capital relationship at that epiphenomenal level.

To return to taxation, there can be no doubt, in retrospect, that all South African governments have taxed mining capital at rates they thought the traffic could bear. Sometimes, they underestimated, helped by the TCM's formidable and unrelenting propaganda programs; occasionally, they might have overestimated capital's ability to pay (though such examples do not readily spring to mind).

THE WHITE MINERS AND THE UNITED PARTY REGIME

Having set out the intractables, or broad constants, of the state-industry relationship, however, it is necessary to reiterate that, within these parameters, the freedom of human will did operate and did make a difference. The example that has been dealt with in this study is white organized mine labor. While there is no doubt that white mineworkers were never remotely powerful enough to harness the South African state for their own ends, one should, nevertheless, ask how well they fared within their limitations. The conventional answer is that by allying themselves to other groups, they were relatively successful. There is some limited truth in this: they did, after all, survive an attack that, some have argued, was intended to replace them *en masse* with black miners.

The manner of their survival under the Pact government, however, left much to be desired. Far from gaining, they lost at the expense of their employers and, less dramatically, even at the expense of their black fellow workers. In the period of economic boom, after 1932, they made something of a recovery, with white real wages and employment level rising slightly faster than those of blacks (see Table 5, Chapter 6, and Table 8, Chapter 7). Nevertheless, amid riches "beyond the dream of avarice," their real wages in 1936 only approximated 1911 levels and fell back thereafter until the war.

The black/white ratio after 1932 moved in favor of the white miner once again, declining by 20 percent between 1932 and 1939. The movement, however, had little to do with the state's action in favor of the white miners or with trade-union pressure. Rather, it was the result of continuing mechanization over this period that required more skilled and supervisory white labor for the operation of mechanical and electrical equipment.[4]

Though the mining unions won a closed-shop agreement with the TCM in 1937,[5] the motivations of the employers seemed to be largely to help resist "a newly-formed organization, said to be racial and political in character"[6] (this referred to the struggle of a rival trade union, the Afrikanerbond van Mynwerkers, to take over control of the white miners and to take over the SAMWU). In the same year, the mineworkers' modest request for a cost-of-living allowance was brushed aside.[7]

The TCM continued to refuse to form an industrial council in spite of mild criticism from, *inter alia*, the 1935 Industrial Legislation Commission, which pointed out that of eighty-nine conciliation boards assembled since the I.C. Act in 1924, twenty-eight were for disputes in the gold mining industry.[8] The Commission also pointed out that there had not been one prosecution of the employers under the I.C. Act in 1933 and 1934, and that employers, in general, were leniently treated when prosecuted and inadequately fined for deterrence purposes.

Not surprisingly, it also reported that workers were apathetic and the unions were less militant, with declining membership.[9] The Secretary for Labour bemoaned this as "a regrettable tendency, since a high degree of organization among employers and employees usually signifies a high degree of compliance with wage-regulating instruments."[10] The co-optation of the trade unions, if it was to work smoothly, needed the unions to continue to represent the majority of the white workers. The unions had to retain some support from the rank and file; otherwise, they ceased even to represent "elements which in some way reflect the sentiment or possess the confidence of the relevant public or mass. . . ."[11]

Thus, the period 1933–1939 is notable for the white miners only in the sense that they accomplished nothing important, even though the profits of the employers and the revenue of the state remained at between 150% and 600% of 1932 levels (see Table 13). The structured access to the state that the white miner (along with

Table 13   How the Cake Was Sliced, 1932–1939

	White miners[a]	Employers[b]	State[c]
1932	963	8/0	4.3 (8.2%)
1933	1,010	15/9	14.5 (33.0%)
1934	1,024	15/0	13.2 (23.8%)
1935	1,014	14/8	14.3 (33.6%)
1936	1,009	13/3	13.6 (23.6%)
1937	976	12/6	13.6 (20.4%)
1938	939	11/9	12.6 (19.5%)
1939	952	12/2	16.6 (27.0%)

Sources: Official Yearbooks; ARTCMs; Leo Katzen, *Gold and the South African Economy*, Cape Town, 1964, pp. 56–57.

[a]Real wage index, 1910=1,000.

[b]Working profit per ton, in shillings and pence. This understates the employers' bonanza to the extent that tonnages increased.

[c]Receipts from gold mining, £ millions (percent of total revenue).

other organized workers) had "won" in 1924–1926 proved once again to be very much an illusory prize. Even after 1932, when the state and capital were awash with cash and the traffic could bear significant wage increases, the white miners' position stagnated. From 1935 to 1938, in fact, the index of real wages of the white miners declined.

What this demonstrated once again was that formal co-optation had given the South African Mine Workers' Union "responsibility for power rather than power itself."[12] This was, of course, a far worse situation for white labor in some ways than before 1907, when neither the state nor the employers had been willing to recognize the organized unions as the white workers' mouthpiece. Then, the unions could more freely use direct industrial action, in the form of strikes, to achieve their goals. Now—for obvious reasons, given the successful state-capital incorporation of the unions—the state and the employers became the ones to insist that the truncated unions spoke for their members.

The post-1933 period did not usher in any significant changes for organized labor outside of the mining industry. Representatives of both capital and organized labor broadly supported the status quo when they gave evidence to the 1935 Industrial Legislation Commission. When the Industrial Conciliation Act was amended in 1937, therefore, the changes merely enabled the councils to extend their scope beyond those defined as "employees" under the act—that is, they were empowered to lay down terms for the employment of blacks. The net effect was to negate the possibility of blacks undercutting white labor in the large organized industries (an amendment to the Wage Act in the same year had a similar effect on labor structures in the unorganized industries).[13]

The state progressively supervised more and more of the organized labor force, and capital experienced progressively less political opposition from labor. Table 14 partially illustrates this process. It refers to nonmining sectors only, as no industrial council has ever been appointed for the mining industry.

Such changes as occurred in the field of labor legislation after 1933, then, made it easier for the state to impose its civilized labor policy on sectors of capital other than the mining employers. These employers, the manufacturing capitalists said by some to have been the hegemonic fraction of capital after 1924 (see Introduction and

Table 14   Institutionalization and Depoliticization: The Case of the Industrial Conciliation Act, 1933–1939

	No. of industrial council agreements registered (A)	Conciliation board agreements and awards (B)	No. of white employees covered by A and B ('000)	No. of whites involved in strikes
1933	22	6	40.2	1,255
1934	29	7	52.4	1,539
1935	28	7	49.3	1,005
1936	35	8	47.9	640
1937	38	5	71.6	1,077
1938	37	6	86.8	92
1939	43	4	97.1	49

Source: Robert Davies, *Capital, State and White Labour*, New Jersey, 1979, p. 270, drawn from Department of Labour Reports.

Chapter 7), continued to bear the burden, with the state bureaucracy, of easing white unemployment and of thus helping the state with its legitimation problems.

THE STATE AND THE ECONOMIC BOOM

The revival of the gold mining industry in 1933 led to an unprecedented boom in the South African economy as a whole. State revenue and mining capital profits rocketed, but, as has been pointed out, organized labor on the mines made extremely meager progress. Even the illusion of power that was bestowed by the process of formal co-optation began to fade. The mining unions lost some members, but more importantly, they lost the last vestiges of militance and coherence even as they gained closed-shop status. By the time of World War II, organized white mine labor was an insignificant force in South Africa, particularly in economic and industrial terms. Formerly the most organized and militant section of the white labor force, it was thoroughly co-opted, depoliticized, and riven by internal dissent and corruption.

The state, for its part, had gained tremendously in stature. It had obtained that "secure minimum of earnings," which, Galbraith argues, enables a state to "preserve the autonomy on which its decision-making depends" without "finding it necessary to appeal to outside suppliers of capital."[14] It had formally co-opted organized labor without any significant sacrifices in sovereignty and had established a *quid pro quo* relationship with mining capital, which ensured that the employers would "take cognisance of the social costs as well as the private costs of the industry."[15]

Almost uniquely among industrial states, South Africa had a series of budget surpluses between 1933 and 1937 as a result of the gold bonanza.[16] It paid off a significant proportion of its foreign debts and began to raise significantly more loans in South Africa, which made it less dependent on foreign capital and gave it an important degree of financial independence:[17] foreign debt as a percentage of total state debt fell dramatically. (See Table 15.) This was highly significant, not only in the state's dealings with the international community of states, but also in its relationship with foreign investors. It was also significant in that the mining industry was the source of much of this debt finance, which further cemented the symbiotic relationship of state and mining capital.

Foreign investment, of course, remained very important and, in fact, poured in at an accelerating rate after 1933, accentuating the boom: it was estimated that £63 million was invested from abroad in the gold fields between 1933 and 1939,[18] well over 60 percent of total foreign investment for the period. While foreign private investment increased, however, the South African state rapidly

Table 15   The State's Public Debt, Selected Years, 1911–1945

	Total debt (A) (£ million)	Foreign debt (B) (£ million)	B as % of A
1911	114.2	104.0	91.0
1915	138.2	123.3	89.2
1920	173.9	123.4	71.0
1925	214.3	139.2	64.9
1930	249.7	156.0	62.5
1935	274.1	156.7	57.2
1940	291.4	106.1	36.4
1945	540.1	18.2	3.4

Source: Union Statistics for Fifty Years, 1910–1960, Pretoria, 1960, Q7/8.

reduced its own financial obligations to foreign lenders. This was vital, especially when one considers how international finance capital can use (and has used, see Chapter 2) the state's public finance position to influence its dealings with private capital.

At the same time, the state's revenue from the gold mines also increased phenomenally: total receipts rose from £4.3m in 1932 to £13.5m in 1933 and did not drop below £12.6m for the rest of the decade (see also Table 11). These receipts, of course, came from the vastly increased taxation of the gold mines. The gold mines did not concede the new tax rates without a tremendous public struggle, but behind the scenes, its leaders were prepared to go along with the state since the increased taxation still left vastly increased profits.

In 1933, John Martin, one of the most senior mining employers and several times TCM President, wrote an apologetic private letter to Patrick Duncan, the Minister responsible for the increased taxation, regretting the terms of a TCM statement on taxation increases "to which you justifiably took exception." He said he did not think there was any difference of opinion between Duncan and "the responsible representatives of the industry."[19] Two years later, Martin once again wrote to Duncan opposing a minimum-wage bill for the mining industry: It would be, he said, "disastrous for the Government to start fixing wages in the primary industries."[20] This time Duncan bowed: the bill was never passed. The relationship of the state and mining capital remained a symbiotic one, though the balance had, to some extent, tilted in favor of the state.

It has been argued that the vastly increased tax bill imposed on mining capital by the state indicates a takeover of the state by national, manufacturing capital and its appropriation of the windfall profits of mining capital. This argument is patently false when applied to the Pact government as the instrument of national capital (see Chapter 1, especially note 35; passim). But to what extent is it true of the United party, which incorporated the old "allies" (some would even say "servants") of mining capital: the Unionist and South African parties?

There is no doubt that the state diverted revenue from the mining industry to other sectors of the economy and that it established marketing arrangements that discriminated in favor of certain sectors—most notably, agriculture. This policy was in line with developments elsewhere, including the agricultural policies of the

New Deal in the United States. But the diversion was nothing new in South African history: since Union in 1910 and before, the mining industry was regarded by the state as both a wasting resource and as the milch cow of the economy, and it was treated as such whenever possible. Its position as a milch cow also ensured it certain privileges: when it was seriously threatened, governments would be forced to act to protect it, even if their actions were politically unpopular (as in 1907, 1914, and 1922). The state also gave the industry a virtual monopoly over foreign migrant labor, a monopoly no South African government has ever seriously challenged.

Thus, although mining capital faced unprecedented rates of taxation in the post-1933 boom, its senior leaders and strategists, such as John Martin, never seriously challenged the state's right to take a large share of the windfall profits resulting from the higher gold price. The tax system, after all, was already moving toward taxing profitability rather than profits (through Robert Kotze's leasing taxation system, established two decades earlier). This plan meant little or no tax in hard times and very high tax in good times; it maximized security and restricted windfall profits.

The state had provided mining capital with a great deal, without which the industry itself would not have been possible: it provided essential help in the establishment of a migrant labor system that covered half of Africa; and it established a system of labor conciliation for organized labor, which has been discussed at length above (Chapters 2 to 5), and which ensured industrial stability. It had also done many other things to encourage the development of the industry, which are beyond the scope of this study. Mining capital, then, though it was (as always) vociferous in its complaints about the taxation of its post-1933 windfall profits, accepted the idea that the services provided in return by the state were well worth the price. In 1934, the state greatly simplified and expanded the mineral rights it was prepared to grant to mining capital. The effects are impossible to quantify, but the new situation comprised a substantial *quid pro quo* for the increased taxation faced by the gold mines.

The state, then, had always been willing to ensure that the gold mining industry would continue to be viable. After 1933, it was also able to use its vastly increased revenue to implement new programs of industrial diversification that virtually ended the poor white and unemployment problems.

The subjugation and co-optation of organized white labor in the 1920s made it possible for both the state and employers to benefit fully from the gold price increase without passing on any significant share of the new prosperity to the white miners or to organized labor in general. The treatment of organized labor in South Africa in the late 1930s should finally put to rest any remaining notion that the unions won a victory in 1924. It should also confirm the importance to the state of the 1924 transformation of the white labor question from an intensely political to a largely administrative issue. The fact that the state's intervention largely stabilized the mining industry by depoliticizing white labor made it that much easier for the state to take an increasingly interventionist role in society in general. The modern South African state finally came of age after the gold price increase of 1932-1934, but the foundations of adulthood had been laid between 1907 and 1924.

NOTES

1. A notable example of both was the massive five-volume study, *Report of the Commission on the Poor White Problem in South Africa,* Stellenbosch, 1932, sponsored by the Carnegie Foundation.

2. Social and Economic Planning Council Reports, Report No. 11, *Economic Aspects of the Gold Mining Industry,* p. 52.

3. C. Potts, "A History of Union Corporation," unpublished.

4. Ranan Lubinsky, "The Role of the Gold Mining Industry in the Growth of the South African Economy, 1933-1939," B.A. honours diss., University of the Witwatersrand, 1974, p. 7.

5. ARTCM, 1937, pp. 61-66.

6. Ibid., pp. 33-34, 50.

7. Ibid., p. 34.

8. UG 37-1935, p. 94.

9. Ibid., p. 88.

10. Ibid., p. 89.

11. Philip Selznik, *TVA and the Grass Roots,* p. 14; Dan O'Meara, "White Trade Unionism, Political Power and Afrikaner Nationalism," in the *South African Labour Bulletin,* Vol. 1, No. 10, April 1975, outlines the corruption of the SAMWU at this stage.

12. Selznik, *TVA and the Grass Roots,* p. 14. It was only much later, under the national party, after 1948, that the SAMWU made anything of a comeback; but even in the 1960s, when the white miners were reputed to be a powerful force, it can be argued that they remained formally co-opted by the state.

13. Davies, *Capital, State and White Labour*, pp. 264–66, 269–70.

14. John Kenneth Galbraith, *The New Industrial State*, New York, 1967, pp. 177–79.

15. *Economic Aspects of the Gold Mining Industry*, p. 57.

16. De Kiewiet, *A History of South Africa*, p. 176.

17. Ibid.

18. S. H. Frankel and H. Herzfield, "An Analysis of the Growth of the National Income of the Union in the Period of Prosperity Before the War," *South African Journal of Economics*, Vol. 12, 1944, cited in Davies, *Capital, State and White Labour*, p. 252.

19. Patrick Duncan Papers, University of Cape Town, A5.1.3, Martin (London) to Duncan (South Africa), 17.7.1933.

20. Ibid., A5.2.9, 3.1.1935.

Epilogue: The Seventies and Eighties

Ça ira, ça tiendra
[That will be, that will last]

—French Revolution Song

L. P. Hartley, the British novelist, has argued that the past is like a foreign country, somewhat opaque, offering "lessons" for ourselves, and the present, which are at best of ambiguous validity. However persuasive this argument may be, it remains true that the past provides a perspective to understanding current affairs that we would be foolish to ignore. This does not mean that it would now be appropriate to update the above text with a potted history of the relationship of state, capital, and organized labor in South Africa from World War II to the present. Organized labor between 1940 and 1970 was largely a non-issue, particularly with regard to the developing symbiotic relationship of state and capital. Labor history in those years, while of intrinsic interest, is of no particular significance to this study.

In the 1970s, however, organized labor again became a vital issue to both state and capital, though it has to be remembered that we are now talking of "another country" and another "organized labor," and that extreme caution must be exercised in drawing analogies. In terms of the above study, a number of general themes are recurring now. The state's legitimation and accumulation imperatives are once again in acute contradiction. The state's technique of blending subjugation and co-optation in meeting potential challenges has come to the fore again. And the state continues to operate in a symbiotic relationship of mutual dependence with mining capital. This epilogue views South Africa briefly in the 1970s

and 1980s with these specific themes in mind and with no preten-
sions of saying anything more comprehensive about the contemporary scene.[1] The terminology and argument of the Epilogue
therefore presupposes familiarity with the argument of this study as
a whole.

It is important first to say a few words about methodology. This
study has attempted to analyze the decision-making process by
looking in detail both at the intentions of the decision makers—particularly as expressed privately and without rhetorical objectives—and the actual outcomes of their policies. These outcomes
include, of course, unintended consequences and have, as far as
possible, been expressed in concrete statistical data. In looking at
the 1970s and 1980s one finds progressively less reliable non-
rhetorical data about the intentions of policy makers. The exegesis
of policy statements, press releases, and the editorializing of the
media, however acutely it may be done,[2] is subject to inherent and
inevitable limitations. This does not mean that such analysis should
be rejected; obviously, it is not always possible (or desirable) to wait
thirty years for the opening of archival evidence. All this means is
that in such situations one should perhaps be more cautious than
ever in judging motives and intentions. What follows, therefore, is
loaded in favor of statistically verifiable "outcomes" and begs some
questions. Little is said about the extent to which these "outcomes"
were intended or unintended consequences of policy. These are important questions, but it would be inappropriate or impossible to
do them full justice here.

PROFILE 1: ORGANIZED LABOR

Some analysts have argued that organized white labor—in particular white mine labor—has maintained a political significance in
South Africa. In the 1948 General Election, the swing to the National party in four key mining constituencies helped defeat the
United party.[3] And, as recently as the 1981 General Election, mining constituencies voted more strongly for the Herstigte Nasionale
Party (HNP) than any other constituencies (up to 30 percent).
While these may be plausible arguments, they say nothing more
than that specific interest groups can exercise disproportionate influence in closely fought elections.

It would be pointless to deny, for example, that the religious parties in Israel have exercised influence because of their crucial role in forming coalition governments; but it would be obtuse to suggest that the Israeli state is therefore a theocracy. Similarly the white miners, and the white workers in general, may exercise an influence on South African elections, but they do not determine the complexion of the state as a whole.

In economic terms, the relative impotence of the organized white labor movement—and the white miners—is even clearer. White miners and white workers as a whole have diminished steadily in proportion to blacks, and the real wages of whites grew more slowly in the 1970s than those of blacks, though the income gap between the races remains huge. This income gap is particularly notable in the gold mining industry, in which blacks started off from a very low base. (See Table 16 and Figure 2.)

Table 16   White and Black Miners' Wages, 1968–1980

	Indexed and deflated by the consumer price index (January 1968=100)		Actual (Rands per month)		White/black wage ratio
	White	Black	White	Black	:1
1968	100.4	98.7	337	16.41	20.54
1969	99.4	99.6	347	17.06	20.34
1970	104.7	98.8	386	17.82	21.66
1971	106.5	99.3	414	18.96	21.84
1972	106.8	107.6	450	21.96	20.49
1973	123.7	133.3	576	29.93	19.24
1974	124.3	193.6	649	48.69	13.33
1975	123.1	285.9	734	81.38	9.02
1976	122.0	301.9	802	95.33	8.41
1977	119.3	307.6	872	108.09	8.07
1978	112.8	317.2	930	124.33	7.48
1979	108.9	324.7	1023	144.82	7.06
1980	112.5	345.9	1191	214.97	5.54

Source: Derived from Chamber of Mines of South Africa statistics.

Note: The wages for whites are of unionized workers. Mine officials, not classified as unionized, experienced a slightly slower growth of wages from a similar base.

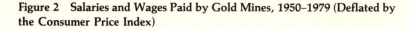

Figure 2　Salaries and Wages Paid by Gold Mines, 1950–1979 (Deflated by the Consumer Price Index)

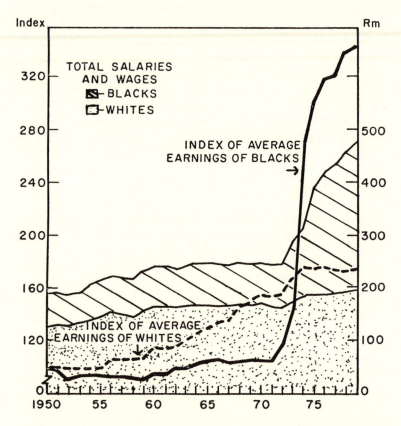

Source: Mercabank, *Focus on Key Economic Issues,* No. 25, March 1980, Johannesburg, 1980.

White miners' wages have always been a significant percentage of total gold mining revenue: 24.6 percent in 1911, 25 percent in 1920, 18.8 percent in 1930, and 16.7 percent in 1940. By 1980 white miners' wages had declined to 5.7 percent of total gold mining revenue. The black:white proportion had also shifted in favor of the blacks, though not dangerously so from the white point of view (up to 9.9:1, or 426,329 to 42,928). But even this position is still under attack.

The steep climb in black wages in the mines is attributable partly to the rapid increase in the gold price, which moved from an average of $40 per ounce in 1971 to $97 in 1973, $159 in 1974, and, after the depressed years of 1975 to 1977 up farther to $193 (1978), $307 (1979), $612 (1980), before a new decline to $462 (1981). The increase in the gold price was the *necessary* condition for the increase in black wages, but the price increase was not a *sufficient* cause. After all, in the post-1933 boom, neither black nor white wages moved in line with the gold price (see Table 13). Moreover, the boom of the 1970s was not accompanied by any notable increases in white miners' wages, for, while black wages increased by 246 percent in real terms, white wages increased by a mere 12.5 percent.

There were two reasons black wages increased so quickly, besides the fact that their extremely low levels were beginning to attract world criticism and to embarrass the industry internationally. First, there was a squeeze on supply, particularly after Malawi withdrew most of her migrant miners in the early 1970s. Moreover, the takeover by Frelimo in Mozambique at the same time posed the threat of even greater losses. In the early 1970s, less than 25 percent of the black labor force on the gold mines was of South African origin, while about 50 percent came from Malawi and Mozambique. Though Frelimo could never afford to withdraw migrant labor from South Africa, the Malawi withdrawals caused some punishing shortages and made the employers acutely aware of their vulnerability to foreign supplies. To attract more South African mine labor, particularly from the urban areas, considerably higher wages were offered. The policy was a success, and by the end of the decade over 55 percent of the black mine labor force was South African, whereas less than 15 percent came from Malawi and Mozambique. (See Figure 3.)

Second, black miners began in the early 1970s to show an activism that had been completely absent since the crushing of their mass strike in 1946. Riots in the mine compounds became frequent occurrences. It was and is by no means clear that these riots were the result of wage grievances; it has even been argued that the riots were caused by increased wages and the narrowing of differentials between different categories of black miners. Certainly, the riots began after black wages started their rapid increase. Nevertheless, the riots occurred in the context of black labor unrest elsewhere,

Figure 3   Sources of Black Labor in Gold Mining, 1950–1979

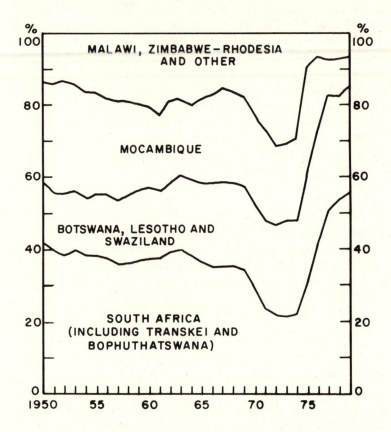

Source: Mercabank, *Focus on Key Economic Issues*, No. 25, March 1980, Johannesburg, 1980.

notably in the Durban strikes of 1973, and no doubt accelerated the trend to higher wages and better conditions in the compounds.

Overall, however, the rate of increase of black mineworkers' wages is likely to slow markedly in the 1980s. The supply squeeze has disappeared because of higher wages and is unlikely to return while black unemployment in the subcontinent remains high. Black wages outside the mines will also vary with supply and demand, pending the emergence of a really powerful organized labor movement.

It has been argued earlier in this study that organized white labor was thoroughly co-opted by the passing of the Industrial Conciliation Act of 1924. But the white mining unions, and, in particular the Mine Workers' Union, continue at least to threaten to go outside the system of institutionalized conciliation procedures. This qualification in no way contradicts the argument: when lions lose their teeth, they do not stop roaring. In fact, they frequently roar all the louder to conceal their impotence. Nor can these elderly lions be ignored completely; the Mine Workers' Union still wins its local victories, and its roar still sends the more ignorant and timorous of the media into shivers of fear about a possible repetition of the 1922 Rand Revolt.

Nevertheless, events of the 1970s have generally confirmed the long decline of the white miners as both a political and an economic force. Though the Herstigte Nasionale Party won its greatest support in the mining constituencies in 1977 and 1980, at times nearly a third of the vote, this has not resulted in any major gains for the white miners. The miners have tried for decades to win a five-day week, but a Government Commission found in 1977 that this would "be too costly to the country at this stage."[4] By 1976, according to Chamber of Mines of South Africa statistics, the officials' associations on the mines (nonunionized) had almost as many members as all the unions put together—18,815 compared to 18,994 unionized men. Of the union men less than half, 9409, were members of the Mine Workers' Union, and most of the balance were members of various "artisan" unions which frequently oppose the views of the MWU, an "industrial" union. Finally, the government made it clear that, while in principle it supports the abolition of all racial discrimination, whether statutory or customary, in the mining industry, it stopped short of committing the state to implement such a change.[5] After 55 years, both state and capital still shy away from the short-term costs of a frontal attack on the shell of the color bar. The white miners can still mobilize a fair amount of popular support on the issue of the color bar, and Dr. Andries Treurnicht's Conservative party will try hard to win the miners from the HNP. But it would be totally unrealistic to expect 18,000 mineworkers, at most, to become a significant political force in the future. Nor can one expect organized white labor outside the mines to become a significant force, either economically or politically.

By contrast, organized black labor—perhaps incorporating some white support—is destined to become one of the major actors in the South African economy and, notwithstanding state efforts at compartmentalization, probably in the polity as well. Black labor on the mines is still largely a migrant force, and, though the Chamber of Mines has now agreed to recognize black unions in certain circumstances, the mineworkers are unlikely to be in the vanguard of the new organized labor movement.

Estimating the size of organized labor in South Africa in the early 1980s is difficult and has to rely to a large extent on the unions' own estimates. At the beginning of 1981 the Trade Union Council of South Africa (TUCSA) was claiming a total of 299,455 members in 60 unions—73,859 whites, 187,180 Indians and Coloureds, 38,416 Africans.[6] Many of the African and Coloured members are organized into "parallel" unions, operating under the wing of their corresponding white unions. TUCSA is avowedly nonpolitical and accepts the existing conciliation procedures within which it operates. The South African Confederation of Labour (SACLA) is an all-white grouping of 18 unions with 134,864 members claimed at the beginning of 1981. Only three years earlier its membership was 250,000. There were several withdrawals by unions which wished to include black members, contrary to the SACLA constitution.

The Confederation of Unions of South Africa (CUSA) is SACLA's black counterpart and claimed 36,019 members as of October 1980. It confines itself to labor organization and to black membership. The Federation of South African Trade Unions (FOSATU) claimed 58,260 members of all races at the end of 1980 and 94,617 by the end of 1981,[7] in ten unions. FOSATU's origins were in the Durban strikes of 1973 and in black unions which left TUCSA in 1976. It was founded in 1979 and has concentrated on converting craft unions into broadly based industrial unions. It has extensive social objectives, but has thus far largely confined itself to industrial methods for achieving these ends. Finally, there are a loosely-bound group of unions which advocate an all-embracing general workers' union and which seek community support in the form of consumer boycotts and general strike funds. They are sometimes known as the "community unions,"[8] and their quasi-syndicalist tactics and political outspokenness has drawn some support away from FOSATU and, in turn, made the latter more politically outspoken.

Overall, organized labor probably had close to 1 million members on its books by the early 1980s, with whites less than 25 percent. This compares with 9,178 in 1910; 135,140 in 1920; 75,496 in 1930; 235,051 in 1940; and 358,625 in 1950,[9] the majority of which were white. Size is less important, however, than the nature of the unions. As recently as 1970, one could have described organized labor as a co-opted movement operating within the established state conciliation procedures and with no aspiration to any form of worker autonomy or activism. This description is clearly no longer accurate since there has been a massive resurgence of strike activity over a wide spectrum of the economy. In 1981, there were 283 strikes and 59 work stoppages nationwide, resulting in the loss of 1,812,434 man-hours.[10] The only comparable figures in the first half of this century are the localized 1922 and 1947 miners' strikes (1.3 million man-hours and 1.4 million man-hours respectively.)

The strikes of the early 1980s were not direct challenges to the state as was the strike of 1922, but strikes must be viewed ominously by the state all the same. It is clear that organized labor in the 1980s, or a significantly large section of it, has not been incorporated or co-opted by the state. In the same way that organized white labor constituted a threat to the state before its co-optation in 1924, organized black labor now constitutes a threat to the South African state. The state is responding to the threat of the 1980s in almost exactly the same way as it did in the early 1920s: with a blend of subjugation (for example, the draconian breaking of the Johannesburg Municipal Workers' strike in July 1980) and co-optation (for example, the Wiehahn Commission blueprint cautiously to incorporate organized black labor). Subjugation and co-optation are not contradictory policies, as some would suggest,[11] but are complementary. The 1924 Industrial Conciliation Act would possibly not have come about without the 1922 Rand Revolt, and the Act would certainly not have worked as well without the Revolt and the state's subjugation of organized labor in 1922. As former President Richard Nixon's aide, Charles Colson, reportedly put it: "If you've got them by the balls, their hearts and minds will follow."

Thus a continued policy of subjugation and co-optation of organized labor, of its leaders and of its mouthpieces in the media can be expected throughout the 1980s. Such a policy poses major problems for the state, which has to tread a wary path between destroying the credibility of the groups it wishes to co-opt and losing ultimate control over areas where it was previously dominant.

The policy also poses major problems for organized labor, which continually must decide whether it can accept the state's gift of fire without burning itself. It must survive to be effective, and it also must use whatever leverage is available to achieve its ends, including "strings-attached" inducements from the state. But it must retain the support of its followers at the same time.

The difficulty of this policy for the government can be seen in the splits in the ruling National party, which arise out of the issue whether organized labor and other groups should be subjugated, or co-opted. Or, in more sophisticated versions of the split, to what extent a policy of subjugation should be followed, to what extent a policy of co-optation. Similar splits have opened up in the labor movement between, for example, the FOSATU and "community" unions over the issue of whether to register as unions under the state umbrella, or to stay aloof.[12] The latter splits have in turn resulted in a rather florid academic debate of great acrimony and passion about the "correct strategy" for organized labor.[13]

The experience of organized labor in the pre-1924 period suggests there is no one correct strategy and that registration will turn out to be important only in the context of various other issues. One has to ask how dedicated and efficient union leadership is and whether it has the resources to survive possible frontal state attacks once it has committed its followers to operating within the formal conciliation machinery. This in turn requires an intimate knowledge of all the protagonists, state, labor and capital and the international context within which they operate. In the early part of this century, organized labor never really stood a chance of an equitable settlement with state and capital: it was too small, vulnerable and dispensable. The struggle of the 1980s promises to be more evenly matched.

PROFILE 2: CAPITAL

Mining capital worldwide is far more concentrated than capital in general, largely because of the nature of mining and its structural requirements. About 150 companies dominate the mining production of all the so-called market economies. They show a high degree of vertical integration and form a fairly close international "fraternity" through interlocking directorates and participation in joint ventures. About 1,250 mines produce 90 percent of total mining output of the "market economies," and nearly two thirds of the major companies are concentrated in the English-speaking countries. The trend to concentration continues to increase, with the growing popularity of massive megaprojects and the growing intervention of states in such projects.[14]

South African mining capital is no exception to this characteristic of mining capital. In fact, it has always been, and continues to be, an extreme example of concentration (see Chapter 2 above). As such, it has put an indelible stamp on the structure of South African capital as a whole. This is not, of course, to argue that the present situation is exactly the same as that of the past, or that past experience can be applied directly to the understanding of present and future. Compare the South African state, economy and capital of 1910 with that of 1980, and the differences are obvious to the most casual observer. To a large extent they can be summarized by one word: diversification. There has been diversification of all three, resulting in change of a very basic nature.

On the other hand, there are continuities that it would be foolish to ignore. Mining capital today, albeit diversified, stands in a very similar symbiotic relation to the contemporary diversified state as pertained sixty years ago, and for many of the same reasons. Its role in the accumulation and legitimation processes is also very similar, as we shall see. Distinguishing the continuities as well as the structural changes illuminates a whole series of contemporary events and problems.

Two major events in the 1970s have changed the shape of South African mining capital. First, the freeing of the gold price gave an enormous impetus to capital expansion, the opening up of new mines, and the diversification into new enterprises by the Mining Houses. One of the results of the rapidly rising gold price was that the cost of producing gold was allowed to rise very rapidly, particularly the cost of black labor, in an industry that previously had always contained costs ruthlessly and efficiently. The situation was a novel one for gold mining capital, but two slumps in the gold price—in the mid 1970s and early 1980s—brought home very clearly that capital was as dependent as ever on a gold price over which it had almost no control.[15] This in turn meant that it remained dependent on the state to protect it in a crisis: the state duly responded by drastically devaluing the currency, the rand, in the mid-1970s and by allowing it to float down in a "dirty" (managed float) in the early 1980s. Devaluation of the currency is a crucial aid to the gold mines because they are paid for their gold in U.S. dollars. Thus, for example, if the gold price in dollars falls less than the rand:dollar conversion rate, the rand receipts of the mines would still be up. Between 1970 and 1981, the average *rand* price received for gold declined only twice, in 1976 and 1981.

The second major event for mining capital in the 1970s was the massive diversification of mining in South Africa. In the early 1970s, the state embarked on an enormous program of infrastructural development, with a major purpose of allowing the competitive export of coal and base minerals to world markets. Two new deepwater seaports were built, Saldanha Bay and Richards Bay, and a third was extensively expanded, Port Elizabeth. Heavy traffic connections to these ports were built or expanded. The result was an exponential increase in non-precious metal exports, particularly of iron ore and coal. This increase tended to be hidden by the gold price bonanza, but in the year 1976–77, as the gold price slumped to nearly half its 1974 level, coal in particular started making a significant contribution to the balance of payments. By 1990, according to a U.S. bank study by Chase Manhattan,[16] South Africa should be the world's largest exporter of steam coal, with exports of 80 million tons compared to Australia's 35 million and the United States's 30 million. South African coal exports were 42% up in 1981, to R977 million, compared to gold's 18 percent decline to R8.6 billion.[17] In the next ten years the gap is likely to narrow considerably.

Diamond and platinum group metals also experienced large price increases in the 1970s. And there was a concerted drive into the processing and beneficiation of minerals in South Africa before their export. Taking advantage of the latest developments in processing technology and of its cheap sources of electrical power (now even relatively cheaper in a post-OPEC world), South Africa put up plants to produce ferro-metals (especially ferro-chrome and ferro-manganese), easily undercutting its competitors worldwide.

The relative increase in nongold mining activity is shown clearly in Figure 4.

The South African mining industry had been large by world standards for many years, but the events of the 1970s established it

Figure 4 Gross Value Added in Mining, 1950–1979 (at Constant 1970 Prices)

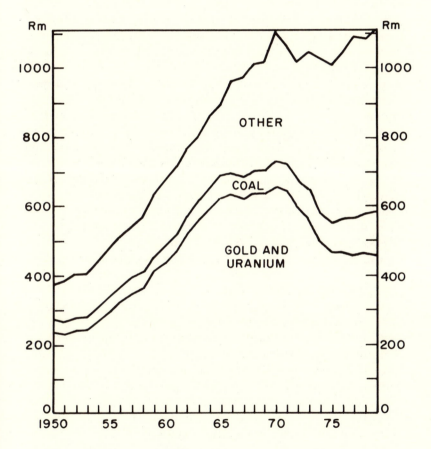

Source: Mercabank, *Focus on Key Economic Issues*, No. 25, March 1980, Johannesburg, 1980.

firmly among the top five producers in the world (the others were the United States, USSR, Canada and Australia). The 1970s also reestablished beyond dispute the primacy of mining capital within South African capital as a whole. With an eye on the 1960s boom of the manufacturing industries fired by state policies of import substitution and on the static gold price then, some have argued that manufacturing had become the dominant sector of capital in South Africa. (Indeed, some would claim that the process started as early as 1925, see Chapter 7). It is true that manufacturing accounted for a rapidly increasing proportion of the Gross Domestic Product in the sixties; but this in no way indicates that it came to dominate capital in South Africa as a whole.

It is a fallacy to link share of GDP directly to degree of influence, and this fallacy becomes clearest when one looks at the relationship of state and capital. Manufacturing and agricultural capital in South Africa have always been basically dependent on the state for subsidies and other forms of support. Overall, they are simply not competitive on international markets. Thus they rely on state protection or hidden subsidies and are permanently beholden to the state. The mining industry, by contrast, has always been internationally competitive and has more than paid its own way. Even when some marginal gold mines received direct state assistance, this assistance was negligible in relation to the contribution of mining capital as a whole to state coffers. The state has also helped by artificially keeping down costs (for example, through its contribution to the migrant labor system), but the state did not need to subsidize mining capital directly. It is of utmost importance to recognize that mining has been by far the dominant source of exports and foreign currency, without which developing countries characteristically experience a foreign exchange bottleneck and stagnating development. South Africa has never experienced such a bottleneck because world demand for gold and, to some extent, diamonds has been virtually insatiable.[18]

The fact that mining capital generally does not need state subsidy means that the particular structural needs of mining capital are given top priority by the state. This does not mean that the state indulges in superficial favoritism on behalf of mining capital. On the contrary, the state has a long tradition of milking mining capital to subsidize manufacturing and agriculture. What it does mean, however, is that the structural needs of mining capital are paramount. It is the goose that lays the golden eggs. It is all very well to appropriate some of the eggs for the welfare of others, but not so many that the species itself becomes threatened. In a real crisis, therefore, the state will tend to back the needs of mining capital. It did so in 1922; and in the mid-1970s when Soweto was in flames, costs were rising steeply, and the gold price was plummeting from $200 an ounce to $107, it did so again by devaluing the rand against the dollar and thereby increasing mining capital's rand receipts. Devaluation did not have similar beneficial effects for the manufacturing and agricultural sectors.

In the 1970s, mining capital moved to shift state policy from support-in-the-last-resort to a greater degree of positive support. It has had a large degree of success, as is clear from the massive infrastructural build-up by the state in the early 1970s discussed above, the major beneficiaries of which were mining capital and the state.[19] But mining capital has plans for the process to go considerably further. In the late 1970s, the Chamber of Mines of South Africa commissioned a major study by the Bureau for Economic Policy and Analysis of the University of Pretoria (the BEPA Report).[20] The report was compiled by the same academic economists who are central to state social and economic planning, led by Professor Jan Lombard, who subsequently became the Prime Minister's chief constitutional advisor.

The purpose of the BEPA Report was to detail the importance of mining in the South African economy overall. It calculated that in 1978 mining accounted directly and indirectly—through its multiplier effects—for 26 percent of total expenditure on South Africa's Gross Domestic Product (GDP). And in 1981, an internal calculation by a Chamber of Mines economist estimated that, in 1980, mining (boosted by an average gold price of $613 an ounce) contributed a full 33 percent of total expenditure on South African GDP, with gold mining alone accounting for 25.7 percent. The gross figures are far less important, however, than the calculations which show how the foreign currency earnings of the mining industry enables the purchase of vital capital goods imports by other sectors of the economy. Mining has a low import propensity, which means that it requires to spend little foreign currency relative to the foreign currency it earns. Manufacturing capital, by contrast, has not been able to pay its way. In 1979, for example, it has been calculated that the manufacturing sector imported R7 billion worth of goods and exported R3 billion. The shortfall of R4 billion in foreign exchange was financed primarily by mining earnings abroad. This calculation was made by the Chamber of Mines of South Africa, admittedly an interested party, but the figures are nonetheless striking.

State and mining capital are clearly considering further major structural changes in the South African economy. Traditionally, manufacturing industry has been given subsidies by the state in an attempt to make it internationally competitive. There is now serious talk within state and mining capital of giving equal incentives to mining to further encourage its exports. This discussion has been largely confined to secret committees and study groups[21] as the issue promises to be politically explosive. There is already a pronounced swing in state policy toward encouraging large concentrations of capital, and the extension of export incentives to mining would dramatically speed up this process. Not surprisingly, all parties are moving cautiously and quietly on the issue.

All this is not, of course, to argue in the terms of the "Fractionalist School" (see Chapter 1), that the mining capital fraction has now gained the upper hand in the eternal struggle with the manufacturing fraction for hegemony within the power bloc. First, mining capital has always been central both to the state and capital as a whole. The electoral shifts emphasized by the "fractionalists" in no way affect this centrality. Second, mining capital is the ultimate owner of a very large part of manufacturing capital. The commanding heights of the economy—other than those controlled by the parastatals such as the Iron and Steel Corporation (ISCOR)— the major heavy industries, the banks and finance houses, and most of the large concentrations of manufacturing capital are predominantly under the direct or indirect control of mining capital.[22] The situation is complicated at times by companies that appear to represent industrial capital being the holding companies of mining companies. But further investigation usually shows that both are controlled by the same group of people and that the initial accumulation of assets and the ongoing drive for further accumulation is based on the priorities of mining capital and its dependents, the financial institutions.

In the seventies, an industrial conglomerate, Barlows, took over an ailing mining group, Rand Mines. It was helped in this takeover by the largest mining group, Anglo American Corporation. Anglo was a large shareholder in Rand Mines but chose to avoid a further growth in mining, which would have been politically unpopular and risky. Instead, it backed the Barlows bid and acquired a large strategic stake in the newly merged company, Barlow Rand. This ostensible takeover by industrial capital, then, can also be seen as a diversification by mining capital into manufacturing capital.

The historical centrality of mining capital has had a number of profound consequences for contemporary South Africa. One has been the unusual ease with which the state has handled foreign multinational companies. The diamond and gold mines were initially financed with European money, but by the second decade of the twentieth century it became clear that the locus of control was to be found in South Africa. This was so even though the mining magnates continued for many years to regard England as "home," and to send their sons to Eton, Harrow, or Oxbridge. For at the same time they were progressively generating and raising a greater proportion of development capital locally, making investment decisions with a view to the needs of the local industry, establishing a more comprehensive relationship of mutual dependence with the South African state and, finally, diversifying into other sectors of the local economy. The reason they took the final vital step is complex but has at least something to do with the state's extreme tolerance of large industrial monopolies and oligopolies, with the Exchange Control policy initiated after Sharpeville in the early 1960s effectively blocking the export of capital from South Africa, and with the fact that it is more difficult to realize and repatriate mining assets than industrial assets.

A final change within mining capital that has had a significant effect on it and on its relationship with the state is the penetration of Afrikaner-dominated capital. Very early in South African history, aspirant Afrikaner capital enlisted the aid of the state for its expansionary aims. The state provided this support not because of its importance to the accumulation process, but rather because it sought legitimation vis à vis the Afrikaner electorate. In 1943, the leader of the National Party, Dr. D. F. Malan, demanded that the state intervene to the maximum possible degree in the economy to help the Afrikaner achieve his rightful share.

It is a measure of the success of the Afrikanerization of capital that in the 1970s and 1980s it is no longer thought necessary to demand state intervention to help Afrikaner capital. In fact, Afrikaner capital interprets state intervention as a threat because blacks will probably be the next group to attempt to harness the state machinery to advance their economic interests.

The last significant sector of capital penetrated by Afrikaner capital was the mining industry. Until the early 1960s there were no substantial Afrikaner mining interests. Then Federale Mynbou took over General Mining Corporation. This takeover also received the support of the head of Anglo-American, Harry Oppenheimer. The usual reason given for this support was that Oppenheimer thought the government and state would be more actively supportive of mining capital if Afrikaner capital had a significant stake in mining capital. He appears to have been correct—the formerly symbiotic but cool relationship of state and capital has developed into a more actively cooperative situation, as is evidenced by the infrastructural and export incentive changes discussed above. Oppenheimer's move helped to "legitimate" the mining industry vis à vis the electorate and freed the state to move actively to support the industry.

Mining capital in South Africa today—and capital in general—is dominated by two massive aggregations of capital: the Anglo American/DeBeers stable, and the Sanlam/Federale Mynbou/General Mining stable. They are no longer rivals in any primary ethnic sense, and the current convergence of their points of view on capital's relationship with the state and organized labor is far more striking than the differences they might have. The Sanlam group accumulated its capital base outside mining, helped by Afrikaner nationalist backing. The group eventually bought into mining with the help of Anglo, and mining is now the foundation of its strength and influence.

To sum up, mining capital continues to be the major source of capital accumulation in South Africa, and appears to have tentative state support to further increase its role. Mining capital's role in the process of legitimation has never been vital, except in a negative sense where its survival needs forced governments to follow highly unpopular policies. This continues to be the case, and the dissatisfaction among white miners and white workers with state policies toward black workers provides a powerful potential source of support to Afrikaner nationalist opposition parties. Even more important, but somewhat further down the road, the ability of mining capital to incorporate organized black miners into mutually agreeable conciliation structures is crucial. The state, however, will undoubtedly play a large role in attempting to regulate this developing relationship and, as was the case over sixty years ago with the white miners, to ensure that the need to keep the mines open and profitable is balanced against the need to incorporate organized black labor into the prevailing labor negotiation procedures.

PROFILE 3: THE STATE

The South African state faces major problems of accumulation and legitimation in the 1970s and 1980s, in the same way that it did in the first few decades of this century. The details, and in some cases the protagonists, are different; but the central issues are the same.

ACCUMULATION

The South African state and the parastatal bodies (such as those producing electricity, steel, oil-from-coal) were responsible for roughly 20 percent of the total economic activity and gross production in the economy in 1977. The public sector was responsible for roughly R12 billion of a R60 billion total, of which R5.6 billion consisted of government services, R3.8 billion of government goods and services, and R3 billion of goods and services provided by public corporations.[23]

The extensive role of the state in the economy is, of course, an international phenomenon today. However, the process started exceptionally early in South Africa. State involvement in the economy was firmly established by the 1920s. "Long before the postwar 'nationalizations' in the west, South Africa had placed all its major utilities and several of its industries under national ownership."[24]

Over recent years the trend has been for greater shares of state participation. The public sector's share of gross domestic product rose from 23.4 percent in 1960, to 30.7 percent in 1975.[25] Proclaimed policy of the government is now to reduce the state role, but it has merely succeeded so far in slowing the *growth* of state participation. State regulation of the economy is possibly as important as its participation in it: large numbers of marketing control

Figure 5   Government Revenue from Gold Mining, 1971–1979

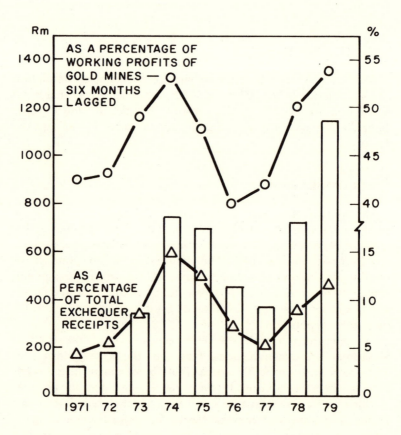

Source: Mercabank, *Focus on Key Economic Issues*, No. 25, March 1980, Johannesburg, 1980.

boards and a vast network of laws and regulations make state intervention in the economy very extensive.

The mining industry, and gold mining in particular, remains a vital direct source of state revenue. Revenue from gold mining taxation and leases rose from R120 million in 1971, to R1.1 billion in 1979 (see Figure 5). Gold provided about 10 percent of total tax revenue in 1979, 14 percent in 1980 and close to 25 percent in 1981. And, as always, it is an indispensable provider of foreign currency: 35 percent of all exports in 1979, 45 percent in 1980, and about 37 percent in 1981. Gold also increased relatively faster in price in the 1970s than South Africa's major imports, including oil. This means that the country's terms of trade—its ability to pay for its imports with its exports—improved, thanks to gold (see Figure 6).

The role of the mining industry has therefore not shown the decline that was anticipated in the 1950s and 1960s. In fact, with the new state commitment to resource exploitation, mining will probably grow in importance to the state and the accumulation process as a whole. This means that the symbiotic relationship of state and mining capital initiated in 1907 will probably continue to remain central, and may even become stronger. The industry will continue to remain a source of state funds for redistribution to other sectors of the economy in good times, and a vital lynchpin to be protected in bad times. And mining capital will continue to complain about high taxes when it is doing well and to scramble for state assistance, direct or indirect, when it is not.

While there are as yet few signs that the rapidly growing state role in the economy is being reversed, the scale of that role is being seriously questioned within the state. It is argued that private sector capitalism is more efficient, generates more employment, and is a more effective accumulator. But far more potent reasons for a cutback in the state role have been advanced by those who increasingly fear a legitimation crisis of the state in the 1980s.

LEGITIMATION

If it could be argued that the South African state in the 1980s is in crisis,[26] then that crisis is one of legitimation. "Legitimation," as has been explained above, is not a mere synonym for the overworked concept of "ideology." To legitimate a state requires an ideology; but it also requires extensive policy measures, particularly in the

Figure 6   The Terms of Trade with the Rest of the World, 1950–1979

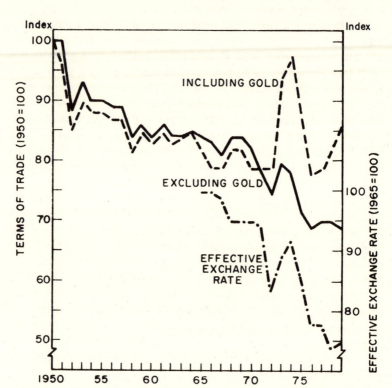

Source: Mercabank, *Focus on Key Economic Issues*, No. 25, March 1980, Johannes-
       burg, 1980.

area of co-optation. A state with a very ill-defined, nebulous ideology may nevertheless have very powerful legitimating institutions.
In fact, the two are often in inverse relationship: the more effective
the legitimating institution (for example, the vote, Parliament), the
less necessity to formulate ideological blue-points.

   Thus one can contrast England, with powerful legitimating instruments and vague (but not therefore weak) ideology, to South
Africa, which has weak legitimating instruments with respect to its
overall population, and a highly defined and systematic (but not

necessarily effective) ideology. The prevailing state ideology in South Africa for about 30 years after 1948 has been that of apartheid—the *policy* of apartheid, of course, predates the ideology by many years.

The policy of apartheid has constituted a very effective, unusually ruthless exercise of power, and continues in the 1980s almost in its entirety. The *ideology* of apartheid, by contrast, has always had only limited success, confined largely to the converted. For the vast majority of the population, the apartheid ideology was not backed up by credible legitimating instruments and thus had little or no effect. Tribal "bungas" or assemblies, and state-appointed headmen, became more and more irrelevant as industrialization gathered pace, and the state never really put significant resources into trying to make them more credible.

In the 1970s and 1980s it has become increasingly more obvious that South Africa's future lies in industrialization rather than a federation of ethnically and anthropologically pure bucolic pseudo-states. Apartheid is no ideology for a state that wishes to be a part of the emerging world industrial economy and urgently needs an exponential growth in the quality and quantity of its skilled labor. This is not to argue that apartheid *policies* are dead: the core policies will be around for a considerable time to come, though the periphery ("petty apartheid") will increasingly be discarded.

The ideology that is being developed by the government to take apartheid's place is the ideology of the free market. Loosely speaking, this calls for the progressive removal of state intervention in the economy and its replacement by the sovereignty of the market, of supply and demand.

Free market *policies,* as was pointed out above, make sense in the context of the state's contemporary accumulation imperatives. But as ideology, the "free market" makes even more sense in terms of the state's legitimation goals. As one of its major formulators points out:

> In addition to sharing the general Western concern with this matter [of excessive state intervention] because of the possible eroding effects on the efficiency of the economic system, the plural character of the population in South Africa adds further urgency to rather fundamental changes in the political

superstructure of government administration in this country. Fortunately it so happens that the principle of limited government which serves economic efficiency so well, also provides the kind of political philosophy that plural societies need. Accordingly, even under the most conservative political assumptions the impact of government on private enterprise will require very careful redefinition.[27]

What this amounts to is the intelligent and cynical recognition that the interventionist state has played its role and needs now to embark on a program of progressive self-emasculation. Whether it will be prepared actually to do anything so painful is debatable, but the logic is inescapable. The state is faced with a very similar dilemma in the 1980s to that of 1907 to 1924: the growing politicization of groups which threaten the very structure of state. These groups have therefore to be co-opted and incorporated into the structures of the state. There are various ways this might be done. Groups might be given industrial rights (unions or the right to strike) and/or political rights. They would, in other words, be depoliticized through the granting of legitimating rights.

One obvious alternative method of depoliticization and legitimation is the one followed in Europe after World War II: increasing state intervention and the creation of a welfare state. In Europe this was an extremely effective way of buying legitimation. In South Africa, the welfare state would be highly unpalatable to both state and capital—who dominate South African society through a symbiotic alliance—and would probably not work anyway due to the logistics of economic resources and demographic patterns.

Another method of depoliticizing issues is to withdraw the state and cut back its role, particularly in the economy. This creates ostensibly nonpolitical zones in which issues are fought out "economically," or even administratively. There are thus excellent economic as well as political reasons for the state to seriously contemplate transforming the ideology of the free market into a partially free market policy.

South Africa was a leader in the early part of the twentieth century in the process of increasing collaboration between state and capital, and the co-optation of organized labor; it is just conceivable that it might become a leader in the late twentieth century in the opposite process, state withdrawal from the economy. It has more pressing reasons to follow these policies than either President Reagan or Prime Minister Thatcher.

This is not to suggest that such a policy will be easy to initiate, let alone successful. The problems of co-opting organized black labor and blacks as a whole in South Africa in the late twentieth century are infinitely more complex than the issue of the white unions at the beginning of the century. To tackle these problems will require massive state intervention (both subjugation and co-optation) at precisely the same time that state withdrawal is being planned. It requires the development of legitimating institutions of a subtlety and range that has never been evidenced in human affairs to date.

The state has been making a considerable effort to clear the way for such a policy. It is trying to structure a new constitution that will result in a less significant state role as a provider and re-distributor of economic benefits. The poor are thus led to blame their poverty on the free (but unequal) market and their own lack of training and ability. These are less explosive scapegoats than the color of one's skin, or the state's policy of political and economic discrimination. The state hopes that if its role as accumulator and distributor are reduced, its vulnerability as a legitimator will be correspondingly reduced.

Closing the gap between free market ideology and policy will be an enormous task, and it is far from clear whether either state or capital had seriously thought through the issue by the early 1980s. It is comparatively simple to manipulate and create institutional structures; but to get them to work can take decades (it did in the case of the incorporation of white labor in 1924). It is also com-paratively simple to advance a mobilizing ideology such as free market ideology; but to get it to work as policy would require radical changes of the most painful kind.

The powerfully symbiotic relationship of state and capital would also need to be fundamentally altered. As the chief free market ideologist, Jan Lombard, put it, many business leaders believe they just cannot live without the special blessing of government. This is an attitude of mind that encourages what he describes as a "monu-mental delusion" that any alliance between private enterprise and government amounts to support of a free market economy.[28] In fact, it's abundantly clear that the symbiotic relationship of state

and capital is posited on, and a contributor to, the massive centralization and monopolization of capital. The powerful and enduring
nature of the relationship means that free market *policy* will be exceptionally difficult to implement. Free market ideology can exist
independently of policy; but without some real advances on the
policy, the state will not be able to use it effectively as a legitimating tool. Real advances would need to include the breaking up of
state and private sector monopolies; in fact, the state continues to
create these, and supervised the separation and monopolization of
the beer and wine industries in the early 1980s.

The lessons of history are always profoundly ambiguous; but the
historical roles of state, capital and organized labor demonstrate the
centrality of legitimation and accumulation in twentieth-century
South Africa, and the extreme difficulty of reconciling the conflicting
needs of the two imperatives. As in the period from 1907 to 1924,
the central task of the state in the 1980s will be to attempt to do exactly this.

NOTES

1. Possibly the best recent attempt is that of John S. Saul and Stephen
Gelb, "The Crisis in South Africa: Class Defence, Class Revolution,"
Monthly Review, Vol. 33, No. 3, July-August 1981, an avowedly partisan
account. See also R. W. Johnson, *How Long Will South Africa Survive*,
Johannesburg, 1977; Simon Jenkins, "The Great Evasion," and "The Sur-
vival Ethic," *The Economist*, 21 June 1980 and 19 September 1981; and
Tom Lodge, "Children of Soweto," in *The Politics of Black Resistance in
South Africa 1945–1980*, London, forthcoming.

2. See Saul and Gelb, *The Crisis in South Africa*.

3. Dan O'Meara, "White Trade Unionism, Political Power and Afrikaner Nationalism," *South African Labour Bulletin*, Vol. 1, No. 10, April
1976.

4. Republic of South Africa, *Report of the Commission of Inquiry into
the Possible Introduction of a Five-Day Working Week in the Mining Industry of the Republic of South Africa*, RP 97/1977, Johannesburg, 1977,
p. 9.

5. Republic of South Africa, *White Paper on Part 6 of the Report of the
Commission of Inquiry into Labour Legislation (Wiehahn Commission)*,
W.P.V.-'81, Pretoria (?), 1981.

6. The Johannesburg *Star*, 27 January 1981, p. 21. Subsequent
membership estimates, unless otherwise stated, are from the same source.

7. South African *Financial Mail*, 18 December 1981, p. 1385.

8. Tom Lodge, *The Politics of Black Resistance in South Africa*, "Children of Soweto."

9. *Union Statistics for Fifty Years*, Jubilee Issue 1910-60, (Pretoria, 1960), G-18.

10. The Johannesburg "Star," International Airmail Weekly, 3 April 1982, p. 1.

11. Saul and Gelb, "The Crisis in South Africa," p. 85.

12. Lodge, *The Politics of Black Resistance*.

13. See, for example, Bob Fine, Francine de Clercq, and Duncan Innes, "Trade Unions and the State; the question of legality," *South African Labour Bulletin*, Vol. 7, Nos. 1 and 2, September 1981; and the three replies to the article in the subsequent edition of the *SALB*, Vol. 7, No. 3, November 1981.

14. Andrew J. Freyman, *The Role of Smaller Enterprises in the Canadian Mineral Industry with a Focus on Ontario*, Toronto, 1978, p. I-1.

15. R. W. Johnson, in *How Long Will South Africa Survive?*, Johannesburg, 1977, Chapter 4, argues that South Africa has influenced the gold price by withholding large amounts of its production. This betrays an ignorance of both the South African state's foreign currency needs and of the world supply position. The United States has the equivalent of more than fifteen years' South African production stored in its vaults, and even the U.S. attempts to manipulate the gold price by selective sales of its gold stocks and IMF stocks were only temporarily effective. The gold market cannot be manipulated with any success by South Africa, unlike the diamond gemstone market, which is extraordinarily effectively controlled by De Beers Consolidated.

16. Johannesburg *Sunday Times*, 24 August 1980.

17. *Mining Journal*, 9 April 1982, p. 271.

18. J. A. Lombard, J. J. Stadler, *The Role of Mining in the South African Economy: A Study Prepared for the Chamber of Mines of South Africa*, Bureau for Economic Policy and Analysis, 1980, p. 57. The study is henceforth referred to as the BEPA Report.

19. R. W. Johnson, *How Long Will Africa Survive?*, p. 319, describes this shift as the "Australian Model": "That is, having developed her manufacturing base in order to become a ranking industrial power, she has been forced to step back a stage and concentrate again upon production of primary raw materials for export."

20. Lombard and Stadler, BEPA Report.

21. A Study Group on Export Incentives was appointed by the Minister of Economic Affairs early in 1977 (The Van Huyssteen Study Group). In March 1978, the Minister appointed a Technical Committee to investigate the practicality of the Van Huyssteen Study Group's radical proposals. The

Technical Committee, in a secret report, reiterated that a basic reevaluation of the relative extent to which manufacturing and agriculture had been favored over mining should be carried out.

22. This can be fairly easily established simply by looking at the subsidiaries and investment portfolios of the Mining Houses and their holding companies, as detailed in their annual reports. See also P. G. du Plessis, "Concentration of Economic Power in the South African Manufacturing Industry," *South African Journal of Economics*, Vol. 46, No. 3, September 1978, pp. 257–70, which concludes: "Should the present situation be allowed to continue unabated the South African economy may in due course be dominated by government enterprises on the one hand and only a very few conglomerates on the other," (p. 269). It could be argued that this is already very much the situation.

23. J. A. Lombard, J. J. Stadler, E. J. du Toit, *Government Participation in the South African Economy*, Pretoria, 1979, p. 4.

24. South African *Financial Mail*, 6 November, 1981, p. 668, reporting a talk by Merton Dagut, economist and senior manager of the bank conglomerate, Nedbank. Nancy Theis, "State Intervention in the South African Steel Industry: The Establishment of ISCOR," Yale University mimeo, 1981, also comments on the very few precedents anywhere for direct state intervention in production. The most prominent of these was, of course, the Soviet Union.

25. South African *Financial Mail*, ibid., p. 668.

26. For example, Saul and Gelb, "The Crisis in South Africa." It is difficult to identify crises until afterwards. South Africanists have been harping on the "Eleventh Hour" Crisis for so long that the cliché is increasingly difficult to credit. On the other hand, like a broken clock, they might well turn out to be correct at some point. If not the 1980s, perhaps the 1990s? But, even though the crisis of survival has not yet arrived, it could easily be argued that the crisis of legitimation has.

27. Lombard, Stadler, Du Toit, *Government Participation in the South African Economy*, p. 4.

28. South African *Financial Mail*, 1 May 1981, p. 503.

Bibliography

This study is based largely on primary sources, the vast bulk of which are unpublished archival sources, only superficially utilized by historians to date. The three most important archival sources are listed below.

PRIMARY

Unpublished Sources

Major archives

Private papers

Oral sources

Published Sources

SECONDARY

Books

Articles, journals, and occasional publications

Unpublished

For a detailed discussion of the State Archives holdings, see Frederick Johnstone's bibliographic notes in *Class, Race and Gold*, and my response in "Quest for a neo-Marxist Approach." The holdings are enormous, very poorly catalogued, and difficult to work with, but they are extremely valuable and relatively untapped.

In spite of his claims to have been the first researcher to study systematically the post-1910 departmental archives (for example, the private papers of the Secretary for Mines), Johnstone has made very sparing use of this source, which I found to be the most valuable. He seems to have used the archives of government commissions far more extensively. These constitute evidence given in public for public consumption.

Citations from the three major archival sources can be easily distinguished by the first group of letters: "MM" and "PM" indicate sources in the State Archives, the collections of the Secretary for Mines and of the Prime Minister's Secretary, respectively; "TCM" indicates a Chamber of Mines source; and "BRA" indicates a Barlow Rand source.

PRIMARY

Unpublished Sources

Major Archives

South African State Archives
South African and Transvaal Chamber of Mines (TCM)
Barlow Rand Archives (BRA)

Private Papers

Chamber of Mines of S. A. *Statement of Evidence to the Commission of Inquiry into Labour Legislation.* Wiehahn Commission, ca. 1977.

Duncan, Sir Patrick. Patrick Duncan Papers. University of Cape Town, A5.1.3.

General Mining and Finance Corporation. Miscellaneous correspondence in Strange Africana Library, Johannesburg Public Library.

Kotze, Sir Robert Nelson. Private papers in possession of his son-in-law, F. G. Hill. Johannesburg, South Africa.

Malan, F. S. Malan Papers in Cape Archives.

South African Defence Force. Office of the Comptroller (Directorate, Documentation Service). Mobilization Plan B. Kompt/DOK D/19/3/5/2, 20 May 1976.

Smuts Papers. S. A. State Archives (unpublished), Vol. 193 (18), No. 16.

Oral Sources

Anderson, C. B. Interview in August 1976 with the son of P. M. Anderson, leading figure in mining industry at the time of the Rand Revolt and for two decades thereafter. C. B. Anderson was several times President of Transvaal Chamber of Mines, as was his father.

Curtis, Jack. Mining engineer, interview July 1976.

Gemmill, James. Interviews with the son of William Gemmill, former General Manager of the Transvaal Chamber of Mines, April 1976. James Gemmill was a former head of the TCM mine labor recruiting organizations.

Gibbs, Tommy. Interview with former Governor Mining Engineer, July 1976.

Hill, F. G. Interviews with son-in-law of late Goverment Mining Engineer, Sir Robert Kotze, December 1975 and August 1976. Hill is a senior mining administrator.

Published Sources

Carnegie Commission. *Report of the Commission on the Poor White Problem in South Africa*, 5 Vols. Stellenbosch, 1932.

Duminy, A. H., and Guest, W. R., eds. *Fitzpatrick, South African Politician: Selected Papers, 1888–1906.* Johannesburg, 1976.

Fraser, Maryna, and Jeeves, Alan, eds. *All that Glittered: Selected Correspondence of Lionel Phillips, 1890–1924.* Cape Town, 1977.

Hancock, W. K., and van der Poel, J. *Selections from the Smuts Papers*, 7 Vols., Vol. 2. Cambridge, 1966, 1973.

Parliamentary Register, 1910–1961. Cape Town, 1970.

Republic of South Africa. *Report of the Commission of Inquiry into the Possible Introduction of a Five-day Working Week in the Mining Industry.* RP 97/1977.

———. *Report of the Commission of Inquiry into Labour Legislation (Wiehahn Commission)*, Part 1 RP 47/1979; W.P.S.-1979 Part 6 RP 28/1981; W.P.V.-1981.

Transvaal Chamber of Mines. Annual Reports.

Transvaal (Colony). *Report of the Customs and Industries Commission.* TG 6. Pretoria, 1908.

———. *Report of the Mining Industry Commission, 1907–1908.* Pretoria, 1908.

———. *A Report of the Transvaal Indigency Commission*, TG 13. Pretoria, 1908.

Transvaal (Colony) Mines Dept. *Report of the Government Mining Engineer, 1902–1910*, annual.

Transvaal (Colony) Parliament. Debates, 1907–1910.

Union of South Africa. Government Gazettes.

———. *Interim and Final Reports of the Low-Grade Mines Commission*, UG 45-1919; UG 34-1920. Cape Town, 1919–1920.

———. *Interim Reports of the Cost of Living Commission*, UG 13-1918. Cape Town, 1918.

———. *Official Yearbooks*, annual.

———. Parliamentary Debates (House of Assembly, Senate).

————. *Public Service List*, annual.

————. *Report of the Committee on Deep-Level Mining*, UG 18-1945. Pretoria, 1945.

————. *Report of the Committee on Gold Mining Taxation*, UG 16-1946. Cape Town, 1946.

————. *Report of the Government Mining Engineer*, annual.

————. *Report of the Industrial Legislation Commission*, UG 37–1935. Pretoria, 1935.

————. *Report of the Low-Grade Ore Commission*, UG 16-1932. Pretoria, 1932.

————. *Report of the Martial Law Inquiry Judicial Commission*, UG 35-1922. Pretoria, 1922.

————. *Report of the Mining Industry Board*, UG 39-1922. Cape Town, 1922.

————. *Report of the Mining Regulation Commission*, UG 36-1924. Cape Town, 1925.

————. *Report of the Select Committee on the Gold Mining Industry*, SC 3-1918. Cape Town, 1918.

————. *Report of the Select Committee on the Gold Standard*, SC 9-1932. Cape Town, 1932.

————. *Report of the Select Committee on the Industrial Conciliation (Amendment) Bill*, SC 9-1930. Cape Town, 1930.

————. *Report of the Select Committee on the Industrial Conciliation Bill*, SC 5-1923. Cape Town, 1923.

————. *Report of the Select Committee on Subject Matter of the Regulation of Wages (Specified Trades) Bill*, SC 4-1917. Cape Town, 1917.

————. *Report of Select Committee on Trading by Mining Companies on Mines*, SC 7-1921. Cape Town, 1921.

————. *Report of the Select Committee on the Union Defence Forces Bill*, SC 10-1921. Cape Town, 1921.

————. *Report of the Witwatersrand Disturbances Commission*, UG 55-1913. Pretoria, 1913.

————. *Social and Economic Planning Council Reports*, Vols. 1–13, especially Report No. 11: *Economic Aspects of the Gold Mining Industry*, UG 32-1948. Pretoria, 1948.

Union Statistics for Fifty Years, 1910–1960, Jubilee issue. Compiled by the Government Bureau of Census and Statistics. Pretoria, 1960.

Newspapers. Johannesburg *Rand Daily Mail*, Johannesburg *Star*, *Cape Times*, *Manchester Guardian*, and *Observer* were among the most useful.

SECONDARY

Books

Abraham, Neville. *Big Business and Government: The New Disorder.* London, 1974.

Adam, Heribert. *Modernizing Racial Domination: South Africa's Political Dynamics,* Berkeley, Calif., 1971.

Arendt, Hannah. *Origins of Totalitarianism.* New York, 1966.

Bachrach, Peter, and Baratz, Morton S. *Power and Poverty: Theory and Practice.* New York, 1970.

Barnes, Denis and Reid, Eileen. *Governments and Trade Unions: The British Experience, 1964–79.* London, 1980.

Barnes, George N. *History of the International Labour Office.* London, 1926.

Blackburn, Robin, ed. *Ideology in Social Science: Readings in Critical Social Theory.* Bungay, U.K., 1973.

Bley, Helmut. *South-West Africa under German Rule, 1894–1914.* London, 1971.

Bosson, Rex, and Varon, Bension. *The Mining Industry and the Developing Countries.* Washington, D.C., 1977.

Bozzoli, Belinda. *The Political Nature of a Ruling Class.* London, 1981.

Brookes, Edgar H., and Macauley, J. B. *Civil Liberty in South Africa.* Cape Town, 1958.

Brookes, Edgar, H. et al. *Coming of Age: Studies in South African Citizenship and Politics.* Cape Town, 1930.

Bruwer, A. J. *Kapitalisme Party-Politiek en Armoede.* Bloemfontein, 1935.

Butterfield, Herbert. *The Whig Interpretation of History.* London, 1931.

Cartwright, A. P. *Golden Age: The Story of the Industrialization of South Africa and the Part Played in It by the Corner House Group of Companies, 1910–1967.* Cape Town, 1968.

———. *Gold Paved the Way: The Story of the Goldfields Group of Companies.* London, 1967.

———. *The Gold Miners.* Johannesburg, ca. 1962.

Cobbe, James H. *Governments and Mining Companies in Developing Countries.* Boulder, Colo., 1979.

Coetzee, J. Albert. *Politieke Groepering in die Wording van die Afrikanernasie.* Johannesburg, 1941.

Consolidated Goldfields. *The Gold Fields, 1887–1937.* Johannesburg, 1937.

Cope, R. K. *Comrade Bill: The Life and Times of W. H. Andrews,* Cape Town, n.d.

Creswell, Margaret. *An Epoch of the Political History of South Africa in the Life of F. H. P. Creswell.* Johannesburg, 1956.

Cutten, Theo E. *A History of the Press in South Africa.* Johannesburg, 1936.

Davenport, T. R. H. *South Africa: A Modern History.* London, 1977.

Davies, Robert. *Capital, State and White Labor in South Africa, 1900–1960: An Historical Materialist Analysis of Class Formation and Class Relations.* Atlantic Highlands, N.J., 1979.

De Kiewiet, C. W. *A History of South Africa: Social and Economic.* London, 1941.

Denoon, Donald. *A Grand Illusion: The Failure of Imperial Policy in the Transvaal Colony During the Period of Reconstruction, 1900–1905.* London, 1973.

de Villiers, André, ed. *English-speaking South Africa Today.* Cape Town, 1976.

Doxey, G. V. *The Industrial Colour Bar in South Africa.* Cape Town, 1961.

Du Toit, P., compiler. *Verslag van die Volkskongres oor die Armeblankevraagstuk gehou te Kimberley 2 tot 5 Okt. 1934.* Cape Town, n.d.

Feldberg, Meyer; Jowell, Kate; and Mulholland, Stephen, eds. *Milton Friedman in South Africa.* Cape Town, 1976.

Fieldhouse, D. K. *Unilever Overseas: The Anatomy of a Multinational, 1895–1965.* London, 1978.

Florence, P. Sargant. *Industry and the State.* London, 1957.

Foster, C. D. *Politics, Finance and the Role of Economics. An Essay on the the Control of Public Enterprise.* London, 1971.

Fourie, J. J. *Afrikaners in die Goudstad, 1886–1924.* Pretoria, 1978.

Frankel, S. H. *Capital Investment in Africa.* London, 1938.

———. *Investment and the Return to Capital in the South African Gold Mining Industry.* Cambridge, 1967.

———. *The Railway Policy of South Africa.* Johannesburg, 1928.

Fredrickson, George H. *White Supremacy: A Comparative Study of American and South African History.* New York, 1981.

Galbraith, John Kenneth. *The New Industrial State.* New York, 1967.

Greenberg, Stanley. *Race and State in Capitalist Development: Comparative Perspectives.* New Haven, 1980.

Gregory, Roy. *The Miners and British Politics, 1906–1914.* Oxford, 1968.

Grosskopf, J. F. W. *Economic Report: Rural Impoverishment and Rural Exodus.* Stellenbosch, 1932. This is Part I of the five-volume Carnegie Commission report, *The Poor White Problem in South Africa.*

Habermas, Jurgen. *Legitimation Crisis.* Boston, 1973.

Hancock, W. K. *Smuts 1: The Sanguine Years, 1870–1919.* Cambridge, 1962. *Smuts 2: The Fields of Force, 1919–1950.* Cambridge, 1968.

———. *Survey of British Commonwealth Affairs,* Vol. 2. *Problems of Economic Policy, 1918–1939.* Part 2. London, 1940.

Hartmann, Heinz. *Enterprise and Politics in South Africa.* Princeton, N.J., 1962.

Herd, Norman. *1922: The Revolt of the Rand.* Johannesburg, 1966.

Horwitz, Ralph. *The Political Economy of South Africa.* London, 1967.

Houghton, D. Hobart. *The South African Economy.* Cape Town, 1973.

Humphriss, Deryk, and Thomas, David G. *Benoni, Son of My Sorrow: The Social, Political and Economic History of a South African Gold Mining Town.* Benoni, 1968.

Hunter, Guy, ed. *Industrialisation and Race Relations: A Symposium.* London, 1965.

Johnstone, Frederick A. *Class, Race and Gold: A Study of Class Relations and Racial Discrimination in South Africa.* London, 1976.

Katzen, Leo. *Gold and the South African Economy: The Influence of the Gold Mining Industry on Business Cycles and Economic Growth in South Africa, 1886–1961.* Cape Town, 1964.

Keefe, David, ed. *Insight into 1981: Transcription of the Simpson-Frankel Investment Conference.* Carlton Hotel, Johannesburg, 28 January 1981.

Kruger, D. W. *The Age of the Generals.* Johannesburg, 1961.

Kubicek, Robert V. *Economic Imperialism in Theory and Practice: The Case of South African Gold Mining Finance, 1886–1914.* Durham, N.C., 1979.

Lacey, Marian. *Working for Boroko: The Origins of a Coercive Labour System in South Africa,* Johannesburg, 1981.

Lanning, Greg, with Mueller, Marti. *Africa Undermined: Mining Companies and the Underdevelopment of Africa.* Harmondsworth, 1979.

Liebenberg, B. J. "The Union of South Africa up to the Statute of Westminster, 1910–1931," in *500 Years: A History of South Africa,* edited by C. F. J. Muller. 2nd edition, New York, 1975.

Lindberg, Leon N.; Alford, Robert; Crouch, Colin; and Offe, Clause, eds. *Stress and Contradiction in Modern Capitalism: Public Policy and the Theory of the State.* Lexington, Mass., 1975.

Lombard, J. A. *Freedom, Welfare and Order: Thoughts on the Principles of Political Cooperation in the Economy of Southern Africa.* Pretoria, 1978.

Lombard, J. A., and Stadler, J. J. *The Role of Mining in the South African Economy.* Pretoria, 1980.

Long, B. K. *Drummond Chaplin: His Life and Times in Africa.* London, 1941.

Miliband, Ralph. *The State in Capitalist Society.* New York, 1969. See also Blackburn.

O'Connor, James. *The Fiscal Crisis of the State.* New York, 1973.

O'Donnell, Guillermo A. *Modernization and Bureaucratic Authoritarianism: Studies in South American Politics.* Berkeley, Calif., 1973.

Patterson, Sheila. *The Last Trek: A Study of the Boer People and the Afri-*

kaner Nation. London, 1957.

Phillips, Lionel. *Some Reminiscences.* London, n.d. [1925?].

Poulantzas, Nicos. *Political Power and Social Classes.* London, 1973.

Price, A. Grenfell. *White Settlers and Native Peoples.* Cambridge, 1950.

Purcell, Susan Kaufman. *The Mexican Profit-Sharing Decision: Politics in an Authoritarian Regime.* Berkeley, Calif., 1975.

Ransome, Stafford. *The Engineer in South Africa.* London, 1903.

Richards, Cecil S. *The Iron and Steel Industry in South Africa.* Johannesburg, 1940.

Rose, Richard, and Peters, Guy. *Can Government Go Bankrupt?* London, 1979.

Routh, Guy. *Industrial Relations and Race Relations.* Johannesburg, 1952.

Roux, Edward. *Time Longer than Rope: A History of the Black Man's Struggle for Freedom in South Africa.* London, 1948.

Sarti, Roland. *Fascism and the Industrial Leadership in Italy, 1919–1940: A Study in the Expansion of Private Power Under Fascism.* Berkeley, Calif., 1971.

Schumpeter, Joseph A. *Capitalism, Socialism and Democracy,* 2d ed. New York, 1947.

Selznik, Philip. *TVA and the Grass Roots: A Study in the Sociology of Formal Organization.* Berkeley, Calif., 1949.

Serton, P. *Suid-Afrika en Brasilië: Sosiaal-Geografiese Vergelyking.* Cape Town, 1960.

Simons, H. J., and Simons, R. E. *Class and Colour in South Africa, 1850–1950.* Harmondsworth, 1969.

Stepan, Alfred. *The State and Society: Peru in Comparative Perspective.* Princeton, N.J., 1978.

Stone, John. *Colonist or Uitlander: A Study of the British Immigrant in South Africa.* Oxford, 1973.

Swainson, Nicola. *The Development of Corporate Capitalism in Kenya, 1918–1977.* London, 1980.

Tatz, C. M. *Shadow and Substance in South Africa.* Pietermaritzburg, 1962.

Thompson, Leonard. *The Unification of South Africa, 1902–1910.* Oxford, 1960.

Thompson, Leonard, and Wilson, Monica. *The Oxford History of South Africa,* Vol. 2. Oxford, 1971.

Transvaal Chamber of Mines. *Tribal Natives and Trade Unionism: The Policy of the Rand Gold Mining Industry.* Johannesburg, 1946.

Transvaal Chamber of Mines, Gold Producers' Committee. *Party Programmes and the Mines: A Business Statement.* Johannesburg, Transvaal Chamber of Mines, June 2, 1924.

Trotsky, Leon. "Bonapartism and Fascism," in *The Struggle Against Fascism in Germany.* New York, 1971.

Tuchman, Barbara, W. *A Distant Mirror: The Calamitous 14th Century.* Harmondsworth, 1979.

Van Biljon, F. J. *State Interference in South Africa.* London, 1939.

Van den Berghe, Pierre L. *Race and Racism.* New York, 1967.

Van der Horst, Sheila. "The Effects of Industrialisation on Race Relations in South Africa," in Hunter, Guy, ed., *Industrialisation and Race Relations: A Symposium.* London, 1965. See also Hunter.

——. *Native Labour in South Africa.* London, 1942.

Van Jaarsveld, F. A. *Afrikaner's Interpretation of South African History.* Cape Town, 1964.

Vatcher, W. H. *White Laager.* London, 1965.

Walker, I. L., and Weinbren, B. *2,000 Casualties: A History of the Trade Unions and the Labour Movement in the Union of South Africa.* Johannesburg, 1961.

Wassenaar, A. D. *Assault on Private Enterprise.* Cape Town, 1977.

Weinstein, James. *The Corporate Ideal in the Liberal State, 1900–1918.* Boston, 1968.

Welsh, David. "English-speaking Whites and the Racial Problem," in de Villiers, André, ed., *English-speaking South Africa Today.* Cape Town, 1976.

Wilson, Francis. *Labour in the South African Gold Mines, 1911–1969.* Cambridge, 1972.

Wright, Harrison M. *The Burden of the Present: Liberal-Radical Controversy over Southern African History.* Cape Town, 1977.

Articles, Journals, and Occasional Publications

Botha, D. J. J. "On Tariff Policy: The Formative Years," *South African Journal of Economics,* Vol. 41, No. 4, 1973.

Bozzoli, Belinda. "The Origins, Development and Ideology of Local Manufacturing in South Africa," *Journal of Southern African Studies,* Vol. 1, No. 2, April 1975.

Choksi, A. M. "State Intervention in the Industrialization of Developing Countries: Selected Issues," World Bank Staff Working Paper No. 341, July 1979.

Clarke, Simon. "Capital, Fractions of Capital and the State: 'Neo-Marxist' Analysis of the South African State," *Capital and Class,* Vol 5, Summer 1978.

Crawford, Archie. "The Present Industrial Situation," SAIF Pamphlet, 1919.

Davies, Robert. "Class Character of South Africa's Industrial Conciliation Legislation," *South African Labour Bulletin,* Vol. 2, No. 6, January 1976.

——. "Mining Capital, the State and Unskilled White Workers in South Africa, 1901–1913," *Journal of Southern African Studies,* Vol. 3,

No. 1, October 1976.

———. "The White Working Class in South Africa," *New Left Review*, No. 82, November–December 1973.

Davies, Robert, and Lewis, David. "Industrial Relations Legislation: One of Capital's Defences," *Review of African Political Economy*, No. 7, September–December 1976.

Davies, Robert; Kaplan, David; Morris, Mike; and O'Meara, Dan. "Class Struggle and the Periodisation of the State in South Africa," *Review of African Political Economy*, No. 7, September–December 1976.

Denoon, Donald. "Capital and Capitalists in the Transvaal in the 1890's and 1900's," *Historical Journal*, Vol. 23, No. 1, 1980.

———. " 'Capitalist Influence' and the Transvaal Government During the Crown Colony Period, 1900–1906," *Historical Journal*, Vol. 11, No. 2, 1968.

du Plessis, P. G. "Concentration of Economic Power in the South African Manufacturing Industry," *S.A. Journal of Economics*, Vol. 46, No. 3, September 1978.

Elvander, Nils. "The Role of the State in the Settlement of Labor Disputes in the Nordic Countries: A Comparative Analysis," *European Journal of Political Research*, Vol. 2, 1974.

Frankel, S. H. "Gold and International Equity Investment," Hobart Paper 45, London, 1969.

Jeeves, Alan. "The Control of Migratory Labour on the South African Gold Mines in the Era of Kruger and Milner," *Journal of South African Studies*, Vol. 2, No. 1, October 1975.

Jessop, Bob. "Recent Theories of the Capitalist State," *Cambridge Journal of Economics*, No. 1, 1977.

Kahn, Ellison. "The Right to Strike in South Africa: An Historical Analysis," *S.A. Journal of Economics*, Vol. 11, No. 1, March 1943.

Kallaway, Peter. "F. S. Malan, the Cape Liberal Tradition, and South African Politics, 1908–1924," *Journal of African History*, Vol. 15, No. 1, 1974.

Kantor, Brian, and Kenny, Henry. "The Poverty of Neo-Marxism: The Case of South Africa," *Journal of Southern African Studies*, Vol. 3, No. 1, October 1976.

Kaplan, David. "The Politics of Industrial Protection in South Africa, 1910–1939," *Journal of Southern African Studies*, Vol. 3, No. 1, October 1976.

Katz, Elaine. "White Workers' Grievances and the Industrial Colour Bar, 1902–1913," *South African Journal of Economics*, Vol. 42, No. 2, 1974.

Legassick, Martin. "Race, Industrialization and Social Change: The Case of R. F. A. Hoernle," *African Affairs*, April 1976.

Lewis, Jon. "The New Unionism: Industrialisation and Industrial Unionism in South Africa, 1925-1930," *South African Labour Bulletin*, Vol. 3, No. 5, March-April 1977.

Marks, Shula. "Scrambling for South Africa," *Journal of African History*, 23, 1982.

Marks, Shula, and Trapido, Stanley. "Lord Milner and the South African State," *History Workshop*, Vol. 8, 1979.

Mawby, Arthur A. "Capital, Government and Politics in the Transvaal, 1900-1907: A Revision and a Reversion," *Historical Journal*, Vol. 17, No. 2, 1974.

Morris, Mike. "The Development of Capitalism in South Africa," *The Journal of Development Studies*, Vol. 12, No. 3, April 1976. See also under Davies.

Nankani, G. "Development Problems of Mineral Exporting Countries," World Bank Staff Working Paper No. 354, August 1979.

O'Dowd, C. E. M. "The General Election of 1924," *South African Historical Journal*, No. 2, November 1970.

O'Meara, Dan. "White Trade Unionism, Political Power and Afrikaner Nationalism" (review article), *South African Labour Bulletin*, Vol. 1, No. 10, April 1975.

Perrings, Charles. "The Production Process, Industrial Labour Strategies and Worker Responses in the Southern African Gold Mining Industry" (review article), *Journal of African History*, Vol. 18, No. 1, 1977.

Ploeger, J. "Op Brandwag - Drie Eeue Militêre Geskiedenis van Suid-Afrika," *Militaria*, Vol. 1, No. 4, 1969.

Poulantzas, Nicos. "Internationalisation of Capitalist Relations and the Nation-State," *Economy and Society*, Vol. 3, No. 2, May 1974.

Saul, John S., and Gelb, Stephen. "The Crisis in South Africa: Class Defense, Class Revolution," *Monthly Review*, Vol. 33, No. 3, July-August 1981.

Schumann, C. G. W. "Report of the Customs Tariff Commission, 1934-1935," *South African Journal of Economics*, Vol. 4, 1936.

Smyth, H. Warington. "Fostering of Productive Industries," *Cape Times*, 3, 5, 6 May 1924.

South African Correspondent. "The Colour Bar Decision in the Transvaal," *Journal of Comparative Legislation and International Law*, Series 3, Vol. 6, 1924.

South African Journal of Labour Relations, Vol. 3, No. 2, June 1979.

Stadler, J. J. "The Gross Domestic Product of South Africa, 1911-1959," *South African Journal of Economics*, Vol. 31, 1963.

Stultz, Newell M. "Who Goes to Parliament?" Occasional paper No. 19, Institute of Social and Economic Research, Rhodes University, 1975.

Thompson, Leonard. "Afrikaner Nationalist Historiography and the Policy of Apartheid," *Journal of African History*, Vol. 3, No. 1, 1962.

Ticktin, David. "The War Issue and the Collapse of the South African Labour Party, 1914–1915," *The South African Historical Journal*, No. 1, November 1969.

Union of South Africa Department of Mines. *The South African Journal of Industries*, 1924 and 1925.

Van der Merwe, P. J. "An Analysis of the Report of the Commission of Inquiry into Legislation Affecting the Utilisation of Manpower," Occasional publication *BEPA*, ca. 1979.

Wojciechowski, M. J. "Federal Mineral Policies, 1945 to 1975: A Survey of Federal Activities that Affected the Canadian Mineral Industry," Centre for Resource Studies, Queen's University, Kingston, Ontario, May 1979.

Wolpe, Harold. "The 'White Working Class' in South Africa," *Economy and Society*, Vol. 5, No. 2, May 1976.

Yudelman, David. "Capital, Capitalists and Power in South Africa: Some Zero-sum Fallacies," *Social Dynamics*, Vol. 6, No. 2, December 1980.

———. "Industrialization, Race Relations and Change in South Africa: An Ideological and Academic Debate," *African Affairs*, January 1975.

———. "Lord Rothschild, Afrikaner Scabs and the 1907 White Miners' Strike: A State-Capital Daguerreotype," *African Affairs*, Vol. 81, April 1982.

———. "Mines: Race Against Time," *South African Financial Mail*, cover story, 28 February 1975.

———. "The Quest for a neo-Marxist Approach to Contemporary South Africa," *South African Journal of Economics*, Vol. 45, No. 2, June 1977.

Unpublished

Bouch, Richard. "The South African Party in Opposition, 1924–1929." Honours diss., University of the Witwatersrand, 1972.

Erickson, K. P. "Labour in the Political Process in Brazil: Corporatism in a Modernizing Nation." Ph.D. diss., Columbia University, 1970.

Garson, N. G. "The Political Role of the White Working Class in South Africa, 1902–1924." Paper given to African Studies Institute conference, 8–10 April 1976.

Greenberg, Stanley. "Race and Business Enterprise in South Africa," Part 2. Mimeographed, Yale University, 1976.

Grey, Pieter Cornelius. "The Development of the Gold Mining Industry of the Witwatersrand, 1902–1910." Ph.D. diss., University of South Africa, 1969.

Hessian, Bernard. "An Investigation into the Causes of the Labour Agitation on the Witwatersrand, January to March 1922." Master's thesis, University of the Witwatersrand, 1957.

Jeeves, Alan. "Competitive Recruiting and Labour Piracy in South-East Africa, 1900–1921." University of the Witwatersrand, History Workshop, February 1981.

Kaplan, David. "The State and Economic Development in South Africa." Unpublished paper presented at seminars at the Universities of Sussex, Oxford, Witwatersrand, and Cape Town, 1974–1975. See also under Davies.

Katz, Elaine N. "Early South African Trade Unions and the White Labour Policy." Paper at the Conference on Southern African Labour History, 8–10 April 1976 at the University of the Witwatersrand.

———. "The Origins and Early Development of Trade Unionism in the Transvaal, 1902–1913." Master's thesis, University of the Witwatersrand, 1973.

Legassick, Martin. "The Mining Economy and the White Working Class." Paper presented at the Conference of Southern African Labour History, Johannesburg, 1976.

Lever, Jeffrey. "Creating the Institutional Order: The Passage of the Industrial Conciliation Act, 1924." Chapter of forthcoming Ph.D. diss., University of Stellenbosch.

Lewis, Jon. "The Germiston by-election of 1932: The State and the White Working Class During the Depression." Paper presented at African Studies Seminar, University of the Witwatersrand, March 1978.

Lubinsky, Ranan. "Depression and Boom: The South African Economy. 1929–1939." Economic history honours paper, University of the Witwatersrand, 1974.

———. "The Role of the Gold Mining Industry in the Growth of the South African Economy, 1933–1939." B.A. honours diss., University of the Witwatersrand, 1974.

Mawby, Arthur A. "The Political Behaviour of the British Population of the Transvaal, 1902–1907." Ph.D. diss., University of the Witwatersrand, 1969.

Mericle, Kenneth S. "Conflict Regulation in the Brazilian Industrial Relations System."Ph.D. diss., University of Wisconsin, 1974.

Meth, Charles. "Shortages of Skilled Labour Power and Capital Reconstruction in South Africa." Paper presented at African Studies Seminar, University of the Witwatersrand, October 1981.

O'Meara, Dan. "Class, Capital and Ideology in the Development of Afrikaner Nationalism, 1934–1948." Ph.D. diss., University of Sussex, 1979.

Ould, C. R. "General Smuts' Attitude to White Labour Disputes Between 1907 and 1922." Master's thesis, University of Witwatersrand, 1964.

Potts, C. "A History of Union Corporation." Unpublished.

Stadler, A. W. "Industrialization and White Politics in South Africa During the Twentieth Century." African Studies Seminar, University of the Witwatersrand, 1974.

———. "The South African Party." African Studies Programme working paper, University of the Witwatersrand, n.d.

Thompson, Leonard, "The Parting of the Ways in South Africa." Unpublished draft ms., Yale University, 1977.

Van Onselen, Charles. "The Main Reef Road into the Working Class: Proletarianization, Unemployment and Class Consciousness Amongst Johannesburg's Afrikaner Poor, 1890–1914." History Workshop, University of the Witwatersrand, 1981.

Yudelman, David. "All the King's Men: Reflections on the 1922 Rand Revolt and Its Historiography." Mimeographed, Yale University, 1973. Lodged with History Department, Yale University.

———. "From Laissez-Faire to Interventionist State: Subjugation and Co-optation of Organised Labour on the South African Gold Mines, 1902–1939." Ph.D. diss., Yale University, 1977.

———. "Slavery and Race Relations in Brazil and the United States: A Case Study in Comparative and Whig History." Mimeographed, Yale University, 1973.

Zarenda, Harry. "The Policy of State Intervention in the Establishment and Development of Manufacturing Industry in South Africa." Master's thesis, University of the Witwatersrand, 1977.

Index

About the Author

DAVID YUDELMAN is presently Senior Research Associate at the Centre for Resource Studies of Queen's University, Kingston, Canada. Born in Johannesburg, he has worked as a journalist and a historian in South Africa and on Fleet Street, and both as a financial analyst and political scientist in South Africa.